HISTORICAL DICTIONARIES OF RELIGIONS,
PHILOSOPHIES, AND MOVEMENTS
Edited by Jon Woronoff

Historical Dictionary of North American Environmentalism

Edward R. Wells
and
Alan M. Schwartz

*Historical Dictionaries of Religions,
Philosophies, and Movements, No. 14*

The Scarecrow Press, Inc.
Lanham, Md., & London
1997

SCARECROW PRESS, INC.

Published in the United States of America
by Scarecrow Press, Inc.
4720 Boston Way
Lanham, Maryland 20706

4 Pleydell Gardens, Folkestone
Kent CT20 2DN, England

British Library Cataloguing in Publication Information Available

Library of Congress Cataloging-in-Publication Data

Wells, Edward R. (Edward Robert), 1964–
 Historical dictionary of North American environmentalism / Edward R.
Wells and Alan M. Schwartz.
  p. cm. — (Historical dictionaries of religions, philosophies, and
movements ; no. 14)
 Includes bibliographical references.
 ISBN 0-8108-3331-X (alk. paper)
 1. Environmental sciences—Dictionaries. 2. Environmentalism—
Dictionaries. 3. Environmentalism—North America—History—
Dictionaries. 4. Environmentalists—Biography—Dictionaries. I. Schwartz,
Alan M. II. Title. III. Series.
GE10.W45   1997
363.7'003—dc21   97-11258

ISBN 0–8108–3331–X (cloth : alk. paper)

CONTENTS

EDITOR'S FOREWORD

Many of the movements in this series deal with vital issues and embrace millions, even hundreds of millions, of members or followers. But none is concerned with so many questions of life and death for humanity as environmentalism. While not everyone participates actively, and some claim they are antienvironmental, no one will be unaffected by whether satisfactory solutions are—or are not—found to a multitude of environmental problems. For such obvious reasons, this *Historical Dictionary of North American Environmentalism* should be of interest to a very broad public—not only activists and professionals but others whose fate is equally affected.

Strangely enough, environmentalism is not a very old movement. Early thinkers and philosophers lived just a few generations ago. Many pioneers are still alive, and founders of major groups remain active. Seminal works appeared a decade or only a few months ago. Yet, it is essential to know this past, how the movement originated, which persons shaped it, and which issues preoccupied it. That provides a more solid basis for understanding what tasks must be tackled at present and what challenges may emerge in the future. These are important purposes, which this volume fulfills with informative entries on significant thinkers, writers, and activists; issues and events; many of the leading groups and organizations; and an array of tasks and challenges. The trajectory is more readily followed thanks to the chronology, while the bibliography offers a welcome introduction to the rapidly expanding literature.

This *Historical Dictionary of North American Environmentalism* was written by two academics who are very familiar with the movement. Alan M. Schwartz is a

professor and director of the Environmental Studies
Program at St. Lawrence University in Canton, New
York. For over two decades he has expanded the program
until it gained national recognition. Edward Robert Wells
holds a lectureship at the Center for Environmental
Programs at Bowling Green State University in Bowling
Green, Ohio. Both authors have lectured and written
widely on environmental issues, and not just within
academia. That may explain why this book is so jargon-
free and accessible to not only activists and professionals
but also the much broader constituency of ordinary people
whose well-being is no less dependent on this movement's
success.

Jon Woronoff
Series Editor

PREFACE

This volume follows in a series of new historical dictionaries of religions, philosophies, and movements. It is neither a dictionary of environmental science nor environmental issues, but rather an attempt to capture the people, places and events that have contributed to the development of environmentalism around the world. Much more complete dictionaries of environmental science, such as the excellent *Encyclopedia of Environmental Studies* (Ashworth 1991) or *The Green Encyclopedia* (Franck and Brownstone 1992), give the reader definitions of extensive lists of terms associated with the environment. Much more complete guides to environmental groups, such as *Your Resource Guide to Environmental Organizations* (Seredich 1991), are also available. This volume differs in that it attempts to place each environmental term within the context of a developing movement.

The task of deciding which event or what person had a key role in the evolution of environmentalism is much like throwing a rock into a pond. The big splash and the first ripple are easily identified. There is universal agreement that people such as Marsh, Muir, and Thoreau, and events such as the publication of *Silent Spring,* are key to the formation of environmental thought. After this "big-splash" core group, the ripples get less distinct; as they radiate from the core, people might include different events and individuals. Most environmentalists would agree that the nuclear accidents at Chernobyl in the Ukraine and Three Mile Island in the United States significantly influenced the future of nuclear energy in much of the world. A substantial debate might arise as to whether or not the grass-roots organization Citizens Clearinghouse for Hazardous Waste is a significant player affecting waste management policies. We have made our judgments, and, thus, this volume should be viewed as a work in progress—a first attempt to identify the most critical factors in the development of modern environmentalism.

Although the primary focus of this volume is the history of North American environmentalism, there are two types of entries in this dictionary that are not purely North American. One kind is international; examples are movements such as ecofeminism and ecotourism, and individuals such as Charles Elton and Thomas Malthus. These events and individuals are, however, vitally important to a work of this scope because they either include North America in their subject (the inequality between the sexes and the association of women with nature) or they shaped environmentalism on this continent (Thomas Malthus' theory on population growth).

The second kind of non-North American entry, which is exclusively about another country, includes events and individuals that have influenced North American environmentalism in some manner. This influence is described in each respective entry. For instance, "Eastern Europe's Environmental Legacy" calls into question the superiority of a centrally planned economy in providing for resource protection as well as demonstrating the need to require environmental impact assessments for government projects.

In all, each entry contained in this book has relevance to North American environmentalism.

In order to facilitate use, terms used in one entry that also appear in a separate entry are set out in bold typeface. Related terms are included at the end of any entry with the words *See also.*

ABBREVIATIONS

ANILCA	Alaska National Interest Lands Conservation Act
ANWR	Arctic National Wildlife Refuge
BBU	Bundesverband für Bürgerinitiativen für Umweltschutz
CAA	Clean Air Act
CCME	Canadian Council of Ministers of the Environment
CEC	Commission for Environmental Cooperation
CEIP	Cooperative Education and Internship Program
CEQ	Council on Environmental Quality
CERCLA	Comprehensive Environmental Response, Compensation and Liability Act
CFCs	chlorofluorocarbons
CITES	Convention on International Trade in Endangered Species of Wild Flora and Fauna
CPA	Canadian Environmental Protection Act
CWA	Clean Water Act
CZMA	Coastal Zone Management Act
DDT	dichlorodiphenyl trichloroethane
DOE	Department of the Environment, Canada
EDF	Environmental Defense Fund
EIS	Environmental Impact Statement
EPA	Environmental Protection Agency
ESA	Endangered Species Act
FIFRA	Federal Insecticide, Fungicide, and Rodenticide Act
FOE	Friends of the Earth
FWS	Fish and Wildlife Service
IJC	International Joint Commission
IUCN	International Union for Conservation of Nature and Natural Resources
IWC	International Whaling Commission
LISA	Low-Input Sustainable Agriculture

NAAEC	North American Agreement on Environmental Cooperation
NAFTA	North American Free Trade Agreement
NEPA	National Environmental Policy Act
NGO	nongovernmental organization
NMFS	National Marine Fisheries Service
NOAA	National Oceanographic and Atmospheric Administration
NPDES	National Pollution Discharge Elimination System
NRDC	Natural Resources Defense Council
PCBs	polychlorinated biphenyls
RCRA	Resource Conservation and Recovery Act
SARA	Superfund Amendments and Reauthorization Act
SEAC	Student Environmental Action Coalition
TOSCA	Toxic Substances Control Act
TVA	Tennessee Valley Authority
UFW	United Farm Workers
UNCED	United Nations Conference on Environment and Development
UNEP	United Nations Environment Programme
WWF	World Wildlife Fund (inside North America) World Wide Fund for Nature (outside North America)

CHRONOLOGY

1626 Plymouth Colony passes ordinances regulating the cutting and sale of timber on colony lands.

1639 Newport, Rhode Island, prohibits deer hunting for six months of the year. First wildlife management law.

1681 William Penn, proprietor of Pennsylvania, decrees that for every five acres of land cleared, one must be left forested.

1785 First ordinance to survey and distribute land in the United States.

1803 Thomas R. Malthus's book *Essay on the Principle of Population* published.

1816 First gas company established in Baltimore, Maryland, produces gas from coal.

1832 George Catlin proposes the creation of a national park.

1836 Ralph Waldo Emerson's *Nature* published.

1849 U.S. Department of the Interior established.

1854 Henry David Thoreau's *Walden* published.

1859 First U.S. oil well drilled in Titusville, Pennsylvania.

1862 U.S. Department of Agriculture established.

1864 George Perkins Marsh's *Man and Nature* published.

1864 Yosemite Valley, California, reserved as a state park.

1872 Yellowstone designated as the world's first national park.

1875 American Forestry Association established.

1876 Appalachian Mountain Club founded.

1879 U.S. Geological Survey established.
Electric streetlamps replace gaslight in New York City.

1881 Division of Forestry created in the Department of Agriculture as a fact-finding agency.

1885 New York establishes the Adirondack Forest Preserve (later Adirondack Park).
Coal surpasses wood as leading U.S. energy source.
Banff National Park, Canada's first national park, established.

1886 New York Audubon Society founded.

1887 Banff National Park created (Canada's first national park).

1888 Boone and Crockett Club founded.

1889 International Boundary and Water Commission created (United States and Canada).

1890 Yosemite designated a national park.

1892 Sierra Club founded by John Muir and others.

1895 American Scenic and Historic Preservation Society founded.

1898 First college-level work in forestry offered at Cornell.
Gifford Pinchot named head of the Division of Forestry.

1899 "Refuse Act" section of the Rivers and Harbors Act signed into law, March 3.

1900 Lacey Act makes interstate shipment of game killed in violation of state laws a federal offense.
Society of American Foresters founded.

1903 First U.S. wildlife refuge established on Pelican Island, off the coast of Florida.

1905 Forest Service created.
Audubon Society becomes national organization.

1906 Antiquities Act permits reservation of areas of scientific or historical interest on federal land as national monuments.
Pure Food and Drug Act enacted.

1908 Grand Canyon of the Colorado made a national monument.
U.S. President Theodore Roosevelt hosts a conference of governors at the White House on the subject of conservation.
British Petroleum discovers first giant oil field in Iran.

1909 Boundary Waters Treaty, between the United States and Canada, signed.
International Joint Commission between the United States and Canada created, January 11.

1913 Hetch Hetchy Valley in Yosemite National Park granted to San Francisco for a reservoir after prolonged controversy.

Martha, the last known passenger pigeon, dies in Cincinnati Zoo.

1915 Rocky Mountain National Park designated.

1916 National Park Service created.
Migratory Bird Treaty between United States and Canada.

1918 United States implements 1916 Migratory Bird Treaty Act from Canada to restrict hunting of migratory species.
Save-the-Redwoods League founded.

1919 National Parks and Conservation Association founded.

1920 Federal Power Commission created.
Federal Water Power Act gives the Federal Power Commission authority to issue licenses for hydropower development on public lands.
Mineral Leasing Act regulates mining on federal lands.

1922 Izaak Walton League of America founded.

1924 The Forest Service designates first extensive wilderness area in the Gila National Forest in New Mexico.

1930 Food and Drug Administration created.
Knutson-Vandenberg Act established.

1933 Tennessee Valley Authority created.

1934 Fish and Wildlife Coordination Act established, March 10.

1935 Soil Conservation Act extends federal involvement in erosion control and establishes the Soil Conservation Service in the U.S. Department of Agriculture.
The Wilderness Society founded by Aldo Leopold.

1936 National Wildlife Federation founded.

1937 Ducks Unlimited founded.
Pittman-Robertson Act makes federal funds available to states for wildlife protection and propagation.

1940 Bald Eagle Protection Act signed by U.S. President Franklin D. Roosevelt, June 8.
The creation of the Fish and Wildlife Service consolidates federal activities in this area.

1942 DDT introduced into the United States.
Alaska Highway completed.
First atomic reactor operated at the University of Chicago.

1944 Public Health Service created by U.S. Congress, July 1.

1946 Atomic Energy Commission created.
U.S. Bureau of Land Management established to consolidate the administration of the public domain.
International Whaling Commission established to regulate the killing of whales.

1947 Defenders of Wildlife founded.
Everglades National Park created.
Federal Insecticide, Fungicide, and Rodenticide Act (FIFRA) established.
Nuclear Regulatory Commission created.
United States changes from a net exporter of oil to an importer.

1948 Federal Water Pollution Control Act enacted to regulate waste disposal.
The Conservation Foundation founded
International Union for the Conservation of Nature and Nature Resources (IUCN), now The World Conservation Union, founded.
Donora, Pennsylvania, air pollution disaster causes 6,000 illnesses and 20 deaths.

1949 Aldo Leopold's *A Sand County Almanac* published.

1950 Oil surpasses coal as the number one energy source for the United States.

1951 The Nature Conservancy founded.

1952 Resources for the Future established.
The Population Council founded.

1953 First National Seashore, Cape Hatteras, North Carolina, designated.
Outer Continental Shelf Lands Act established (amended in 1990).

1956 Echo Park Dam scheduled for construction in Dinosaur National Monument deleted from the Upper Colorado River Storage Project, marking a major victory for wilderness preservation and the national park system.

1957 International Atomic Energy Agency created.
Price Anderson Act signed into law.
Student Conservation Association founded.
First U.S. nuclear power plant to be hooked up to the electricity grid.

1959 Trout Unlimited founded.

1960 Hazardous Substances Act established, July 12.
Multiple Use-Sustained Yield Act established, June 12.
Six Middle Eastern countries form the Organization of Petroleum Exporting Countries (OPEC).

1961 Federal Maritime Commission created.
World Wildlife Fund (WWF) founded.

1962 U.S. President John F. Kennedy hosts a White House conference on conservation.
Rachel Carson's *Silent Spring* published.

1963 First U.S. Clean Air Act.
Glen Canyon Dam built.

1964 Land and Water Conservation Fund passed (amended in 1986).
Wilderness Act establishes the National Wilderness Preservation System.

1965 Rachel Carson Council founded.
Solid Waste Disposal Act signed into law.
Environmental group "Scenic Hudson" given standing to sue in court.

1966 National Historic Preservation Act passed.

1967 Environmental Defense Fund (EDF) founded.
Fund for Animals founded.

1968 Wild and Scenic Rivers Act established.
Garrett Hardin's "Tragedy of the Commons" published.
John Muir Institute of Environmental Studies created.
National Trails Act established.
Paul Ehrlich's *The Population Bomb* published.

1969 Friends of the Earth founded by David R. Brower.
Santa Barbara, California, oil spill.
The Population Institute founded.
Union of Concerned Scientists founded.

1970 Clean Air Act amendments require the setting of national ambient air quality standards to be set.
National Environmental Policy Act (NEPA) approved.
Council on Environmental Quality (CEQ) established by NEPA.
Environmental Action founded.
Environmental Protection Agency (EPA) created.
First "Earth Day" celebrated, April 22.
League of Conservation Voters founded.
National Oceanographic and Atmospheric Administration created.
Natural Resources Defense Council (NRDC) founded.
United Nations established Man and the Biosphere Program.
United States oil production peaks.

1971 Barry Commoner's *The Closing Circle* published.
Greenpeace founded.
International Institute for Environment and Development created.
Save the Whales founded.
Sierra Club Legal Defense Fund founded.
Department of the Environment, Canada, established.

1972 Amendments to FIFRA focus on environmental consequences of pesticides.
Center for Science in the Public Interest founded.
Convention concerning the Protection of the World Cultural and Natural Heritage agreement signed in Paris.

Convention on the Prevention of Marine Pollution by Dumping of Waste and Other Matter (London Dumping Convention) adopted in London.

DDT banned.

Marine Mammal Protection Act established (amended in 1988).

Marine Protection, Research, and Sanctuaries Act enacted.

National Coastal Zone Management Act (CZMA) enacted.

Negative Population Growth founded.

The Club of Rome's issuance of *The Limits to Growth* triggers worldwide debate.

United Nations Conference on the Human Environment held in Stockholm.

Stockholm Declaration (Declaration of the Conference on the Human Environment).

Clean Water Act (Federal Water Pollution Control Act Amendments).

Great Lakes Water Quality Agreement signed.

Oregon passes first beverage bottle recycling law in the United States.

1973 Endangered Species Act (ESA) enacted in United States.

Inform founded.

Tallgrass Prairie Alliance founded.

The Cousteau Society founded.

U.S. production of natural gas peaks.

Trust for Public Land founded.

United Nations Environment Programme established.

Congress passes Trans-Alaska Pipeline Authorization Act.

Canadian Wildlife Act passed.

1974 Environmental Policy Institute founded.

Forest and Rangeland Renewable Resources Planning Act established.
Institute for Local Self-Reliance founded.
Safe Drinking Water Act signed into law.
Sikes Act signed into law.
Worldwatch Institute founded.
Chemist Sherwood Roland suggests that CFCs may be depleting ozone layer.

1975 Convention on International Trade in Endangered Species of Wild Fauna and Flora (CITES) adopted.
Hazardous Materials Transportation Act established.
Edward Abbey's *Monkey Wrench Gang* published.
Brown's Ferry nuclear plant accident.
Nuclear Regulatory Commission created.

1976 Barry Commoner's *The Poverty of Power* published.
Federal Land Policy and Management Act established.
Fishery Conservation and Management Act established.
National Forests Management Act established.
Polychlorinated biphenyls (PCBs) banned in manufacture and most uses in the United States.
Resource Conservation And Recovery Act (RCRA) signed into law.
Toxic Substance Control Act (TOSCA) created.

1977 U.S. Department of Energy created.
First oil flows through Alaska Pipeline.
Love Canal in Niagara Falls, New York found contaminated with 2/2,000 tons of toxic chemicals.
Sea Shepherd Conservation Society founded.
Surface Mining Control and Reclamation Act signed into law.

1978 National Recycling Coalition founded.

New York State evacuated 240 families from the area around Love Canal toxic waste site.

1979 Ames Test developed.
Convention of the Conservation of Migratory Species of Wild Animals (Bonn Convention or Migratory Species Convention) signed in Bonn, Germany.
James Lovelock's *Gaia: A New Look at Life on Earth* published.
Three Mile Island nuclear power plant accident, Harrisburg, Pennsylvania.
Valley of the Drums uncovered.
Oil supplies decrease because of Iran's Islamic revolution; oil prices skyrocket.

1980 U. S. Synthetic Fuels Corporation created, June 30.
Alaska National Interest Lands Conservation Act passed.
Arctic Wildlife Refuge created.
Comprehensive Environmental Response, Compensation and Liability Act (CERCLA) (Superfund) enacted.
Earth First! founded.
Supreme Court in the Diamond v. Chakabarty case allows patent of genetically altered life-forms.
James Watt appointed U.S. Secretary of the Interior.
Love Canal designated as the first federal environmental disaster area.
Pacific Whale Foundation founded.
World Conservation Strategy published.
Coalition on Acid Rain, a Canadian environmental group, formed.

1981 Global Tomorrow Coalition founded.

1982 Convention of the Law of the Sea signed.
Earth Island Institute founded.
Great Lakes United founded.

Rocky Mountain Institute founded.

World Charter for Nature adopted by the United Nations General Assembly.

1983 U.S. government offers to buy entire town of Times Beach, Missouri, because of dioxin contamination.

U.S. Public Interest Research Group founded.

World Commission on Environment and Development created by United Nations (disbanded in 1987 after publication of its final report, *Our Common Future).*

1984 Leak of toxic gas causes worst industrial accident in history, killing 2,500 people in Bhopal, India.

1985 Rails to Trails Conservancy founded.

French agents sink *Rainbow Warrior,* Greenpeace's research vessel.

Nine nations sign the Bucharest Declaration, committing themselves to cooperate on water management and pollution control of the Danube River.

1986 Emergency Planning and Community Right-to-Know Act (EPCRA) enacted.

Superfund Amendments Reauthorization Act (SARA) enacted.

U.S. Synthetic Fuels Corporation discontinued.

Meltdown at Chernobyl nuclear power plant in the Soviet Ukraine.

Times Beach, Missouri, evacuated and bought by the U.S. Environmental Protection Agency because of dioxin contamination.

Fire in a chemical warehouse in Basel, Switzerland, releases tons of a poisonous pesticide into the Rhine River, killing most life for hundreds of kilometers.

1987 Clean Water Act amendments focus on updating standards for toxic substances.
Conservation International founded.
Endangered Species Act (ESA) amended, mandating conservation programs for endangered species and a means to protect ecosystems.
Montreal Protocol on Substances that Deplete the Ozone Layer established and signed (amended in 1990).
Our Common Future (Brundtland Report) published. This United Nations-endorsed report called for new economic growth to be based on sustained development.
Canadian Environmental Protection Act enacted.

1988 Student Environmental Action Coalition (SEAC) founded.
European Community directive requiring environmental review of major projects goes into effect.
Chico Mendes, a prominent Brazilian environmentalist, was murdered by a rancher infuriated by Mendes' efforts to preserve rain forests.
Canadian Council of Ministers of the Environment formed.

1989 *Exxon Valdez* runs aground in Alaska's Prince William Sound, causing the world's largest oil spill.

1990 Clean Air Act amendments emphasize new market techniques such as emissions trading.
Twentieth Anniversary of Earth Day celebrated by 200 million people in 141 nations.
U.S. President George Bush signs Clean Air Act on November 15 requiring cuts in automobile and utility emissions as well as new marketplace methods for pollution reduction.
Convention on International Trade in Endangered Species of Wild Fauna and Flora issues ban in trade of ivory.

Canada/United States Air Quality Agreement signed.
Canadian government issues the Green Plan.

1991 Thirty-nine nations agree to Madrid Protocol, which creates a moratorium on mining in Antarctica.
People of Color Environmental Summit held in Washington, D.C., to promote environmental justice.
The U.S. Environmental Protection Agency (EPA) launches a program to convince chief executive officers of the 1,000 largest U.S. companies that lighting efficiency will reduce pollution and raise profits.
The German government announces the creation of an environmental research center to investigate the massive problems in heavily polluted cities in East Germany.
The U.S. Senate backs an EPA proposal to fine other government agencies for environmental violations.
The last of 700 Kuwaiti oil well fires set during the Iraqi invasion of 1990 was capped. The Kuwaiti government estimated 25-50 million of barrels of oil were spilled in the desert.
London reports its worst air pollution day since record-keeping began in 1976.
Norway canceled its whale hunt for the first time since the sixteenth century. One year later, it resumed.
A German government report estimates the cost to clean up eastern Germany's central industrial belt at 11 billion U.S. dollars. Emissions from some plants in the region were still at 100 times the western German limits.
A three-judge panel in Alberta, Canada, issues a precedent-setting ruling declaring environmental cleanup takes priority over repaying creditors in bankruptcy case.
U.S. President George Bush presents a national energy plan that stresses domestic production increases and only modest efforts to increase conservation and efficiency.
Germany begins the world's most ambitious program of mandatory recycling with recycling goals of 80 percent

for plastics and paper and 90 percent of glass, tin, and aluminum.

For only the second time in history, the Mexican Secretariat for Urban Development and Ecology (SEDUE) declared in Mexico City a second-stage air pollution alert, denoting very dangerous air quality.

After 1,465 children are treated for breathing problems, the Chilean government closes 188 factories and bans 40 percent of the cars from its capital, Santiago.

1992 United Nations Conference on Environment and Development (Earth Summit) held.

Albert Gore's *Earth in the Balance* published.

Basel Convention, forbidding countries to dump waste in or transport waste through countries without their permission, ratified by 20 countries.

Secretaria de Desarollo Urbano y Ecologia (SEDUE) eliminated and Mexican environmental programs are placed under newly created Secretariat of Social Development (SEDESOL).

Representatives from 143 countries sign Global Warming Pact. Environmentalists unhappy because agreement sets no specific limits for greenhouse gases and no timetables.

U.S. Food and Drug Administration declares genetically altered food is not intrinsically unsafe and needs no special approval before entering the market.

The first-ever swap of pollution rights took place between two U.S. electric utilities, under provisions of the U.S. Clean Air Act.

The gray wolf is removed from the endangered species list.

A threatened tourist boycott persuaded the State of Alaska to cancel a proposed killing of several hundred gray wolves.

United States puts into effect a ban on the importation of yellowfin tuna captured in encircling nets that also kill dolphins.

The Pacific Fishery Management Council cuts commercial salmon harvest in U.S. waters to the lowest level ever.

Draft Biological Diversity Treaty to be presented at the Rio Earth Summit approved by 98 countries. The United States, United Kingdom, and Japan express reservations and threaten not to sign.

Ninety-three nations agree to speed up the phaseout of ozone-destroying chemicals and eliminate them by 1996 instead of 2000—the year agreed to in the Montreal Protocol (1987).

The 112-member Convention on International Trade in Endangered Species of Wild Fauna and Flora (CITES) rejects a proposal from five African nations to relax the international ban on ivory trade.

1993 The U.S. Environmental Protection Agency (EPA) held its first auction of credits for pollution of sulfur dioxide, thus, initiating economic strategies to curtail pollution.

The North American Agreement on Environmental Cooperation, a side agreement to NAFTA, signed.

India's Supreme Court orders the closure of over 200 factories whose pollution was damaging the Taj Mahal.

Japan protests the Russian practice of dumping low-level nuclear waste into the Sea of Japan.

The United States signs a convention protecting biodiversity developed at the Rio Earth Summit, thus reversing the Bush administration's policy.

Government of China bans purchase, transport, and sales of rhinoceros horns and tiger bones.

Six European nations sign pact to protect the Black Sea.

The Clinton administration proposes a "no net loss" of wetland policy to prevent further loss of this type of productive habitat.

Canada closes five commercial fishing areas on its east coast indefinitely to conserve depleted fish stocks.

The Convention on Biological Diversity Pact, agreed to at Rio Earth Summit, becomes international law.

Hundreds of thousands of people become sick in Milwaukee, Wisconsin, due to the contamination of the public water supply.

Canada initiates policy requiring businesses to report type and amount of all hazardous waste produced.

World Bank sets new policy that allows public scrutiny of environmental assessment documents for proposed projects.

The first segment of the Los Angeles subway system opens amid hopes it will lessen auto traffic and reduce smog.

U.S. and Canadian zoos announce the Giant Panda Conservation Plan to increase captive breeding of this endangered species and reduce number of animals on loan from China.

Environmental agreement signed as part of the North American Free Trade Agreement (NAFTA) distinctively linking trade and environmental issues.

United States and Mexico pledge to clean up border pollution.

1994 United Nations Conference on Population and Development held in Cairo, Egypt.

The U.S. Supreme Court rules that incinerator ash from municipal waste incinerators is subject to toxic waste regulations and cannot be put into normal landfills.

The Environmental Working Group, a U.S. nonprofit group, states 3.5 million people face elevated cancer risk from pesticides in drinking water.

The United States and Canada agree to close the Georges Bank fishing grounds off Nova Scotia for six months to allow fish stocks to replenish.

United States announces plan to cut fishing off New England coast by 50 percent to protect stocks.

Asian Republics of the Commonwealth of Independent States establish Aral Sea Protection Fund.

Governor of Florida signs Everglades Forever Act to preserve the Everglades National Park.

U.S. President Bill Clinton signs California Desert Protection legislation, creating two new national parks—Death Valley and Joshua Tree.

Canada announces plans to seize foreign vessels depleting endangered fish off Georges Bank even if they are beyond 200-mile limit.

U.S. President Bill Clinton signs executive order to combat environmental racism.

U.S. Environmental Protection Agency (EPA) report declares dioxins to be a probable cancer-causing substance.

The bald eagle is removed from the endangered species list and reclassified in the less urgent threatened category.

The International Whaling Commission declares Antarctica as a permanent whale sanctuary.

Norway says it will defy a worldwide ban on whaling.

1995 Canada seizes Spanish fishing boat in international waters to protest overfishing off its shores.

The Australian cabinet agreed to protect 264 forest areas from logging as part of a plan to improve the country's forest reserve system.

The World Bank and international conservation groups announce a plan to establish or improve 155 Marine Protection Areas to safeguard marine biological diversity.

China jails man for 18 years for killing a rare giant panda.

Governments from more than 100 countries approve a United Nations Global Fishing Pact aimed at slowing the depletion of world fish stocks.

Athens, Greece, begins a ban of automobiles in the city's historic business district to combat pollution, which is damaging the city's classical artifacts.
Wolves reintroduced to Yellowstone National Park.
Australia drops a proposal for a carbon tax, which would have encouraged a reduction in greenhouse gases.
A United Nations summit of more than 120 countries (Conference of the Parties to the United Nations Framework Convention on Climate Change) meets in Berlin to discuss global warming.

1996 Theo Colburn's book, *Our Stolen Future,* sequel to *Silent Spring,* published. Colburn makes national news with assertions that low levels of pollutants can mimic hormones and cause birth defects and behavior problems.
In a precedent-setting effort at ecological restoration, the United States floods the Grand Canyon to restore beaches. The effort is successful.
Republicans in the U.S. 104th Congress are unsuccessful in rolling back environmental legislation and greatly weakening the regulatory power of the Environmental Protection Agency.
World Meteorological Association reports Earth's protective ozone layer was briefly depleted by a record 45 percent during the winter of 1996.
With less demand for spying, U.S. surveillance satellites turn toward investigating environmental threats such as erupting volcanoes and desertification.
At presidential convention the Green Party of the United States in its first presidential convention nominates consumer advocate Ralph Nader as its candidate.
Owners of the Connecticut Yankee nuclear power plant do not restart after maintenance, citing the poor economics of nuclear power.
Voters in Maine turn down referendum that would outlaw the practice of clear-cutting.

INTRODUCTION

Thirty years ago a work like this would not have been considered. Although many of our entries pre-date the 1960s, "environmentalism" as we know it today did not exist until later in the decade. However, a spirit of connectedness with the earth is present in many ancient and contemporary cultures. In her 1994 book, *The Way of the Earth*, T. C. McLuhan examines a variety of cultural-spiritual traditions and how they have viewed human-earth relationships. The sixth-century B.C. Chinese sage Lao-tzu, whose writings provide much of the religious doctrine for Taoism, believed that unspoiled nature represented an ideal. He stated:

> Man models himself on Earth,
> Earth on Heaven,
> Heaven on the Way
> and the Way on Nature.
> (McLuhan 1994, p.18)

Medieval Rhineland mystic Hildegard of Bingen (1098-1179) believed that humans and all of life are derived from Mother Earth. She wrote:

> The earth is at the same time mother, she is mother of all that is natural, mother of all that is human. She is the mother of all, for contained in her are the seeds of all. The earth of humankind contains all moistness, all verdancy, all germinating power. It is in so many ways fruitful. All creation comes from it. Yet it forms the basic raw material for humankind.
> (McLuhan 1994, p.16)

In the modern Western world, environmentalism has its roots in several genres of nature appreciation; these include wildlife ecology, literature of the natural world, conservation, and others. Environmentalism promotes the belief that an antagonism exists between humans and the natural environment because the life support system is degrading at an alarming rate and it holds humans responsible for the majority of these ravages. It asserts that humans have the power to reverse these trends and create a sustainable future.

The forerunners to contemporary environmentalists are writers who recognized the value of human-earth relationships. They spoke of humanity's niche in the universe and regarded the natural world as sacred. Humanity's place was not, as many had supposed, to dominate and control the earth to suit the needs of people. Nineteenth-century poet and philosopher Ralph Waldo Emerson wrote that poets know nature better than any woodsman because they can know nature in a nondestructive way. In his poem "Woodnotes I" he wrote:

> When the pine tosses its cones
> to the song of its waterfall tones,
> Who speeds to the woodland walks?
> To birds and trees who talks?
> Caesar of his leafy Rome,
> There the poet is at home.
> He goes to the river-side,
> Not hook nor line hath he;
> He stands in the meadows wide,
> Nor gun nor scythe to see.
> Sure some god his eye enchants:
> What he knows nobody wants.
> In the wood he travels glad,
> Without better fortune had,
> Melancholy without bad
> Knowledge this man prizes best
> Seems fantastic to the rest:

> Pondering shadows, colors, clouds;
> Grass buds and caterpillar-shrouds.
> (Spiller 1975, p. 38)

Following Emerson, Henry David Thoreau witnessed forests cut at increasing rates in the middle decades of the 19th century. Fearing that one day Americans would lose their natural world, he wrote in *Walden* "Spring":

> We need the tonic of wildness—to wade sometimes in marshes where the bittern and the meadow-hen lurk, and hear the booming of the snipe; to smell the whispering sedge where only some wilder and more solitary fowl builds her nest, and the mink crawls with its belly close to the ground. At the same time we are earnest to explore and learn all things, we require that all things be mysterious and unexplorable, that land and sea be infinitely wild, unsurveyed and unfathomed by us because unfathomable. We can never have enough of Nature. (Thoreau 1930, p. 211)

Later in the century, a new generation of predecessors to modern-day environmentalism was ushered in with John Muir who wrote and fought for preservation in the late 19th century until his death in 1914. During his life, Muir enjoyed considerable popularity for his travel manuscripts. Unlike his predecessors whose appreciation of nature was selective, Muir delighted in complete and continual wilderness. That is, while Emerson and Thoreau relished both the offerings of civilization and nature, Thoreau preferring to "keep a foot in both worlds," Muir preferred complete submergence in wildness. He states in *My First Summer in the Sierra* (1911):

These blessed mountains are so compactly filled
with God's beauty, no petty personal hope or
experience has room to be. Drinking this
champagne water is pure pleasure, so is breathing
the living air, and every movement of limbs is
pleasure, while the whole body seems to feel
beauty when exposed to it as it feels the campfire
or sunshine, entering not by the eyes alone, but
equally through all one's flesh like radiant heat,
making a passionate ecstatic pleasure-glow not
explainable. (Muir 1987, p. 131)

After Muir, many expressed an ethical attitude that humans
must develop to treat the earth with care and respect. Aldo
Leopold wrote in the final chapter of *A Sand County Almanac*:

The "key-log" which must be moved to release
the evolutionary process for an ethic is simply
this: quit thinking about decent land-use as solely
an economic problem. Examine each question in
terms of what is ethically and esthetically right, as
well as what is economically expedient. A thing is
right when it tends to preserve the integrity,
stability and beauty of a biotic community. It is
wrong when it tends otherwise. (Leopold 1966,
pp. 261-262)

Environmentalists began to recognize that if you want to
preserve nature, it is not enough to merely preserve habitats
and places; nature must be protected in a pristine condition.
Human activities both inside and outside of natural areas can
affect the well-being of those areas. As John Muir said, "When
we try to pick out anything by itself, we find it hitched to
everything else in the universe." In 1962, Rachel Carson
recognized that when you apply pesticides (a term she believed
was misleading; she preferred to call them "biocides" because

their purpose is to "kill life"), you are making the earth unfit for life. Her book, *Silent Spring* (1962), targeted dichlorodiphenyl trichloroethane (DDT) and other pesticides which were legally used at the time of her writing. She maintains that while pesticides appear to be a quick and easy solution to predation by insects, they are wrought with long-term problems including cancer and other illnesses that plague farm workers and the unknowing consumer. These chemicals are profitable to the companies that produce them, but deadly for those who come into contact with them. The last chapter of *Silent Spring* begins with a cultural challenge. Carson wrote:

> We stand now where two roads diverge. But unlike the roads in Robert Frost's familiar poem, they are not equally fair. The road we have long been traveling is deceptively easy, a smooth superhighway on which we progress with great speed, but at its end lies disaster. The other fork of the road—the one "less traveled by"—offers our last, our only chance to reach a destination that assures the preservation of our earth. (Carson 1962, p. 244).

While Carson was writing on the dangers of pesticides, others began to notice that environmental problems expanded beyond specific industrial culprits. Many American and European writers believed that an environmental crisis was beginning, which was a problem of the culture itself. Secretary of the Interior under U.S. President John F. Kennedy, Stewart L. Udall, wrote about the evolution of American attitudes toward the natural world in *The Quiet Crisis* (1963). Documenting the actions and writings of such players as Thomas Jefferson, George Perkins Marsh, Gifford Pinchot, Theodore and Franklin Delano Roosevelt, and John Muir, Udall stated that:

America today stands poised on a pinnacle of
wealth and power, yet we live in a land of
vanishing beauty, of increasing ugliness, of
shrinking open space, and of an overall
environment that is diminishing daily by pollution
and noise and blight. This, in brief, is the quiet
conservation crisis of the 1960s. . . .This book is
an attempt to outline the land-and-people story of
our continent. (Udall 1963, p. viii)

Two decades later, as the recognition of an environmental
crisis had spread across disciplines, physicist Fritjof Capra
broadened environmental scholarship to include the physical
sciences. From his perspective, a change in worldviews or
paradigms would be needed to change the relationship of
humans with the earth. In *The Turning Point* (1983) he argues
that mechanistic science and enlightenment philosophy
destroyed the organic view of the world shared by western
cultures and replaced it with a relationship between humans
and nature as one of control and domination. He continued,
however, that the rise of the science of ecology and "new
physics," would restore the organic relationship of
connectedness and relatedness. He called this new view the
"systems paradigm." Capra stated that modern physics shows:

that we cannot decompose the world into
independently existing smaller units. As we
penetrate into matter, nature does not show us any
isolated basic building blocks, but rather appears
as a complicated web of relations between the
various parts of a unified whole. As Heisenberg
expresses it, "The world thus appears as a
complicated tissue of events, in which connections
of different kinds alternate or overlap or combine
and thereby determine the texture of the whole."
(Dobson 1991, pp. 43-44)

Writers like ecotheologian Thomas Berry support Capra's notion and also believe that the environmental crisis results from a dysfunctional relationship with the earth. The story of human domination and control of the planet, he argued, became realized most in the Enlightenment philosophy beginning in the 16th and 17th centuries. Berry said that "new physics" and ecology provide the basis for a new creative story. In *The Dream of the Earth* (1988) Berry stated:

> We must now, in a sense, reinvent the human as species within the community of life species. Our sense of reality and of value must consciously shift from an anthropocentric to a biocentric norm of reference. (Berry 1988, p. 21)

Writer of the American West, Edward Abbey, had a more direct approach to the environmental crisis. Abbey's literary and polemical writings provided the motivation for the founding of Earth First!, a direct action environmental group that fights for preservation of wild lands. In *Desert Solitaire* (1968), Abbey argued that industrialization of nature was a primary cause of environmental destruction. He stated:

> There is a cloud on my horizon. A small dark cloud no bigger than my hand.
> Its name is Progress. (Abbey 1968, p. 48)

Many of Abbey's writings reflect how wilderness is a necessary part of civilization and that the national park system has a responsibility to maintain pure wilderness. As quoted by Dave Foreman in *Confessions of an Eco-Warrior* (1991), Abbey calls on individuals, acting out of an ethical duty to prevent destruction of wild lands. He wrote:

> At some point we must draw a line across the ground of our home and our being, drive a spear into the land, and say to the bulldozers, earthmovers, government and corporations, "this far and no farther." If we do not, we shall later feel, instead of pride, the regret of Thoreau, that good but overly-bookish man, who wrote, near the end of his life, "If I repent of anything it is likely to be my good behavior. (Foreman 1991, p. 117)

The failure of government agencies to maintain wilderness caused Dave Foreman, Howie Wolke, and others to join together to form Earth First!—a group that vowed to take any means necessary to defend "Mother Earth." Occasionally, defending wild lands required active involvement in preventing destruction or "throwing a monkey wrench" into the violence wrought against nature. Dave Foreman offered principles to men and women who decide to defend wild nature:

> —Monkeywrenching is nonviolent
> —Monkeywrenching is not organized
> —Monkeywrenching is individual
> —Monkeywrenching is targeted
> —Monkeywrenching is timely
> —Monkeywrenching is dispersed
> —Monkeywrenching is diverse
> —Monkeywrenching is fun
> —Monkeywrenching is not revolutionary
> —Monkeywrenching is simple
> —Monkeywrenching is deliberate and ethical
>   (Foreman 1991, pp. 113-115)

David Brower, called "the most effective conservation activist in the world," has spent the last half of the twentieth century fighting for protection of the environment. He continues to offer creative solutions to the environmental crisis.

In his 1995 book (cowritten with Steve Chapple) *Let the Mountains Talk, Let the Rivers Run: A Call to Those Who Would Save the Earth,* he called on each of his readers to find their own method for improving the natural world. Referring to a poem with Johann Wolfgang Goethe that posits that magic is found in boldness, Brower ended his book with:

> Do you have the magic in you? You bet. Magic is that little genetic genius that has been evolving for three billion years: It connects us all to each other and to everything that has come before and that still lives on the planet. That is some magic, and it was formed in wilderness. Let us begin. Let us restore the earth. Let the mountains talk, and the rivers run. Once more, and forever. (Brower and Chapple 1995, p. 196)

In addition to the individuals that have influenced cultural responses toward the natural world, significant events have awakened societies to the relationship between isolated environmental "events" and the continuing environmental crisis. Events such as Love Canal in Niagara Falls, New York, awakened the American public to the danger of hazardous waste and the need to remediate polluted sites. As a result of this event, Superfund was adopted to clean hazardous waste sites. The December 2, 1984, explosion at Bhopal, India, alerted the world to industrial accidents.

Some countries now face such significant pollution problems that it will be years before such basic needs as air and water are safe to breathe and drink. For example, due to an absence of pollution control devices on coal-burning industrial and power plants, air pollution in Poland is 50 times the legal limits and motorists often must turn on their lights during the day to be able to see. In addition to several other environmental problems that confront the country, nearly one-half of its cities have no wastewater treatment system and nearly all of its river water is too polluted to drink. As the world becomes aware of what can happen to a country where economic growth and industrialization are pursued without consideration of environmental quality, many societies are becoming increasingly aware of environmental limits.

While unlimited industrial growth has caused significant harm to some countries, rapid population growth threatens others. Fortunately for China, the most populated country in the world with nearly 1.2 billion people, the government has taken drastic measures to reduce population growth rates. For instance, it discourages couples from marrying at a young age and having more than one child. Sterilization, contraceptives, and abortion are offered free. While these government programs have been met with much success in limiting population growth, critics disapprove of abortion and point out that coercive techniques are unethical. There is also considerable documentation that overcrowded orphanages provide unhealthy living conditions, many children are left to starve to death, and infanticide is common due to cultural preferences for male children. By the mid-1980s, virtually all of the countries of the world agreed that population growth must be slowed, yet the debate about how fast this should happen and by what means will rage for decades to come.

Environmental problems once affected only the places that created the pollution. Today we find a set of international, even global, problems. Environmental problems that have become the world's shared problems include loss of biodiversity, the global warming threat, stratospheric ozone depletion, and acid rain, among others. These problems are what Garrett Hardin calls a "tragedy of the commons." Hardin described a scenario where several cattle grazers share a grazing commons. Each cattle owner can graze as many animals on the commons as he or she chooses. Acting out of self-interest, each owner maximizes her or his lot and grazes more animals. As a result, the commons is destroyed. In the current situation, the tragedy occurs when each country, acting out of self-interest, uses the commons (air, water, soil, and wildlife resources) as much as it chooses, with little regard for long-range consequences. While each player's disregard may not destroy the commons, their combined actions are ecologically devastating. All the world suffers the consequences.

Other environmental events represent a struggle between two goods: jobs for people vs. animal preservation. This is exemplified in the Pacific Northwestern forests of the United States. The logging industries argue that if they cannot continue their logging practices, jobs will be forfeited. Environmentalists argue that if the forests are not preserved, the endangered northern spotted owl will become extinct. Further, since the owl is an indicator species, if its numbers decline, the health of the entire ecosystem will suffer. Environmental issues like this can result in increased support and antagonism toward environmentalism. Thus, environmental events such as the U.S. Endangered Species Act or efforts to save Brazilian rain forests do not always lend support for environmentalism, and today we see forces against environmentalism, such as the "wise-use movement" in the United States, mobilizing worldwide. Indeed, activists such as Chico Mendes in Brazil have been killed for their pro-environment beliefs.

Events that provided nearly unqualified support for alternative sources of energy are nuclear power plant accidents at Three Mile Island and Chernobyl. In the case of Three Mile Island, an accident of tremendous proportions was narrowly averted, making Americans rethink the place of nuclear power in the country's energy scheme. In the case of Chernobyl, every nation on the planet became aware of the dangers of nuclear power when radiation was spread over the globe. This accident caused 31 deaths; 259 people were hospitalized with radiation sickness; one-half of the 30,000-person clean-up crew later died from radiation sickness; over 250,000 people were evacuated from the vicinity; and millions of people were exposed to high- and low-level radiation.

Events like Chernobyl and others addressed in this reference have surely increased environmental awareness and forced people to question the worldview that dominates industrial society. Thus, in this book, we also address alternative ideas that have been proposed to change the role of our species as Aldo Leopold stated in *A Sand County Almanac,* "from conqueror of the land-community to plain member and citizen of it." Some of the ideas for remaking society that we consider are bioregionalism, ecofeminism, social ecology, and deep ecology.

Finally, in *The Dream of the Earth,* Thomas Berry offered his prescription for reinhabiting the planet. He stated:

> In relation to the earth we have been autistic for centuries. Only now have we begun to listen with some attention and with a willingness to respond to the earth's demands that we cease our industrial assault, that we abandon our inner rape against the conditions of our earthly existence, that we renew our human participation in the grand liturgy of the universe. (Berry 1988, p. 215)

THE DICTIONARY

A

ABBEY, EDWARD (1927-1989) Novelist and writer of the American southwest. Notable works include *Desert Solitaire, The Monkey Wrench Gang, The Journey Home,* and *Down the River.* An enigmatic figure, Abbey has offended nearly every group on the sociopolitical spectrum. Critics have labeled him a fascist, racist, sexist, elitist, crackpot, reactionary, and so on. In spite of this, Abbey has many admirers.

In the environmental arena, he served as a spokesman for, and defender of, the land; an outspoken critic of government land management; an opponent of development; and an outspoken critic of government and land management. In his collection of journals (1951-1989) entitled *Confessions of a Barbarian,* Abbey wrote on June 25, 1959, of how Ralph Newcomb and he floated through Glen Canyon which, at the time, was threatened with development. Abbey stated:

> How much dynamite, we wondered aloud to each other, would be needed to destroy the dam? How delightful and just, we imagined, to have our dynamite so integrated into the dam's wiring system, that when the president or the secretary of the interior and the Four Corner's governors, together with their swarms of underlings, the press and hordes of tourists had all assembled for the Grand Opening, it would be the white pudgy finger of the biggest big-shot, pressing the little

black button on the be-flagged switchboard, that would blow to hell and smithereens the official himself, his guests, the tourists, the bridge and Glen Canyon dam. A sad and hopeless fantasy. (p. 152)

Abbey's own book, *The Monkey Wrench Gang*, provided the impetus for the formation of direct action groups such as Earth First! To Abbey, wilderness offers freedom from government, political oppression, and domination of any kind. He was viewed by many conservatives as subversive, by many liberals as vulgar (as when he stated that he'd rather kill a man than a snake), and by countless people from around and outside of the political spectrum as a symbol for preservation of wilderness. (See also **EARTH FIRST!**)

ACID RAIN CONTROVERSY This environmental problem occurs when sulfur dioxide (mostly from coal plants) and oxides of nitrogen, from auto exhaust and power plants, enter the atmosphere. These oxides are transported by winds, and as they mix with moisture, they convert to sulfuric acid and nitric acid. When the acids fall to the earth as precipitation, they are damaging to both terrestrial and aquatic systems, lowering the pH of each so that many life-forms can no longer survive. Normal precipitation is slightly acidic—5.0-5.6 on the pH scale. Typical rain in the eastern United States, for instance, is often more than 10 times as acidic, with a pH of 4.3. Besides ecosystemic damage, acid rain damages the built environment, eating away at statues, buildings, tombstones, metals, and car finishes. Sulfur and nitrogen, the chemicals responsible for acid rain, contribute to human respiratory diseases. Dutch scientists blame acid rain for declining numbers of titmouses, nuthatches, and other songbirds.

The controversy over this issue arises from the fact that prevailing winds transport acid pollution. Canadian officials estimate that up to one-half of Canada's acid rain problem originates in the Ohio River Valley of the United States. After a decade of Canadian complaints, the U.S. government responded with the 1990 **Clean Air Act**, which addressed acid pollution. It called for the United States to reduce sulfur dioxide emissions by 50 percent of the 1980 level by the year 2000 and to make modest reduction in nitrogen oxide emissions. In 1997, studies by the U.S. Environmental Protection Agency and Canada's Department of Environment questioned whether the reductions agreed to in 1990 will be enough to prevent further damage to lakes in both countries.

The problem of acid rain showed the world that pollution created in one place could affect a different region, even in another country.

ADIRONDACK PARK Six million acres of northern New York State, a mix of public and private lands, make the Adirondack Park the largest state park in the United States. The land within the park had been devastated by lumbermen. In 1892, the state legislature designated 3 million acres of public and private land to create the park. The park has expanded over time to twice its original size. The public land was protected in 1894 by an amendment to the New York State Constitution, designating all public lands within the park, known as forest preserve lands, as forever wild. The private lands, in 1973, came under one of the most stringent and controversial land use plans ever created, which greatly limited development. (See also **FERNOW, BERNHARD**)

AGENDA 21 (See **UNITED NATIONS CONFERENCE ON ENVIRONMENT AND DEVELOPMENT**)

AGENT ORANGE   Named for orange-striped storage containers in which the chemical was held, it was a defoliant used during the Vietnam War. Agent Orange cleared trees and brush that provided cover to the Vietcong and North Vietnamese troops, and it destroyed the farmlands that fed the enemy. The United States used more than 6 billion gallons of the defoliant during the war.

Agent Orange is a mixture of chemicals including the currently used 2,4-D and 2,3,7,8 tetrachloradibenzo-p-dioxin, otherwise known as TCDD—a known toxic carcinogen and linked to such diseases as soft-tissue sarcoma, Hodgkin's disease, and skin and liver disorders. The average exposure per veteran to this dioxin was approximately two ppm. War veterans suffered health ailments due to exposure. Many claim their children are suffering birth defects due to their exposure. Veterans—some 250,000 claimants—brought a lawsuit against the producers of the chemical and settled out of court for $180 million.

AGROFORESTRY   Agroforestry "combines agriculture and/or livestock with tree crops and/or forest plants," usually on an environmentally sustainable basis. Swidden agroforestry involves clearing small areas of rain forest and planting annual crops along with perennial tree crops. As soil fertility depletes, the land is left to regenerate. This practice has sustained native peoples, including Amazonian tribes and rain forests, for many generations.

Although agroforestry has been practiced mostly by remote rural peoples, it also provides income for larger populations. A Peruvian society of 2,000 makes products from forest trees and sells them in Lima markets. Java farmers export teak trees to foreign markets after they grow them along with subsistence crops. (See also **BIODIVERSITY CRISIS; MENDES, CHICO**)

AIR QUALITY ACT (See **CLEAN AIR ACT**)

**ALASKA NATIONAL INTEREST LANDS CONSERVA-
TION ACT (ANILCA)** This act was a result of the
controversy between environmentalists, who wanted to
save as much Alaskan wilderness as possible, and oil
companies, who sought to exploit the vast quantities of
crude oil underlying parts of the state. On December 2,
1980, President Jimmy Carter signed the ANILCA, which
protected 375 million acres in the state, in both the
National Wilderness Preservation System and the Wild
and Scenic River System. (See also **WILD AND SCENIC
RIVERS ACT**)

The act created a controversy which continues to rage.
This act did not include 1.4 million acres of coastal plain
as wilderness. It left the use of this land open to be
determined after a study of the potential for oil
development. In 1994, the U.S. Congress tried to open
this area for oil development, but this attempt was vetoed
by President Bill Clinton. As of 1997 this area was neither
open for oil development nor permanently protected.

ALASKA PIPELINE Initiated by U.S. oil companies that
sought to tap oil under Alaska's North Slope, this pipeline
would transport oil from Prudhoe Bay southward to the
City of Valdez on the Prince William Sound (from north
to south coasts of Alaska). Although Congress was
initially hesitant to permit the pipeline, after OPEC's 1973
oil embargo, the need to provide a secure supply of
domestic oil became critical. Thus, on November 16,
1973, Congress passed the Trans-Alaska Pipeline
Authorization Act, which authorized pipeline construction.

This federal activity was required in the 1970 **National
Environmental Policy Act** (NEPA), which mandates that
an environmental impact statement be written on any

activity with a potential to significantly impact the natural environment. However, in an unprecedented move, Congress exempted the pipeline from NEPA requirements. Several groups opposed to the pipeline filed lawsuits for different reasons. Seven native Alaskan villages sued the oil companies because they felt the oil line would disrupt their cultural lifestyle, especially if an accident were to occur. Further, the **Wilderness Society, Friends of the Earth,** and the **Environmental Defense Fund** filed suit to reduce the pipeline's right-of-way down to 25 feet on either side as required by a 50-year-old state law.

The pipeline, completed June 20, 1977, ran 372 miles below ground and 400 miles above in a harsh arctic environment characterized by permafrost. While environmental impacts have been minimal, the 1989 oil spill by the **Exxon Valdez** raised questions about the abilities of scientists and engineers to transport oil in the rugged ecosystem without future accidents occurring. Finally, many environmentalists are concerned that as the pipeline ages, environmental disasters will become more probable: in 1990, external corrosion along the pipeline was, in fact, detected.

The pipeline continued to transport less and less oil throughout the 1990s and this decline in Alaskan oil production has increased the pressure to develop the **Arctic National Wildlife Refuge.**

ALBRIGHT, HORACE (1890-1987) An influential motivator of the National Park System in the United States, Albright served as assistant under the first director, **Stephen T. Mather,** before succeeding him. He was integral in getting the park bill passed in 1916, fighting opposition from the Chief of the Forest Service, **Gifford Pinchot.**

ANIMISM This philosophy promotes that everything in the natural world has a spirit consciousness and that the entire planet is permeated by a life force that holds the world together. Although it is historically most closely associated with pagan polytheistic cultures, the European Gottfried Leibnitz wrote in the late seventeenth and early eighteenth century that the distinction between living and nonliving things was misleading; he believed everything was interconnected. In the seventeenth century, Baruch Spinoza expressed the philosophy of pantheism: that everything was alive and permeated with God. Spinoza's philosophy valued the entire system of the world, instead of just one or another species such as humans. There was no "tree of life" or hierarchy in this system. The most popular expression of animism in recent times is among existing Native American peoples.

ANTARCTICA   This continent occupies one-tenth of the earth's land surface, although its size fluctuates by up to 50 percent between summer and winter seasons. The environmental controversy over Antarctica lies in the potential for its having significant fuel and nonfuel resources buried deep beneath its frozen surface. The ecosystem is fragile; its untainted condition supports the world's most abundant penguin population, and its summer ozone hole threatens animal and plant life. Environmental groups from North America and around the world continue the fight to protect this pristine frozen wilderness. Several countries have proposed designating the continent of Antarctica as an International Park, thus ensuring its protection. (See also **OZONE DEPLETION**)

   In 1959, 16 countries committed themselves to managing the land for nuclear-free peaceful purposes and nondestructive scientific research by signing the Antarctic Treaty. Pressure by many countries that wanted to explore Antarctica's resource potential resulted in another agreement, called the Montreal Protocol. This agreement, signed in 1991, banned environmentally damaging exploration for 50 years.

Environmentalists fought against exploration for several reasons: oil rigs would be operating in perhaps the world's roughest waters; drifting icebergs could decimate drilling rigs; oil spills, if carried ashore, would destroy colonies of penguins, birds, and seals; spills would kill algae—the base of the marine food chain; and oil in cold water persists 100 times longer than it does in warm water.

While several of the world's nations promote the continent an international peace park, many more are determined to develop the resources of this last continent of "pure" wilderness.

ANTARCTIC TREATY (See **ANTARCTICA**)

ARAL SEA Once the fourth largest lake in the world by area, the Aral Sea has shrunk in size and become salinated because of withdrawals for irrigation combined with high evaporation rates. Located in the central Asian deserts of Uzbekistan and Kazakhstan its feeder rivers have been the Amu Darya and Syr Darya Rivers.

The environmental deterioration of the Aral Sea began after World War I when the newly formed Soviet Union decided to irrigate cotton with water from the sea's tributaries. Irrigation increased and more than doubled in the 1960, with completion of the Kara Kum Canal. This decreased flows in the Amu Darya and Syr Darya Rivers decreased by 90 percent with little water reaching the Aral Sea. By the early 1970s, water shortages were the norm, and by 1990, 40 percent of the surface area and two-thirds of the sea's water volume was lost. Surface water levels dropped and once thriving fishing villages found themselves 40 kilometers (25 miles) from the water's edge.

The Aral Sea's legacy is one example of how un-planned economic growth can cause irreparable environmental damage and, in the long run, the destruction of both environmental and socioeconomic welfare. Although climatic and other conditions differ, environmentalists in both Canada and the United States use the Aral Sea example to demonstrate how overuse of a resource base can have disastrous consequences. American scientists and environmentalists cite the Aral Sea as an example of what might happen if water is diverted from the Great Lakes to the American west where precipitation is scarce and aquifers are drying up. Proponents of this diversion argue that this water will sustain American farming and grazing interests in the years to come. (See also **WISE USE MOVEMENT**)

ARCTIC NATIONAL WILDLIFE REFUGE (ANWR) This refuge, containing more than 20 percent of all land in the U.S. National Wildlife Refuge System, has been an issue of heated debate since the latter part of the 1980s. Two million acres in the northeast corner of Alaska comprise the plain of the ANWR. In 1960, President Dwight D. Eisenhower established an 8-million-acre wildlife range; 20 years later, the area was expanded to 19 million acres. In 1980, the **Alaska National Interest Lands Con-servation Act** set aside 1.4 million acres of the coastal plain to investigate its resource potential. In addition, 90 percent of the northern slope had already opened to development. Although Canada protected its portion of the coast in 1984, resource extraction potential along the U.S. coast denied preservation.

Since 1985, oil companies have asked the U.S. federal government to allow oil development on the remaining 1.4-million-acre plain. Both Presidents Ronald Reagan and George Bush supported the proposal, although Congress prevented this activity. Conservationists have been pressuring Congress to designate the entire coastal plain as wilderness, permanently exempting the region from development.

A report by the U.S. Department of the Interior stated that, while there is less than a 50-percent chance of finding economically recoverable oil in the area, it would yield no more than a 200-day supply at U.S. consumption rates.

Conservationists warn that, while this ecosystem teems with diversity, it is extremely vulnerable to disruption. Due to cold temperatures, ecological regeneration is very slow and because of the condition of permafrost, virtually the entire coastal plain is classified as wetlands. Wildlife residents at the refuge include musk oxen, which were reintroduced after their extermination at the end of the nineteenth century; polar bears who hunt on the offshore ice and come ashore to dig winter dens; millions of waterfowl representing 130 species; and the porcupine caribou, which number about 180,000. The caribou migrate from northwest Canada's Brooks Range to the ANWR in late May to give birth to their young.

Protecting the calving ground is important to the native Gwitch-in and Athabaskan Indians. These peoples have subsisted on the caribou for generations and rely on the animal for food, clothing, and tools. At nearby Prudhoe Bay, which was developed for oil extraction, calving of the caribou has ceased and remnants of exploitation will be visible on the landscape for decades. Pollutants have also contaminated the ecosystem.

While oil development threatens the coastal plain, many elected leaders in the United States have fought against exploration and have offered methods of protecting the area. The Canadian government also made its objections known to the U.S. government. Bills have been introduced to raise automobile fuel efficiency, create incentives for alternative energies, and classify the ANWR as wilderness. In 1996 the Republican-controlled U.S. Congress succeeded in including the opening of ANWR in a budget bill but that bill was vetoed by President Bill Clinton. As of 1997, the stalemate which resulted in no oil development continued.

ARCTIC WATERS POLLUTION PREVENTION ACT (c.A-12, Volume I) This act, passed by the Canadian Parliament in 1970, but not put into effect until 1972, established a 100-mile pollution control zone in Arctic waters. Canada thus claimed jurisdiction, though not sovereignty, over the environmental regulation of the entire area. The act sets standards for ships entering these waters and asserts Canada's right to prevent the entrance of ships not meeting those standards. It also prohibits the deposition of any waste in Arctic waters. This attempt to control waters beyond its territorial sea, in what is considered by most countries to be international waters, is an example of Canada's assumption of the role of custodian of the world's environmental interests. It should be noted, however, that the United States does not recognize this law and views it as an illegal regulation of international waters.

ASWAN DAM Built in the early 1960s, this dam promised great economic benefits for Egypt by providing electricity to the city of Cairo. Many warned, however, that like large-scale hydroelectric dams in the United States, the project would do considerable ecological harm and that the negative effects of damming would greatly outweigh the benefits derived from it. Before the dam, the Nile would flood its banks each year in late summer and early fall and replenish Egyptian farmland with nutrients for cropland. The silt picked up by the flowing water was then deposited in the Mediterranean Sea where it fed phytoplankton, which comprise food for fish.

Soon after the dam was built, ecological problems arose: periodic flooding of farmland ceased so farmers imported nitrogen fertilizers; and the sardine fisheries of the eastern Mediterranean failed because of the absence of nutrient-rich silt. The dam caused the water level of Lake Nassar to rise to a level near the 3,000-year-old Ramses Temple at Abu Simbel. The temple was dismantled and moved to a site 200 feet above its original level—a very costly project. Other effects include a higher incidence of an often fatal disease, schistosomiasis, due to an increase in irrigation water with the disease-carrying snails. This project has often been used by U.S. environmental and others as a classic example of unplanned side effects of large-scale hydroelectric projects. (See also **JAMES BAY HYDROELECTRIC PROJECT**)

AUDUBON, JOHN JAMES (1785-1851)   Haitian-born as Jean Rabin, Audubon's name is most often associated with artistry and his appreciation of nature. Unlike other painters who photographed their subject or painted them in their natural setting, Audubon shot birds and animals and took the specimens back to his studio to paint. Nevertheless, this American artist and naturalist brought an appreciation of the animal world home to a public that would otherwise never have had the opportunity to witness many of the creatures that occupied North America. Future generations of Americans also came to appreciate animals that had become absent from the continent.

His most famous book, *Birds of America*, was finished in 1837 after hunting birds in the Florida bayous and keys beginning in 1820. Next he traveled across the continent and spent time at such places as Fort Union in Yellowstone where he collected specimens for *Quadrupeds of North America* (1854) in which he included 155 plates and descriptions.

Although he killed the subjects for his paintings, he was greatly disturbed by the wanton destruction of the North American wildlife and wild areas he witnessed. He complained that nature was disturbed wherever he went and lashed out at those who would destroy the natural world. The **Audubon Society**, founded in 1886, took its name from John James Audubon.

AUDUBON SOCIETY First originated in 1886 in New York, this organization was formed to stop poachers and commercial hunting of birds and wildlife. The society was started by a group of New York ornithologists, led by **George Bird Grinnell**, and expanded to include responsible hunters and conservationists. It was named after the nineteenth-century naturalist, **John James Audubon**. In its early years, this conservation organizaion campaigned against the use of bird feathers on women's hats. This crusade proved successful when, in 1913, a tariff law prohibited the importation of feathers.

Since its early years, the Audubon Society has pursued land management interests. It has launched battles against oil pollution on the seas and agricultural runoff pollution in rivers and lakes.

The Audubon Society became a national group in 1905. It now boasts over half a million members. The National Audubon Society, founded by 35 groups protesting the killing of plumed birds for use in hats, coalesced into one group. Still known best for its interest in preserving birds, other wildlife, and their habitat, the Audubon Society has branched out into a wide range of concerns that surround wildlife conservation. Conservative on the political spectrum among environmental groups, the society calls itself "The Voice of Reason." Programs to further its goals include nature education in its Audubon Nature Centers, maintaining sanctuaries for important wildlife, especially bird species, and litigation to protect endangered species and their habitat. Among the society's most notable achievements in its role as protector of bird species are the establishment of the first bird sanctuary, lobbying in favor of the ban on **DDT**, and passage of the **Migratory Bird Treaty**.

AUSTIN, MARY HUNTER (1868-1934)   An author of 30 books on feminism, mysticism, conservation, and "aesthetic patterns in the landscape" (Wild 1979, p. 82). In books such as *Land of Little Rain* (1903), Austin wrote about human responsibility for the land. Attaching her personal philosophy to action, she became a land preservation activist. She spoke of the ecological disaster that would result from diverting water from the Owens River valley to Los Angeles. She also witnessed the destruction of the native Inyo culture in the name of progress and taming nature in the American west.

In his book, *Pioneer Conservationists of Western America* (1979, Peter Wild offers that "Mary Hunter Austin prepared the way for **Aldo Leopold, Joseph Wood Krutch, Edward Abbey**, and others who have insisted that the time is well past to change the nation's exploitive ways. Such writers have moved the country to see the arid West with more appreciative eyes" (Wild 1979, p. 91).

B

BACON, FRANCIS (1561-1626)   Francis Bacon, English philosopher, is known as the father of modern science. He defined the inductive scientific method. This method, he said, sought to wrench the truths from nature. After these truths were discovered, humans would no longer stand in awe of an otherwise mystical world. He stated, "By careful study we uncover the secrets of Nature, which can then be used to control the material world" (Bowler 1993, p. 88). Some claim by stripping nature of its symbolic and divine qualities Bacon justified the right of humans to exploit nature since it was placed on earth for the use of man. Bacon paved the way for a mechanistic philosophy that was modeled on his method.

BANFF NATIONAL PARK Canada's first national park, established in 1885, is located in the Rocky Mountains 125 km west of Calgary. Originally created to preserve its sulfur hot springs for public use, its majestic peaks, glaciers, waterfalls, and spectacular wildlife make this the most frequently visited park in Canada.

BARTRAM, JOHN (1699-1777) Mid-18th-century U.S. botanist who, alongside his son **William Bartram,** undertook several descriptive scientific writings interpreting natural works of God. Bartram was a traveling botanist who established the first botanical garden in America which is now preserved in Philadelphia as a city park.

Although he generally had a romantic, appreciative view of the natural world, his descriptions were not without their ambivalence. Once, after traveling a great distance in the Appalachians, he described the mountains surrounding him as "dreary" and that perhaps the best condition for humans was in civilization.

BARTRAM, WILLIAM (1739-1823) Late-18th-century U.S. botanist who traveled throughout the southeast United States, interpreting natural works. Similar to his father **John Bartram,** he was seduced by sublime landscapes as he traveled and discovered many American natural wonders. For 4 years, beginning in 1773, he traveled 5,000 miles in the South, discovering and recording much of the natural wonders he encountered, including the Florida rivers, wild orange groves, swamps and lagoons, fish, snakes, reptiles, and especially birds. He also wrote about the Cherokee and Seminole cultures and rituals. These descriptions and others, contained in his *Travels*, remain some of the most accurate of that time period.

Through his writings, Bartram popularized botany and communicated his descriptions to Europe of American scenes. His enthusiastic renderings inspired such Europeans as William Wordsworth and Samuel Taylor Coleridge.

BENNETT, HUGH HAMMOND (1881-1960) Called the "father of soil conservation," Bennett was an early U.S. crusader for soil conservation. Working as a scientist in the Bureau of Soils, Bennett recognized that, while soils in the forests were soft and fertile loams, those that had been plowed several times were often clay textured with little topsoil. By 1918, he determined that hundreds of thousands of acres of fertile topsoil were lost each year to erosion caused by poor farming practices. In 1928, he wrote that, while many knew a problem existed, few recognized that erosion of the top few inches of soil could devastate the U.S. agricultural system. Bennett and W. R. Chapline noted specific areas where topsoil was completely eroded after taking thousands of years to form. On a national scale, they estimated that 15 million acres of once-fertile soil had been rendered useless for agriculture.

Bennett's warning went ignored, even through the early years of the 1930s Dust Bowl. He estimated that the annual cost of erosion in diminished productivity alone was at least $400 million. By 1935, the U.S. Congress created a permanent Soil Conservation Service in the Department of Agriculture under Bennett's direction. Bennett continued to proclaim the need for farmers to maintain soil fertility and a sufficient amount of topsoil by using various protection methods and for states to form their own soil conservation districts. Bennett's programs included some 147 demonstration projects containing 25,000-30,000 acres per project, in addition to soil-conservation nurseries, research stations, and Civilian Conservation Camps. More than 50,000 farmers requested assistance in soil conservation methods. Nonetheless, in 1947, Bennett noted that the country was losing 3 billion tons of soil each year to water and wind erosion. Bennett worked zealously for the protection of soils his entire career.

BERGER COMMISSION OF INQUIRY The discovery of large quantities of oil and gas off Alaska's north slope in the late 1960s brought about increasing pressure for development and for a pipeline to bring the oil to the lower 48 states and population centers in Canada. In 1973, a proposal was made by Arctic Gas to build a pipeline down the Mackenzie Valley in Canada. The prime minister asked Justice Thomas Berger to conduct an inquiry into this proposal. The Berger Commission of Inquiry into the Alaska Pipeline looked at both environmental considerations and aboriginal land claims issues. It recommended a 10-year moratorium on any construction activity leading to construction of the Alaskan pipeline. Berger is perhaps best remembered for his innovative public hearing process which took him to virtually every aboriginal village in the path of the proposed pipeline. This degree of public participation in decision-making has been cited as a model for other large-scale projects.

BERLIN MANDATE (See **UNITED NATIONS FRAMEWORK CONVENTION ON CLIMATE CHANGE)**

BERRY, THOMAS (1914-) U.S.-born ecotheologian, author, and cultural historian. A major late 20th-century contributor to the link between spirituality and ecology. Arguing that the universe is itself a sacred creation, Berry unites religions in a common valuing of the earth. In a work of particular significance, *The Dream of the Earth* (1988), Berry urges that we will continue to destroy the earth as long as we are under the illusion that we know what is best for the planet. He demands that we must learn to listen to the earth and recognize an earth answer to an earth problem. He coins the term *New Story,* which refers to the evolving scientific understanding of the cosmos set in a spiritual context. Just as science is defining the physical meaning of the cosmos, so the sacred story of the unfolding universe must be realized. The New Story requires a paradigm shift or consciousness transformations that will lead the human species into a sustainable relationship with the universe. The new "Ecozoic" era will then replace the current "Technozoic" era, which has sought to overcome the limits of the planet through technological inventions. In the Ecozoic era, guided by the New Story, an understanding of mutually enhancing human-earth relationships will be recognized.

BERRY, WENDELL (1934-) A 20th-century poet, novelist, writer, farmer, and ecotheologian, Wendell Berry is a native of Kentucky and spokesperson for conservation and sustainable agriculture. Two significant works, *The Gift of Good Land* (1981) and *The Unsettling of America* (1977), advocate a culture in which humans are earthly stewards. This requires a sustainable agricultural system that depletes neither soil quality nor people. Believing in the attainable harmony of nature, culture, and agriculture, he argues that when one of the three is disturbed, the others are necessarily harmed.

Berry promotes a culture of farmers not unlike the noble yeoman championed by Thomas Jefferson. Accordingly, good agriculture requires small, diverse farms, and diversity sustains ecological health and human lives. The good farms and farmers he has seen leads him to believe that ecologically and culturally responsible farming is possible. However, he fears that—with the disappearance of the family farm, fading public respect for the farmer, and dominance of industrial agriculture—society becomes less sustainable, a culture of agriculture becomes a fading dream, and sustainability becomes possible only in agrarian societies.

BHOPAL On December 2, 1984, the world's worst industrial accident happened in Bhopal, India, at the Union Carbide plant. The company manufactured pesticides with the deadly gas methyl isocyanate. A major leak occurred and resulted in an explosion. The explosion killed 2,500 people immediately, and about the same number died from aftereffects. An additional 20,000 persons were blinded, and the livers, kidneys, and nervous systems of 200,000 more were damaged.

In addition to the human lives that were lost, the gas leak contaminated water supplies and soils, causing widespread ecological damage. While the accident could have been prevented by spending approximately $1 million to improve plant safety, $570 million was spent in cleanup and lawsuits.

The enormity of this accident caused regulators in the United States to examine operations at a similar facility in West Virginia and focus more regulatory attention on hazardous chemical manufacturers.

BIERSTADT, ALBERT (1830-1902) Born in Dusseldorf, Germany, Bierstadt at the age of 2 moved to New Bedford, Massachusetts. His career as an artist did not begin until he was 20 years old when he began training in Dusseldorf. As his talents developed, he was most attracted to natural scenes and wilderness.

Bookchin believes that in order to dismantle this power structure, small, self-reliant, decentralized communities must become the norm. These communities would be democratic in form, with each member fully participating in community decisions and small-scale production.

By changing our antiecological society, there would be no need for further reliance on improving ecological technologies. In his 1962 book, *Our Synthetic Environment*, Bookchin wrote that modern technologies grow out of the corporate structure and are increasingly replacing the natural world with a "synthetic environment." We are shaping the earth and its processes to suit human needs, or more particularly, the needs of the marketplace. His view puts technology in the service of community and demands that technologies agree to ecologically sound principles based on nonpolluting energies.

BOONE AND CROCKETT CLUB (See **GRINNELL, GEORGE BIRD; ROOSEVELT, THEODORE**)

BOULDING, KENNETH (1910-1993) U.S. economist and social thinker who has engaged in research on peace, systems analysis, economic theory, economics and ethics, and environmental economics. Boulding coined the term "Spaceship Earth" to suggest that the planet is a closed system; it has a limited amount of resources that must be managed wisely. Exponential population growth would soon deplete the planet's resources for all passengers. Even the "first-class passengers," he pointed out, will suffer in the end as they are on the same spaceship as second-class passengers. He noted that the familiar photograph of Earth against the background of space transmits the reality that our planet is frail and vulnerable. In the 1960s, he was an early proponent of moving from our throwaway economy to a sustainable-earth economy.

Boulding thought that the late 20th-century challenge must be the abolishment of war. He referred to the technological destructive capacity of humanity and realized that war can no longer be an alternative to solving conflicts. He wrote:

It is a fundamental principle that what exists must be possible. Stable peace has existed now in many nations for at least 150 years. It must clearly be possible. In that, there is great hope for the human race and this incredibly beautiful planet." (Miller, G.T. 1992, p. 308)

BOUNDARY WATERS TREATY In the early 1900s problems involving water levels and water apportionment between the United States and Canada showed the need for a dispute resolution mechanism. In 1909, the United States and Great Britain (acting for a then not fully sovereign Canada) signed the Boundary Waters Treaty. Under this agreement, each country pledged that the boundary waters would not be polluted on either side to the injury of health or property of the other. The treaty was one of the most significant international agreements on the environment up to that time and served as a model of international environmental dispute resolution. It also established the **International Joint Commission** to control water-level disputes between the countries and prepare reports on environmental issues about which both countries needed information and/or advice.

BROWER, DAVID R. (1912-) Appointed as Executive Director of the **Sierra Club** in 1952, Brower served this office until 1969, when he became founder of the **Friends of the Earth** (1969), **League of Conservation Voters** (1970), and the **Earth Island Institute** (1982). As a promoter of sustainable and fair economies, Brower once stated:

> It is cruel to pretend that the world's developing countries can reach the standard of living of the world's wealthy countries. . . . It is also clear that the wealthy countries can no longer maintain their standards of living. So we have to do something else. We can learn to live lightly on the earth. (Miller, G.T. 1992, 7th ed., pp. 7-9)

In the mid-1950s, Brower was involved in preventing the **Echo Park Dam** in Dinosaur National Monument. Brower took pictures of the **Hetch Hetchy** Dam in the Yosemite Valley and contrasted these with the scenes of lush grasses, towering trees, and spectacular cliffs of Dinosaur National Monument. The photographs were then matched with pictures taken before the **Echo Park Dam** project. Brower further presented evidence that the Echo Park Reservoir, if constructed, would lose a great amount of water through evaporation and that there were more suitable sites for dam construction for the Colorado River Storage Project.

Brower also led a fight to prevent a dam on the Colorado River in the Grand Canyon. This time, Brower financed full-page ads in the *New York Times* and other national publications. His victory in this endeavor was punctuated by his ousting as Director of the Sierra Club when the board of directors determined he was too extreme for the group.

David Brower continues to write books and speak in the name of environmental preservation.

BROWN, LESTER R. (1934-) U.S. born president of the **Worldwatch Institute** and a prophet of the ecological catastrophe that looms on the horizon due to humanity's disregard for fundamental natural processes. In his various publications with Worldwatch, he keeps the public abreast of the declining quality of the natural environment: deserts expanding, soils eroding, wildlife and ozone disappearing, temperature rising, and life-support systems deteriorating. These trends have led Brown to the conclusion that we can no longer rely on future generations to solve our problems; rather, we have only a few years to reverse our path.

In 1984, he and the Worldwatch Institute started an annual publication entitled *State of the World,* which assesses pressing problems and issues of the day. This book is distributed worldwide, and is published 23 languages. In 1993, *State of the World* added a supplement called *Vital Signs,* which monitors worldwide trends in agricultural output, atmospheric conditions, economics, energy trends, etc. In his 1981 book, *Building a Sustainable Society*, Brown presented what he sees as the requirements of a society: one that satisfies current needs without jeopardizing those of future generations. In his coauthored book with Sandra Postel and Christopher Flavin, *Saving the Planet* (1991), he again addressed the issue of creating a world economy that sustains itself and the ecosystem it inhabits. The book prescribed redesigning energy, tax, and economic systems to be more harmonious with natural systems than the current throwaway culture.

BROWN'S FERRY NUCLEAR PLANT A nuclear power plant located on the Tennessee River near Decatur, Alabama. It was constructed by the Tennessee Valley Association to serve as a model power plant. Beginning operation in August 1974, it supplied electricity needs for up to two million people.

On March 22, 1975, two workers were repairing air leaks in the cable-spreader room through which cables passed into the reactor building. One of the repair checks required holding a lit candle to see if the flame flickered. While one worker was doing this, some polyurethane insulation around a cable caught fire even though local fire fighters arrived to douse the flames, the fire spread for seven-and-a-half hours. Still, nearly all of the plant's safety systems that were designed to bring cooling water to the reactor core were rendered inoperative. While there was no meltdown or serious injury, this event focused attention on the catastrophic effects that may ensue due to simple human errors.

BUCHAREST DECLARATION (See **DANUBE DELTA**)

BUENFIL, ALBERTO RUZ (1945-) A Mexican environmental activist whose book *Rainbows without Borders: Toward an Ecotopian Millennium* (1991) discusses alternative living and sustainable societies. He is the founder of Huehuecoytl, an intentional ecovillage in the mountains of Mexico.

BUNDESVERBAND FÜR BÜRGERINITIATIVEN FÜR UMWELTSCHUTZ (BBU) (See **FEDERAL ASSOCIATION FOR CITIZEN ACTION GROUPS FOR ENVIRONMENTAL PROTECTION**)

BURROUGHS, JOHN (1837-1921) Popularizer of natural history as a literary genre and champion of wilderness preservation. Burroughs teamed up with **John Muir** in their crusade to establish **Yosemite Park**. He became an early U.S. conservationist and was concerned about the power of humans to alter the environment for all creatures. He noted that, while other organisms have natural checks placed upon them by ecosystemic constraints such as climate ranges, predators, and parasites, humans have no such check. Accordingly, he argued against the dominant anthropocentrism shared by

most of American society as well as fellow conservationists. Due to his immersion into wild places and the
respect he developed for the natural world, in 1920 he
wrote, "creation is no more exclusively for [humans] than
for the least of living things" (Burroughs 1920, p. 32).

C

CALDICOTT, HELEN (1938-   )   Australian-born inter-
nationally acclaimed antinuclear activist, environmentalist,
author, and Nobel Peace Prize nominee. A pediatric
physician by training, she resigned in 1980 from Harvard
Medical School to devote her efforts to environmental
concerns, which included exposing what she described as
the lunacy of the U.S.-Soviet nuclear arms buildup. She
cofounded Physicians for Social Responsibility, Women's
Action for Nuclear Disarmament and International
Physicians to Save the Environment.

Her books, *Missile Envy* (1986), *Nuclear Madness*
(1994*)*, and *If You Love This Planet* (1992), are renowned
and continue to enjoy popularity. *If You Love This Planet*
called attention to the earth's declining life-support system
and its demise due to human activities. Although a
physician, Caldicott is committed to social activism,
arguing that like-minded thinkers must organize politically
to force corporations and governments to be accountable
for their actions. Caldicott uses both sound scientific
reasoning and compassion in arguing against the
destructive madness of nuclear capabilities.

CALIFORNIA CONDOR The largest bird in North America,
with a three-meter wingspan, the California condor was
once abundant throughout the western United States and
parts of Canada and Mexico. By 1900, its range had been

reduced to wild areas of the West, and its population had fallen significantly. As with many species, the condors' numbers declined because its adaptations were not compatible with humans: its habitats were destroyed; it was overhunted and poisoned; and its food source shrank. Additionally, as with most large birds, its reproduction rate was low; condors produce an egg every other year high on a rocky cliff or in a cavity of a large tree. Being extremely sensitive to humans, mothers often abandoned their nests if frightened by intruders.

By 1930, a sanctuary was established in the Sisquoc Canyon of the Los Padres National Forest near Los Angeles for the only six condors surviving in the wild. In 1986, lead poisoning suddenly claimed the lives of three and in April 1987, the last condor was captured and taken to the San Diego Zoo where it joined 26 other birds in captivity.

Many biologists argue that restoration efforts are fruitless with such a small gene pool. They argue that the $4 million spent on condors could be better used elsewhere. Even if the population numbers climbed, there are increasingly fewer available areas that can sustain this bird species.

CANADA/UNITED STATES AIR QUALITY AGREE-MENT In December 1990, one month after President George Bush signed the **Clean Air Act** amendments into law in the United States, the governments of Canada and the United States signed a bilateral air quality agreement. This agreement was the culmination a 10 years of discussion, debate, and disagreement between the two nations over the issue of acid rain. In signing the agreement both countries committed to supporting programs aimed at producing cleaner air through the reduction of sulfur oxides and nitrogen oxides, which are the precursors of **acid rain**. Fulfillment of this agreement is monitored by a committee of government representatives that issues reports biannually.

CANADA WATER ACT (c. C-11, Volume II) Because of the great power of provinces in Canada this act was an enabling rather than a regulatory piece of legislation. It authorized the minister of the environment to provide funds and research assistance to provinces and to help them reduce water pollution. It did not create countrywide regulations as did the **Clean Water Act** in the United States.

CANADA WILDLIFE ACT (c. W-9, Volume III) In Canada, proprietary ownership of wildlife rights belongs to the provinces. The federal government has jurisdiction over wildlife on federal lands and migratory animals. In 1973, the federal government passed the Canada Wildlife Act, which authorizes the Canadian Wildlife Service to engage in joint management programs with the provinces. This act provides a basis for migratory bird sanctuaries and national wildlife areas that today encompass about 1 percent of all Canadian lands.

CANADIAN COUNCIL OF MINISTERS OF THE ENVIRONMENT (CCME) In Canada, responsibility for many areas of environmental protection is in the hands of the provinces and not the federal government. This group, comprising the environmental ministers of each of Canada's 10 provinces and the Northwest Territories, grew out of the Canadian Council of Resource and Environment Ministers in 1988. The CCME fosters information exchange, consultation, and debate about environmental issues leading to cooperative federal-provincial initiatives. One of the more important tasks of the CCME is to help establish federal-provincial equivalency agreements for various pollutants as required under the **Canadian Environmental Protection Act.**

CANADIAN ENVIRONMENTAL ASSESSMENT ACT A law established in Canada in June 1992 that facilitates public participation in the environmental assessment of projects to be carried out by, or with the assistance of, the government of Canada. This act, like the **National Environmental Policy Act** in the United States, recognized that the activities of government are substantial contributors to environmental degradation. The requirement that an environmental impact statement be released before the implementation of any government project would at the least alert citizens to potential environmental harm. This act did not ensure that there would be no adverse environmental impact from government projects but did act as a "look before you leap" review.

CANADIAN ENVIRONMENTAL PROTECTION ACT (c. 10, 4th Supplement) A broad-ranging pollution prevention and abatement law. In 1987 it became clear to the government of Canada that the lack of federal jurisdiction in matters of water pollution and air pollution was creating environmental problems throughout the country. The government passed this act on the grounds that the presence of toxic substances was a national concern, that toxic substances were not always contained within provincial boundaries, and that Canada needed to fulfill international obligations. The act used the federal power of product regulation to regulate toxic substances, to establish nationally consistent levels of environmental quality, and to take proactive and remedial measures for environmental protection.

CANCER ALLEY (See **ENVIRONMENTAL JUSTICE**)

CAPRA, FRITJOF (1939-) A 20th-century U.S. theoretical physicist who writes extensively on human-earth relationships in books such as in *The Turning Point* (1982) and *The Tao of Physics* (1983). *The Tao of Physics* addresses parallel worldviews shared between Eastern mystics and Western physicists. The book outlined a way of viewing human-earth relationships that was much more harmonious and sustainable than the present dominant paradigm. Similarly, *The Turning Point* addressed the implications for "new physics" on impending cultural transformations.

Capra is explicit in stating that the only thing that separates humans from other species is their ability to develop a self-consciousness and reflect upon themselves. He believes that humans should see themselves as part of a whole—a life force with a reality different from its parts. Further, each species is unique—with its own attributes that stabilize the planet. In *Belonging to the Universe* (1991) a book coauthored with David Steindl-Rast, Capra stated that our species must overcome conventional theology and integrate a new theology of relatedness with other species and the earth. In a reinterpretation of the Old Testament, he stated that Adam and Eve were placed in Eden to tend the garden rather than dominate it. Capra believes that humans must realize that the earth is self-organized and has survived this way for billions of years; the garden did not need a caretaker, but because we have done it so much harm, it requires one now.

CARSON, RACHEL (1907-1964) U.S. author and biologist of the middle decades of the 20th century. Her best-known work, *Silent Spring*, written in 1962, warned about the overuse of pesticides; it made her a pioneer in the environmental movement. This book, along with other books such as *The Sea Around Us* (1951), were devoted to defending the natural world against environmental pollution produced by industrial society. Carson's writing suggested an urgency and immediacy to disasters that would befall the world if change did not begin soon.

In *Silent Spring*, Carson attributed the marked increase in cancer in the 20th century to be a result of all of the new combination of carcinogenic chemicals that enter the environment—in increasing amounts—each day. She argued that insecticides should properly be called "biocides" because they literally "kill life." At the same time, they are rendered ineffective by evolution as pests develop immunities to poisons. In fact, "destructive insects often undergo a 'flareback' or resurgence, after spraying, in numbers greater than before" (Carson 1962, p. 18). She recounts that one of the first uses of **DDT** was the wartime dusting of many thousands of soldiers, refugees, and prisoners to combat lice. The body stores it in fatty substances. Scarce residues on foodstuffs of any chlorinated hydrocarbon are potentially dangerous as it is stored. As more food is ingested, the DDT is magnified in body fat. Carson showed that, although DDT was a representative dangerous pesticide, its toxicity was no match for other deadlier chemicals such as Chlordane, Heptachlor, Dieldren, Aldrin, and Endrin.

While Carson exposed many of the misconceptions of irresponsible pesticide use, lawsuits by pesticide companies were threatened and later dropped after the companies were unable to disprove her claims. *Silent Spring* brought Carson the respect and recognition for the first of several works of proliferating literature that argued for environmental reform. She died in 1964 without knowing the impact that her writing would have on environmentalism. Many consider *Silent Spring* to be the beginning of the modern environmental movement and perhaps the most significant book on the environment in the 20th century.

CARTER, JIMMY (1924-) When Jimmy Carter was elected president of the United States in 1976, he told Americans that the country must conserve energy, protect resources, and preserve natural resources and land. These views were criticized by many who feared that such acts would sacrifice growth in the economy. Among Carter's accomplishments in office were the National Energy Policy Act, which decontrolled gas and petroleum, increased government research into alternative energies, and added environmental safeguards; the Surface Mining and Control Reclamation Act, which prevented industry from strip mining public lands and required mitigation of damages to lands; and **Superfund**, which helped to clean up hazardous waste sites.

Jimmy Carter also was responsible for the greatest single act of wilderness preservation in world history. On December 2, 1980, he signed the **Alaska National Interests Lands Conservation Act**. This historic legislation protected 104 million acres of Alaska. The National Wilderness Preservation System oversees 56 million acres of this land, tripling the amount of wilderness lands in the country.

CATLIN, GEORGE (1796-1872) U.S. artist of the American West and Native Americans and spokesperson for preservation. Catlin was an impetus for the idea of a national park and spoke of the need to intentionally preserve areas like **Yellowstone**. He reasoned that a national park, "containing man and beast, in all the wild[ness] and freshness of their nature's beauty," would preserve Indians, buffaloes, and wilderness as well as serve the benefits of "refined citizens and the world, in future ages!" (Catlin 1913, pp. 294-295). He considered

Native Americans a part of the natural landscape and foresaw the demise of this civilization that he so much appreciated.

Catlin studied and sketched natives during his summer excursions in 1929 and the early 1930s, and produced paintings in his studio in New York. He had a keen sense for recognizing the vital interrelation between the destruction of indigenous cultures and a vanishing landscape. His paintings presented Indians as part of the landscape rather than a dominant or distinguishing element. He equated the decline of the Native American population with the destruction of the buffalo. Most of his paintings were of Indians, and his works express the sympathy he felt toward their plight. Catlin wanted to rescue the history of these native cultures in his paintings before they had completely vanished.

CHAVEZ, CESAR (See UNITED FARM WORKERS)

CHERNOBYL On April 25, 1986, the worst nuclear power plant disaster in history rocked the Soviet Ukraine, sending radioactive debris and dust high enough in the air to encircle the planet. The accident occurred during a routine maintenance test in one of the reactors. The plant's engineers conducted a test to determine how long the turbine generators would produce electricity—after the normal electrical supply was interrupted—to run the water pumps, which are necessary to keep the reactor cool.

After the power levels were reduced, technicians disconnected power regulators and emergency cooling systems, which would have automatically shut off the reactor. Twenty-four hours later, the flow of steam to the turbine was halted, and the cooling pumps slowed, so very little coolant reached the core. In absence of emergency systems, a massive heat buildup in the reactor core triggered an uncontrolled chain reaction, and Unit

Number 4 reactor exploded. More radioactive material was released than in Hiroshima and Nagasaki, and fires inundated the area.

Some of the consequences of the disaster are that 375,000 people were forced to leaves their homes, 160,000 square kilometers (62,000 square miles) are still radioactive, and between 1985 and 1995 the number of cases of thyroid cancers increased 10 times, especially among children. The total cost of the accident is approximately $400 billion.

This event shook public confidence in the nuclear industry worldwide and prompted many countries with nuclear power, especially the United States, to question reliance on nuclear energy. Public support for nuclear power dropped sharply in North America and around the world following the Chernobyl accident.

CHIPCO MOVEMENT (See **BIODIVERSITY CRISIS**)

CHINA'S ONE-CHILD PROGRAM With 1.2 billion people in 1994, China contained one-fifth of all the world's people, and in that year produced 22 million newborns. Over centuries, China has experienced several population fluctuations, and their current one is a toward lower population growth. The last major decrease in growth resulted from the "Great Leap Forward" program in the 1950s, when 20 million starved to death.

Between 1950 and 1980, death rates dropped sharply and life expectancies were extended from 47 to 70 years. The most recent population boom of the 1960s is attributed to Chairman Mao Zedong's belief that wealth increased at a rate consistent with the size of the labor force. Mao's death in 1976 signaled a new era under Premier Deng Xiaoping who saw population growth as the most important obstacle retarding economic growth.

China has since adopted dramatic techniques to bring population under control by persuading married couples to have only one child. Birth control specialists and production teams monitor couples, give them free contraceptives and medical advice, and guarantee a secure job future for the child, while securing good housing for parents. Penalties for those who have more than one child include pay and service cuts and public reprimands.

While this program has had dramatic success in reducing growth, there are protests from those that argue that these policies are oppressive. Further, infanticide is thought to be common as male children are favored in families. In recent years China has eased its one-child mandate.

Many North Americans are concerned with China's growth and population policy for several reasons. What happens in China, with one-fifth of Earth's humans, will surely have great consequences. More people equates to increased energy use because coal, China's main energy source, has a high carbon content. China can alone significantly increase greenhouse gases in the atmosphere, leading to global warming.

Second, China's sheer number of people require vast amounts of resources. This demand may increase as the country industrializes further. This demand for resources will surely lead to habitat destruction with resultant declines in biodiversity.

Third, its one-child program and accusations of a high rate of infanticide have alarmed human rights groups in North America.

CITIZENS CLEARINGHOUSE FOR HAZARDOUS WASTE, INC. This organization was founded in 1981 by Lois Gibbs, a U.S. citizen activist who became an environmental leader following her involvement with the **Love Canal** toxic waste site in New York State. The organization compiles, condenses, and disseminates information on hazardous waste, so that the information might be used by local environmental groups and decision makers. It assists local activists in their fight against unwanted hazardous waste producers, including industrial plants, incinerators, and landfills. In its brief history, it has worked with over 8,000 communities to protect citizens from exposure to toxic waste.

CLEAN AIR ACT (CAA) (42 U.S.C. 7401 ET SEQ.) In 1970, the Clean Air Act amended the Air Quality Act of 1967. This legislation served to "protect and enhance the quality of the Nation's air resources so as to promote public health and welfare and the productive capacity of its population." The act set national primary air quality standards which defined levels of air quality necessary to protect public health and secondary ambient air quality standards to maintain visibility and protect crops, buildings, and water supplies. National ambient air quality standards were mandated for seven major pollutants: sulfur dioxide, carbon monoxide, particulates, hydrocarbons, nitrogen oxides, photochemical oxidants, and lead.

In 1977, amendments were added to recognize issues of serious deterioration of nonattainment areas, implement a concept of emission offset, encourage innovative control technologies, prevent industries from benefiting from noncompliance with requirements of the act, discourage the use of tall smokestacks as a mitigation technique, force federal facilities to comply with state pollution control requirements, and design guidelines for future **Environmental Protection Agency** standards.

The 1990 Clean Air Act Amendments contained several important provisions including: reducing CFC emissions by up to 50 percent by 1999; requiring industries to use best available technologies to reduce industrial emissions of toxic chemicals; requiring cities not meeting federal emissions standards for ozone to meet such standards between 1993 and 1999; reducing auto emissions of hydrocarbons and nitrogen oxides; requiring large diesel trucks and buses to cut emissions of particulate matter; requiring oil companies to sell cleaner burning gasoline in the 9 dirtiest cities by 1995, and to phase in the sale of alternative energy vehicles in California; and requiring coal-burning plants to cut annual sulfur dioxide and nitrogen oxide emissions. The amendents moved environmental regulation into a new era with a controversial provision that allowed companies to market emission quotas to reduce pollution in the most efficient and least costly way possible. This market approach to reducing pollution will no doubt serve as a model for future rewrites of other pollution legislation, including the **Clean Water Act**.

CLEAN AIR ACT (1971) (c. C-32, Volume II) Because of the great power of the provinces in Canada this act was a enabling rather than a regulatory piece of legislation. It authorized the minister of the environment to provide funds and research assistance to provinces and industries in order to reduce air pollution. It did not create countrywide regulations as did the **Clean Air Act** in the United States. This relatively weak act was replaced with the **Canadian Environmental Protection Act** in 1987.

CLEAN WATER ACT (CWA) (33 U.S.C. 1251 ET SEQ.) Passed in 1972 as the Federal Water Pollution Control Act, this act created the National Pollutant Discharge Elimination System (NPDES) and became the primary mechanism for water pollution control programs designed to eliminate the discharge of pollutants into navigable waters. It also set water quality goals to protect fish and wildlife while providing for recreation; prohibited discharge of toxic pollutants; constructed publicly owned waste-treatment facilities; established statewide water-treatment management plans; developed technologies to eliminate pollution discharge; and developed programs for controlling nonpoint sources of water pollution that cannot be traced back to a single direct source.

One provision of the act developed effluent standards for source-specific existing and new sources of water pollution. Each point discharger must receive a permit specifying the amount of each pollutant that a facility can discharge. The act required discharge permits based on best practical control technology to reduce pollution and set national goals of best available, economically achievable technology for toxic substances and zero discharge for priority toxic pollutants. Third, because of the act, by 1988 all municipalities had at least secondary sewage treatment due to the provision for state grants to aid them in developing pollution control programs.

The 1972 act was renamed the Clean Water Act of 1977; it was amended in 1981, and in 1987 it was amended further and renamed the Water Quality Act. Later amendments focus on controlling nonpoint source pollution, protecting wetlands and aquifer recharge areas, and allowing interested parties to sue polluters that exceed NPDES permits.

CLEMENTS, FREDERIC L. (1874-1945) U.S. pioneer in the study of grassland ecology on prairies. Along with Rosco Pound, he devised a method to characterize natural vegetation by marking off "quadrats," or squares, to define a sample of the vegetation for an area. These areas, often just one meter square, specifically defined every plant. This also allowed them to study succession by clearing a quadrat and then monitoring the succession of plant species that grew toward a "climax" community.

Clements went on to develop a philosophy of "dynamic ecology" that expressed the change and evolution of a landscape. Donald Worster noted that:

[Clements] also insisted stubbornly and vigorously on the notion that the natural landscape must eventually reach a vaguely final climax stage. Nature's course, he contended, is not an aimless wandering to and fro but a steady flow toward stability that can be exactly plotted by the scientist. (Worster 1994, p. 210)

This view has been criticized as it assumes that only one kind of community for each climatic region in the world is possible.

At the heart of Clements's paradigm was the view that a plant community was itself a superorganism and followed laws that transcended the individual organism. That is, the plant community itself grew, developed, and matured just like an individual organism. This holistic philosophy provided the impetus for regional prairie land management: after land was overtaxed by farming or other uses that caused degradation, it could restore itself if set aside for a period. The Dustbowl of the 1930s, however, cast doubt upon Clements's philosophy.

CLIMATE CONVENTION (1992) (See **GLOBAL WARMING**)

CLUB OF ROME A group of influential U.S. scientists and business leaders formed this group in 1972 to study the limits to economic growth. In 1972, it published a volume called **The Limits to Growth,** which presents models showing the world's resource use and how exponential population growth would tremendously outstrip its ability to sustain itself. The book was widely distributed around the world, selling over 9 million copies in 29 languages. It used mathematical models, developed at the Massachusetts Institute of Technology by Jay Forrester, Donella Meadows, Dennis Meadows, Jorgen Randers, and their associates, to project population trends, resource depletion, food supplies, and capital investments.

Five variables were analyzed: population, pollution, nonrenewable resource use, industrial output per capita, and food output per capita. Analyzing the interrelationships between these variables, the group concluded that, if present trends continue, the limits to physical growth on this planet would be reached within 100 years, resulting in worldwide economic and ecological collapse. This study set off an intense debate over the desirability of continual economic growth.

Twenty years later, in 1992, the study was updated in *Beyond the Limits: Confronting Global Collapse, Envisioning a Sustainable Future.* This study reaffirmed its earlier position and noted that some limits were already overshot. The developers of the model stressed that conclusions are projections rather than predictions. Thus, they recognized opportunities confronting our species today that would help us sustain our species and planet through the next century.

COALITION ON ACID RAIN This Canadian environmental nongovernmental organization (NGO), formed in 1980, lobbied in both Canada and the United States for pollution controls to stop **acid rain.** Like many environmental NGOs in Canada it received funding from the Department of the Environment. Its highly visible lobbying campaign in Washington, D.C., was unprecedented for a Canadian group. The activities of this group helped keep acid rain Canada's number-one environmental priority throughout the 1980s. The coalition's efforts also helped spread an awareness of Canadian concerns to Americans.

COLE, THOMAS (1801-1848) Cole's family moved from his birthplace in England to the upper Ohio River Valley in his 18th year. In 1825, he began painting the landscapes of the Catskill Mountains and became enthralled with his subject. Cole was a primary force behind the Hudson River School of painters—an unaffiliated group of artists who painted the wilderness of the eastern United States. His landscape paintings celebrated the magnificence of American nature as he illustrated both the sublime and the beautiful to express creation and revelation in some form. For Cole, the task of the artist was to reveal the hidden glory in the sublime and the sanctified.

Cole's paintings are largely a response to the ravages of man against nature. He wanted to preserve the wild on canvas because the picturesque in nature was being destroyed by civilization's overuse of resources. His 1836 series of paintings entitled "Course of the Empire" depicted various stages of a civilization, starting from discovery and settlement, progressing through a pastoral society to a thriving civilization with an apparent booming economy and a landscape donned with magnificent architecture. The series ends with scenes of a fragmented landscape and broken shards of buildings strewn across a deserted landscape. The last painting, however, shows the landscape returning to its original wilderness condition.

Thomas Cole remains one of the most celebrated landscape painter in U.S. history. Nonetheless, like many of his 19th-century romantic contemporaries, he continually expressed an ambivalence toward the natural world. He was simultaneously pulled by the cultural offerings of civilization and the natural beauties of wilderness.

COMMISSION FOR ENVIRONMENTAL COOPER-ATION (CEC) (See NORTH AMERICAN AGREE-MENT ON ENVIRONMENTAL COOPERATION)

COMMONER, BARRY (1917-) A prominent figure in the U.S. environmental movement beginning in the late 1960s. His book, *The Closing Circle* (1971), placed him among the familiar names in the movement. This study dealt with threats to ecosystems and human society. He discussed the impact of such pollutants as detergents, pesticides, and fertilizers on the then "dying" Lake Erie.

Commoner placed blame on the industrialized world in both *The Closing Circle* and *Making Peace with the Planet* (1990). For example, the United States with only 5 percent of the world's population uses more than one-third of the planet's resources and contributes pollution at about the same level as resource consumption. He pointed out that industries produced synthetic products that destroy and persist in ecosystems and require a heavy dependence on artificial energy. To solve these and other environmental problems, he prescribed a concerted approach to deal with science, politics, the private sector, public policy, and individual rights.

COMPREHENSIVE ENVIRONMENTAL RESPONSE, COMPENSATION AND LIABILITY ACT (CERCLA) (42 U.S.C. 9601 ET SEQ.) This 1980 act amended the Solid Waste Disposal Act by inventorying inactive hazardous waste sites, protecting the public from such sites, and responding to negligent hazardous waste disposal practices. Also known as "Superfund," this law and its amendments in 1986 and 1990, responded to the release of hazardous waste by establishing a Hazardous Substance Superfund, funded by U.S. federal and state governments and taxes on chemical and petrochemical industries. Monies are used to clean up contaminated sites and pay for property damage. The act also established regulations controlling inactive hazardous waste sites by making liable parties financially and legally responsible to pay up to three times the cleanup costs. Further, a national inventory of hazardous waste sites is conducted.

It is generally recognized that the cost of cleanup has been far greater than anticipated. Superfund was first established as a $1.6 billion pool, and was raised to $9.6 billion in 1986. Nonetheless, by 1989, the Environmental Protection Agency estimated that more than 32,000 sites were in need of remediation, while the General Accounting Office put the number of sites between 103,000 and 425,000. By 1992, EPA estimated the cost of cleaning up Superfund sites at $77 billion. Emergency cleanup had to be carried out at virtually all 1,300 priority sites by 1995, but only 56 sites were cleaned up enough to be removed from the priorities list. Environmentalists and industry both agreed more money must be spent on actual cleanup and less on litigation. (See also **SUPERFUND AMENDMENTS AND REAUTHORIZATION ACT**)

CONFERENCE OF THE PARTIES TO THE UNITED NATIONS FRAMEWORK CONVENTION ON CLIMATE CHANGE (See **UNITED NATIONS FRAMEWORK CONVENTION ON CLIMATE CHANGE**)

CONSERVATION FOUNDATION   (See **WORLD WILDLIFE FUND**)

CONSERVATION INTERNATIONAL   Headquartered in Washington, D.C., this conservation organization founded in 1987, conducts its projects in 20 countries around the world. It couples ecosystem preservation activities with support for sustainable community-based development. The most publicized of the group's activities was orchestration of the first "debt-for-nature" swap by purchasing part of Bolivia's national debt in exchange for protection of Amazon wilderness. It has duplicated debt-for-nature swaps in at least 7 other countries and has also helped to establish biosphere reserves in several countries. Conservation International is hoping to be the catalyst for another innovative agreement, specifically profit-sharing ventures between tropical countries and pharmaceutical companies who are interested in medicinal plants.

CONVENTION ON INTERNATIONAL TRADE IN ENDANGERED SPECIES OF WILD FAUNA AND FLORA (CITES) In 1975, 81 nations signed the CITES, thereby prohibiting trade of endangered species or their products. Since 1975, many other countries have signed and it had 124 signatories as of 1995. In January 1990, 119 nations banned international trade of African elephant products. CITES regulates international trade of 675 species of animals and plants whose survival is threatened by trade. Permits are granted if trade will not be detrimental to the survival of the species. While this law sounds stringent on paper, endangered species trade continues due to the difficulty of checking what leaves and enters countries. The **World Wildlife Fund** estimates that illegal trade amounts to $2 to $5 billion annually.

In the United States, the **Endangered Species Act** is the implementing legislation for CITES. Enforcement authorities are distributed among the **Fish and Wildlife Service**, the Animal and Plant Health Inspection Service in the Department of Agriculture, the National Marine Fisheries Service in the Department of Commerce, and the Customs Service in the Department of the Treasury.

COOPERATIVE EDUCATION AND INTERNSHIP PROGRAM (CEIP) FUND This organization, founded in 1972, provides linkages between the environmental community and the business community by placing qualified applicants in paid environmental internships in a wide variety of employment areas. Sponsors of CEIP internships range from Fortune 500 companies (IBM, Chrysler) to government agencies, and nonprofit environmental groups. The group also sponsors environmental education activities, which include seminars, workshops, publications, and so on. Since its founding, the CEIP Fund has placed over 4,000 individuals in paid professional opportunities.

COUNCIL ON ENVIRONMENTAL QUALITY (CEQ) This council in the U.S. government's executive branch was created by the **National Environmental Policy Act** of 1970. Its duties were to "formulate and recommend national policies to promote the improvement of environmental quality." The council has no regulatory function but rather advises the president on environmental matters. The CEQ is also mandated to publish an annual Environmental Quality Report on the state of the environment. An active CEQ produced many useful reports in the 1970s but was reduced by over 80 percent by President Ronald Reagan, and only partially restored by President George Bush. The Clinton administration proposed replacing the CEQ with a White House Office of Environmental Policy, but this proposal was withdrawn after complaints by key congressmen. The CEQ continues to exist, maintaining its important function of preparing regulations and offering guidance to government agencies for the preparation of environmental impact statements.

COUSTEAU SOCIETY Founded by Jacques-Yves Cousteau in 1973, the 150,000-member Cousteau Society is a leader in marine research and education. The society is best known for the production of award-winning films that focus on the marine environment. The society also sponsors field study programs and education centers, and produces two publications—Dolphin Log and Calypso Log—to further its educational mission. In addition to its educational activities, the group also conducts marine research around the world.

CUYAHOGA RIVER In the late 1960s, a few highly visible pollution episodes in the United States helped to galvanize public opinion about the need to address environmental issues. One of the most dramatic was the burning of the Cuyahoga River, which runs through Cleveland, Ohio. The concentration of phenols and oil pollution in the river reached levels high enough to allow the river to catch fire and burn for 8 days in 1969. Two bridges over the river burned, and flames reached heights of 5 stories. The media attention to this event triggered a demand for improved water quality, which eventually led to the passage of the Clean Water Act (then called the Federal Water Pollution Control Act) of 1972.

D

DALY, HERMAN E. (1938-) Twentieth-century environmental economist and senior environmental economist at the World Bank who is credited with bringing the discussion of "sustainable economy" to the public. He characterizes a steady-state economy as one which maintains a constant amount of people and physical wealth and is sustained by a low rate of throughput of matter and energy.

In *For the Common Good: Redirecting the Economy Toward Community, the Environment, and a Sustainable Future* (1989), cowritten with John B. Cobb Jr., Daly introduced the term "index of sustainable economic welfare" (ISEW) to address shortcomings in the Gross National Product as a measure of wealth and economic well-being. GNP, he argued, should be renamed gross national cost (GNC) because it is based on the cost of taking resources from the environment and through pollution and overuse, destroying the quality of resources. While GNP increases are viewed favorably by most economists and politicians, Daly argued that the quality of life had decreased. The ISEW demonstrated that, since 1976, the well-being of life in the United States had decreased, declining 12 percent between 1977 and 1988. To progress toward a sustainable economy, the physical and ecological limits of the planet's resources must be realized.

These required economic changes can come about through a concerted effort by professionals of many disciplines: natural and physical scientists to develop technologies conforming to limits; social scientists to reform unsustainable social institutions; and philosophers, theologians, and educators to stress the once-cherished values of stewardship and distributive justice.

DDT (See DICHLORODIPHENYL TRICHLOROETHANE)

DEBT-FOR-NATURE SWAPS An idea proposed by Thomas Lovejoy, U.S. biologist and former assistant secretary of the Smithsonian Institution, in 1984 to link environmental protection with debt owed by lesser developed countries. If a country's debt is relieved, the country in turn agrees to fund preservation and/or social programs.

Swaps work as follows: the debtor country owes a debt to another country or bank. An international nongovernmental organization, or NGO, such as the **Nature Conservancy, World Wildlife Fund,** or **Conservation International,** purchases the debt at a significant discount. For example, if a country is owed $15 million, which it doubts will be repaid, it sells the debt to the NGO for $5 million. The debt is forgiven, and the debtor and the NGO enter into an agreement that a certain number of acres will receive protection.

The three international NGOs listed above have participated in these swaps. Debt-for-nature swaps have worked successfully for debts owed by Bolivia, Ecuador, Costa Rica, and the Philippines. While this idea will not solve all the problems associated with the **biodiversity crisis**, it surely helps.

DEEP ECOLOGY A philosophical view first articulated by Norwegian philosopher **Arne Naess** in 1972 and later expanded into a cornerstone of the green movement by **Bill Devall** and **George Sessions** in their 1985 book *Deep Ecology*. The view centers on the importance of all living organisms. This biocentric view holds that natural areas must be preserved, not for any utilitarian value but for their intrinsic value. This view is in sharp contrast to the actions of many environmental groups who, deep ecologists would argue, are only concerned with minimizing negative environmental consequences and without radical rethinking of the real problems. Deep ecologists would view actions to reduce air pollution or build more environmentally benign waste disposal facilities as shallow ecology. Deep ecology is closely associated with bioregionalism, which stresses a return to a simpler life centered in a self-sufficient region.

DEFENDERS OF WILDLIFE This U.S. group, founded in 1947 as the Defenders of Furbearers, broadened its mission and changed its name to include all wildlife. Its focus is on the preservation of habitat, predator protection, and appreciation of wildlife. It uses education, and when necessary, litigation to achieve its goals. Although maintaining a Washington, D.C., office, some of its best-known work has been crafted by its field offices located in the western United States. Recent victories for the organization include a compromise program to couple wolf protection with incentives for western ranchers, who might be threatened by the reintroduction of the wolf.

DEPARTMENT OF THE ENVIRONMENT, CANADA (DOE) This Canadian federal agency was formed in 1971. It includes the Atmospheric Science Service; the Environmental Protection Service; the Land, Forest, and Wildlife Service; the Water Management Service; the Policy, Planning and Research Service; and the Finance and Administration Service. This department has regulatory authority like the Environmental Protection Agency in the United States, but, in addition, it is responsible for larger questions of integrated resource management. Because of the much greater power of Canadian provinces compared to states in the United States, the powers of the DOE are more limited. The effectiveness of this department has been further hampered by the high turnover rate of leadership; the DOE has had 16 different ministers during the period 1971-1993.

DEVALL, BILL (1938-) U.S. environmentalist, sociologist, and activist who has worked with **Earth First!** and the **Sierra Club**. His research has examined several aspects of the environmental movement, including its philosophical and psychological motivations, as well as its relationship to politics and social movements. His book, *Deep Ecology*, coauthored with **George Sessions** in 1985, brought Devall to the forefront of U.S. environmentalism and environmental philosophy. The authors stated that deep ecology:

> attempts to articulate a comprehensive religious and philosophical worldview. The foundations of

deep ecology are the basic intuitions and experiencing of ourselves and Nature which comprise the ecological consciousness. For deep ecology, the study of our place in the earth household includes the study of ourselves as part of the organic whole. (Sessions and Devall 1985, p. 65)

Devall argued against reform environmentalism that operates in the dominant social paradigm and supports deep ecology, which rejects the dominant paradigm of human dominance, appreciates the intrinsic worth of nature, and is committed to biocentric equality.

Devall and Sessions recognized two fundamental norms embraced by deep ecology: biocentric egalitarianism and self-realization. Biocentric egalitarianism maintains that all living things, including rivers, mountains, and ecosystems, have equal intrinsic value. Self-realization is defined in wider circles than the individual self or ego. In their context, the term refers to an identification of the individual with the rest of the human and nonhuman world. It transcends cultural definitions of self and integrates the individual with the universe. (See also **EARTH FIRST!; SIERRA CLUB**)

DEVOTO, BERNARD (1897-1955) Mid 20th-century U.S. conservationist and writer of western history. Bernard DeVoto was ushered in to the conservation movement while an English professor at Northwestern and Harvard. In fact, his books, *The Year of Decision: 1846* (1943), *Across the Wide Missouri* (1947), and *The Course of the Empire* (1952), helped to establish western U.S. history as its own discipline. His writings praised the pioneer and natural beauty of western wilderness, but dismissed the rugged individualist and romantic cowboy notions that westerners bestowed upon themselves.

His praise of the West was tied to a conservationist philosophy. He warned of overgrazing rangelands, clear-cutting forests, and strip mining unspoiled lands. He wrote that, like easterners, westerners were controlled by greed and profit. He pleaded with citizens to reject the proclamations of big business and politicians who sought to destroy the natural resources that made the West a paradise.

As a result of his views, he was asked to sit on the advisory board for national parks. His articles in the *Saturday Evening Post, Reader's Digest, Colliers,* and *Fortune* drew criticism from developers who pressured magazines to stop publishing his articles. This only invigorated DeVoto to go on to publish 40 articles aimed at convincing the U.S. Congress to withdraw lands from the private sector. DeVoto's death in 1955 weakened the voice of public lands conservation.

DICHLORODIPHENYL TRICHLOROETHANE (DDT)

DDT is a synthetic, chlorinated hydrocarbon insecticide that is highly toxic. It has been found in high concentrations in nursing mothers and causes disorders in the nervous system. It is also both carcinogenic and mutagenic.

Brig. Gen. James S. Simmons, U.S. Army, applauded the capabilities of DDT in its control of the spread of malaria among U.S. soldiers and its assistance in relief of insect damage to U.S. farms. The chemical was, in fact, responsible for saving millions of lives in the tropics as it effectively eliminated mosquitoes carrying malaria. Upon the discovery in 1939 by entomologist Paul Mueller that it was a potent insecticide (winning him the Nobel Peace Prize in 1948), DDT was considered a miracle chemical promising to rid farmers of insect problems. It appeared to be the perfect chemical: low cost, effective, persistent, and with broad killing capacity. These attributes cause the chemical to be an environmental threat that Americans still confront.

From the 1940s through the 1960s, an estimated 4 billion pounds of DDT was used. In the late fifties, speculations were raised about its danger to birds in concentrated spray areas. For example, a population of 1,000 pairs of western grebes at Clear Lake, California, in 1948 ceased to exist as a breeding population by 1954. Besides causing thinning egg shells in birds like the American bald eagle and the peregrine falcon, scientists found that DDT biomagnified up the food chain. When dumped into a lake to control a gnat population, DDT was found in concentrations of 14 ppm in algae and up to 1,600 ppm in birds.

The battle to ban DDT in the United States was one of the earliest and most significant victories of the modern environmental movement. **Rachel Carson**, in *Silent Spring* (1962), raised serious questions about the chemical's safety and charged that DDT and other pesticides were responsible for the destruction of wildlife and humans. The chemical was banned in 1972 for use in the United States, but there is approximately one billion pounds of DDT remaining in the biosphere. Because it is persistent and bioaccumulates, the residue in the biosphere is a continuing environmental threat to life forms of all kinds.

Even though the United States has banned DDT from its own farms, the country continues to manufacture and distribute it to other countries. When the United States imports produce from other countries, the chemical returns and Americans ingest it as residue on the food.

DOUGLAS, WILLIAM O. (1898-1980) A speaker and activist for the rights of the underprivileged, Supreme Court Justice William O. Douglas stood for the defense of the U.S. environment. In the early 20th century, his ideas of "equal rights for nature" were considered un-American by developers, and radical to many Americans. He viewed the wilderness as a place of kindness that improved one's health and strength while the city represented all that was negative about people. Douglas's father died when he was six, leaving the family to live in poverty. Douglas contracted polio early in his life. These setbacks challenged him and cultivated a sense of kinship with others of a like kind; he never abandoned the rights of the less fortunate, stating "he who has a long purse will always have a lawyer, while the indigent will be without one" (Wild 1979, p. 143). Early in his life, Douglas viewed poverty-stricken people similarly to the natural world, arguing that neither were given the equal voice they deserved.

In spite of his accomplishments in the U.S. justice system, Douglas never lost his craving for contact with the mountains. With dismay, he saw his source of nourishment destroyed by dams, highways, and clear-cut forests. He painstakingly saw that "the public domain was up for grabs and its riches were being dispersed by the federal bureaucracy to a favored few" (ibid., p. 146). He fought against future development with the same vengeance that he fought for civil rights. His books celebrated the natural abundance of the country and the unpardonable sin of its destruction. More notable among his 25 books are *A Wilderness Bill of Rights* (1965) and *Farewell to Texas: A Vanishing Wilderness* (1967). While his Washington colleagues scoffed at his outspoken activism, he marched in protest with other environmentalists; he spoke against damming the Columbia River; he lashed out at the **Fish and Wildlife Service** for its plans to poison fish in the Wind River; and he criticized the **National Park Service** for its design to build communities in **Yellowstone**.

Douglas's most effective defense of the environment was delivered from his position as Supreme Court justice. In *Sierra Club v. Morton,* he rekindled the philosophy of Aldo Leopold's "Land Ethic," stating that organisms are endowed with rights just as humans. Like **Aldo Leopold,** Douglas argued for the extension of rights to the land just as, over the years, rights were extended to women and other races. He argued that the **Sierra Club** should have standing in court as the legal spokesman for the environment.

Douglas retired from the Court in 1975, giving the environmental movement momentum and ideas on which to base future arguments in defense of nature.

DUBOS, RENE (1900-1982) Dubos's contributions to the U.S. environmental movement are ambiguous, but significant. Although he died in 1982, his call to "think globally, act locally" remains an important and familiar adage of contemporary environmental concerns. A microbiologist by training, Dubos led the way in developing antibiotic drugs. He also carefully prescribed their use as he believed that complete mastery over microorganisms could have catastrophic ecosystemic results. As an ecologist, he championed the idea of human modification of nature through a careful process that respects earth processes. He stated that when humans began agricultural societies, some 10,000 years ago, they forever severed their relationship to the biological world and that appreciation of nature since then has been purely intellectual.

Writing in 1976 in an article entitled "Symbiosis Between the Earth and Humankind," Dubos averred that wilderness may not be the best condition for humanity; rather, a gardenlike environment carved out by proper technology would be the best condition for people. He refers to the modified landscape of northern France and other parts of Europe to be works of art. In such an environment, soils can be made more fertile, and aesthetically pleasing plants and animals could thrive in an unpolluted system of clean air and water, while renewable resources support a sustainable community.

Dubos is not without qualification of this thesis. In *Only One Earth* (1972*)*, which he coauthored with Barbara Ward, he wrote that humans "may find the wilderness a great teacher of the kind of planetary modest man most needs if his human order is to survive" (Dubos and Ward 1972, p. 114). Thus, he promotes both wilderness to nourish the human spirit as well as modified landscapes without destroying the physical and biological foundation that supports society to satisfy human needs. He distanced himself from "crude" anthropocentrism, which holds that humans are the center of value in the universe, from what he called "enlightened anthropocentrism," which acknowledges that, in the long run, human good and planetary good coincided with one another. He recognized the ability of humans to alter severely the life-support system of the planet when he wrote:

> This is the hinge of history at which we stand, the door of the future opening onto a crisis more sudden, more global, more inescapable and more bewildering than any ever encountered by the human species and one which will take decisive shape in the lifespan of children already born. (Ibid., p. 12)

DUCKS UNLIMITED A North American conservation group that began in 1937. It holds that protecting wetlands and waterfowl resources is a moral imperative. The motivation of the founders was to protect waterfowl resources primarily to provide ample hunting opportunities. Its achievements are significant as a conservation organization. For instance, by 1996, it protected 7.35 million acres of waterfowl habitat across the United States, Canada, and Mexico and restored 397.298 acres of waterfowl habitat across the continent.

The organization boasts more than 35,000 volunteers and maintains full-service regional offices staffed by biologists, engineers, and fund-raisers in Sacramento, California; Bismarck, North Dakota; and Jackson, Mississippi. Additional offices are located in South Carolina, New Jersey, Minnesota, New England, and Washington, D.C. The organization integrates volunteers, staff, and public and private supporters.

Ducks Unlimited is one of the world's foremost wetlands and wildlife conservation organizations, protecting more than 600 species of wetland-dependent wildlife, as well as 250 endangered or threatened species of wildlife, fish, and plants throughout North America.

E

EARTH DAY In 1970 U.S. Senator Gaylord Nelson proposed a day be set aside to celebrate the earth and protest the despoliation of the earth's environment. During that first Earth Day, held on April 22, 1970, about 20 million Americans in 2,000 communities took to the streets to demand better environmental quality. This event has been celebrated in late April ever since and now involves people throughout the world. **Denis Hayes**, an Earth Day organizer, estimates that over 200 million people in 140 countries participated in Earth Day 1990, the 20th anniversary of this celebration. Earth Day has helped keep environmental issues before the people of the world and, thus, plays an important role in raising environmental consciousness.

EARTH FIRST!   One of the most militant environmental groups that supports a variety of nonviolent actions including civil disobedience. Although "founded" in 1980 by **David Foreman**, the group is more of a movement than an organization. It has no membership, no president, and no paid leadership. The guiding principle of Earth First! is biocentrism—defending the intrinsic value of natural systems over human activities that disrupt these systems. Earth First! not only supports existing wilderness and opposes new dams, but wants to create new wilderness by closing existing roads, and creating new free-flowing rivers by removing existing dams. Although individual groups of Earth First! are autonomous, some task forces within the organization include the Rainforest Action Group, A Biodiversity Project, an Overgrazing Task Force, and an Off Road Vehicle Task Force.

The militant activities of Earth First! are claimed to be inspired by *The Monkey Wrench Gang* by **Edward Abbey** and are thus known as monkeywrenching.

EARTH IN THE BALANCE (See GORE, ALBERT)

EARTH ISLAND INSTITUTE Founded by **David Brower** in 1982, after he left both the **Sierra Club** and the **Friends of the Earth**. This group was founded to be in the vanguard of new conservation programs and to link conservation issues to issues of human rights and economic improvement for Third World countries. The institute funds small short-term programs for preservation and restoration of key habitats around the world. While a spin-off group, the Earth Island Action Group, focuses on legislative advocacy, the **Earth Island Institute** works toward project implementation to bring about progress in the area of environmental protection and human rights. Among its projects are sponsorship of conferences on The Fate of the Earth, the Japan Environmental Exchange to sponsor exchanges of environmentalists between the United States and Japan, and the Environment Project on Central America.

EARTH SUMMIT (See **UNITED NATIONS CONFERENCE ON ENVIRONMENT AND DEVELOPMENT**

ECHO PARK DAM A proposed dam brought into the arena of environmental controversy in 1950. The proposal by the Army Corps of Engineers was to dam the Green River at Echo Park in the 320-square-mile Dinosaur National Monument on the Colorado-Utah border. The monument received its name after dinosaur fossils were discovered in the area. The proposed Echo Park Dam was part of a ten-dam Colorado Storage project. The project sought to provide a steady and reliable source of water for the western United States.

An effective environmental campaign was launched against the project by **David Brower** and the **Sierra Club, the Wilderness Society,** and many other groups and individuals. They reasoned that, if a dam was permitted to be constructed at this national monument, which had virtually the same protection as a National Park, there was nothing to stop further development projects on other protected lands. Against this constituency, a coalition of politicians, developers, and chambers of commerce promoted the realization of the "American Dream" in the West.

As a result of the preservationists efforts, which included tactics such as taking out full-page ads in the *New York Times* to encourage people to write to their senators and voice opposition to the projects, the dam was taken out of the project bill, which became law in April 1956.

ECOFEMINISM   An alternative perspective in viewing human-earth relations. Although a school of thought embracing liberal feminism, marxist feminism, radical feminism, and socialist feminism, ecofeminism itself and these other perspectives share certain common themes. First, the destruction of the earth is a result of patriarchal and androcentric values and institutions. Second, the earth is feminine, i.e., a nurturing Mother Earth that should be loved and respected. Third, sustainable solutions to environmental malaise will not be realized until interdependencies in the natural world are embraced and androcentric concepts and institutions are discarded.

Elizabeth Dodson Gray suggests that, in place of a hierarchical society, ecofeminism emphasizes complementary and symbiotic relationships between men and women, humans and nonhumans, and culture and nature. She calls for a new religious covenant that rejects dualism and the fragmented reality it creates, and instead celebrates harmony, wholeness, diversity, and interconnectedness. Ynestra King, among others, writes that the domination of nature and women are mutually reinforcing. (See also **MERCHANT, CAROLYN**)

ECOLOGICAL RESTORATION   A movement begun in the United States in the late 1970s by Steve Packard. Packard discovered a prairie remnant in the Chicago although the landscape was dominated by opportunistic species and covered with trash. He organized a volunteer group to restore the prairie species. Since that time, ecological restoration of native biodiversity has spread throughout the continent. Academics, as well as citizen groups, who draw from a wide constituency have contributed time and effort toward research of various methods to restore damaged ecosystems.

ECONET One of the first sophisticated computer networks dedicated to the interests of the environmental community. The Institute for Global Communications operates this system, which allows individuals with access to a computer and a modem to communicate with people with similar interests around the world. Individuals must pay a modest fee to the Institute for Global Communications to acquire an Econet I.D. number.

ECOSOLAR A group that began in 1990 to plan for sustainable development and protection of sea turtle habitat in and around Oaxaca, Mexico. Prior to this time, turtle slaughterhouses and foreign businesses dominated the economic life of this community. Just two years after its founding, this small group performed a detailed environmental land-use plan of the area, began to promote Mazunte as an area for ecotourism, helped to establish native housing and businesses, and led the way in establishing low-impact technologies and the use of local materials, workers, and enterprises to promote environmental restoration and preservation. (See also **MAZUNTE, MEXICO**)

ECOSOPHY (See **NAESS, ARNE**)

ECOTOURISM William P. Cunningham defined ecotourism as:

> a combination of adventure, travel, nature appreciation, and cultural exploration in wild settings that appeal to those who want something more exciting and intellectually stimulating than simply basking on a beach. (1994, p. 187)

Ecotourism has become a multibillion-dollar industry around the world. Most often, tourists from the industrialized world visit a region of native culture (often in tropical rain forest areas) and spend their time hiking, photographing nature, canoeing, camping, enjoying wildlife safaris, and learning about other cultures—their arts, customs, and relationships with the land. Afterward, they often return home with native artworks, clothing, and souvenirs.

The revenues that are generated from tourists can then be used for land protection. Instead of indigenous people cutting forests to sustain their lives, they host tourists at a much more profitable rate. Wildlife is also protected in this enterprise. One wildlife biologist estimated that a hunted lion generates $8,500 if shot in Kenya's Amboseli National Park, while preserving one lion for ecotourists is worth $515,000.

While ecotourism appears to be a win-win situation for natives, tourists, and natural areas, it is nonetheless controversial. Visitors often have negative effects on native culture. Their purchases often deplete natural resources; in Nepal, for example, visitors overuse firewood for camping and have created a fuel-wood shortage for natives. In some areas, facilities for tourists may adversely affect the ecosystem the tourists come to visit.

Thus, while ecotourism bolds the potential to aid in habitat preservation, if not done carefully it could also destroy the very resource that attracts the ecotourist.

EHRLICH, PAUL (1932-   ) Ehrlich, a population biologist born in Philadelphia, Pennsylvania, taught most of his life at Stanford University in California. He has written numerous books on biology, ecology, and the environment, and coauthored, with his wife, Anne, the controversial *The Population Bomb*. Published in 1968, this book has sold more than 20 million copies. Since that time, he has been in the center of debates on global warming, biodiversity, nuclear winter, and other environmental topics. Many of Ehrlich's critics point to him as one of the doomsday sayers of the environmental movement, and note that many of his dire predictions of overpopulation have never come to pass. He responded to this criticism with *The Population Explosion* (1968) which points out that, in addition to overpopulation problems, we must contend with industrial pollutants causing ozone depletion and global warming, and, in spite of an increase in agricultural output, the world's rain forests are being destroyed at unprecedented rates. In sum, Ehrlich argued that the root of environmental problems are in overpopulation multiplied by excessive resource consumption and pollutants from using these resources.

Paul Ehrlich has been in the forefront of linking population growth with environmental destruction, and a leader in calling for population control.

EISELEY, LOREN (1907-1977) Born in Lincoln, Nebraska, Eiseley received his Ph.D. from the University of Pennsylvania in 1937. He taught anthropology and sociology at the University of Kansas and at Oberlin College before becoming chair of the anthropology department at the University of Pennsylvania in 1947. Eiseley also served on the National Research Council and on the advisory board on national parks for the U.S. Department of the Interior.

Eiseley produced collections of essays exploring the mysteries of humans and nature and humanity's view of itself in relation to the natural world. *The Firmament of Time* (1966) discusses humanity's view of itself and the natural world as it has been influenced by anthropology, biology, and geology. In *The Immense Journey* (1957), Eiseley blends scientific knowledge with imaginative vision to tell the story of humanity's historical adaptations to its environment. In *The Unexpected Universe* (1969), he tells of the nature of life with poetic and scientific insights and precision. Eiseley uses the concepts of desolation and renewal to explain the symbolic aspects of the universe.

ELTON, CHARLES SUTHERLAND (1900-1991) Born in England, Elton was instrumental in establishing animal ecology as a discipline. Between 1925 and 1931, he studied the fluctuations of fur-bearing animals in the Canadian Arctic over extended time periods. His book, *Animal Ecology* (1926), popularized the concept of the ecological "niche" that is defined as a species role in an ecosystem. He argued that species can be understood by studying their function in the larger, biotic community. Elton also popularized the concepts of food chains and food webs, producers, primary and secondary consumers, reducers and decomposers, ecological pyramids, biomass, and territorialism.

He found colder, arctic climates easier to study due to their low species diversity and, therefore, easier species identification. Dismissing the notion of "balance of nature," Elton explained that organisms continually compete with one another and that it is difficult—if not impossible—to determine the ecosystemic impacts that one species' population increase or decrease would have on the entire system. This work encouraged **Aldo Leopold** to formulate his game management plan.

EMERSON, RALPH WALDO (1803-1882) Nineteenth-century U.S. poet, environmental philosopher, social critic, and religious leader. He was critical of industrial society and favored an agrarian lifestyle. While recognizing the contributions that industry bestowed on Europe, particularly the "bounteous" wealth it earned for the British. He also noted the pollution that would deteriorate the natural world in the United States.

The natural world, according to Emerson, was a revelation of the Divine. Experiencing nature was, thus, important to understanding the order or perfection of creation. He stated in *Nature* (1836):

> Standing on the bare ground . . . all mean egotism vanishes . . . the currents of the Universal Being circulate through me; I am part or parcel of God. . . . In the tranquil landscape, and especially in the distant line of the horizon, man beholds somewhat as beautiful as his own nature. (Emerson 1975, p. 182)

Nature explained the philosophy of Transcendentalism. According to Emerson's transcendental philosophy, all humans contain the divine spirit or "Oversoul." The Oversoul permeates nature and humans gain wisdom and spiritual renewal by breaking the shackles of industrial society and coming into closer contact with nature. By doing so, the nobler wants are served, namely, the love of beauty. This romanticized notion was mostly admired from his library or garden rather than contact with wilderness. **John Muir** discovered this after inviting Emerson on a hike only to hear the latter's caution not to be engulfed in wilderness.

ENDANGERED SPECIES ACT (ESA) (16 U.S.C. 1531-1542) In 1973, it became the world's most stringent environmental law. The act outlawed U.S. trade or import of any product made from an endangered species unless it would be used for an approved scientific purpose or enhance the survival of a species. The act designated 9 ports to facilitate throughput of all commercial shipment of wildlife and wildlife products, although, due to the excessive trade and few inspectors, it is likely that illegal trade makes it through port inspection.

The act also provides protection in the United States and abroad for species that are *endangered* (a species numbering so few that it may become extinct in its range) and *threatened* (a species that may become endangered due to its rapidly declining numbers),. The National Marine Fisheries Service (NMFS) and the **Fish and Wildlife Service (FWS)** identify and list the species that cannot be hunted, killed, collected, or injured in the United States. The act further prohibits any federal project that would jeopardize endangered or threatened species.

Once listed, habitats of endangered and threatened species are preserved and the FWS and NMFS plan a recovery strategy. However, due to inadequate funding, few recovery plans have been implemented. By the early 1990s, approximately 1,200 species were listed as endangered or threatened, while 4,000 were waiting for consideration and about 270 recovery plans had been implemented. As of 1997 this act was still up for reauthorization. Environmentalists argued for strengthening this act with more emphasis on preserving ecosystems, while property rights advocates want to see the act substantially weakened.

ENVIRONMENT CANADA (See **DEPARTMENT OF THE ENVIRONMENT**)

ENVIRONMENTAL DEFENSE FUND (EDF)   The EDF utilizes science and litigation to stem pollution in the United States. Founded in 1967, its first major contribution was a scientific study of the movement of **DDT** through food chains. Although not the first such study, many give EDF a piece of the credit for the U.S. ban on DDT use. With its large staff of lawyers, EDF is known for lawsuits to protect air and water quality, and the prevention or elimination of toxic chemicals in the environment. In 1990 EDF parted company with many other environmental groups by building the concept of pollution trading into the U.S. clean air policy. Its dual role of litigation and emphasis on market forces to reduce pollution make this group somewhat unusual. With over a quarter million members, it is a powerful force in crafting pollution legislation. (See also **CLEAN AIR ACT**)

ENVIRONMENTAL IMPACT STATEMENT (EIS)   A written document explicitly detailing the environmental consequences of a given action. The **National Environmental Policy Act (NEPA)** requires this document for all major federal actions significantly affecting the environment. According to NEPA, the document must contain certain key items, including a summary of findings, alternatives to the proposed action (including a no-action alternative), and a full description of the environmental impacts expected should the project go forward. EISs are prepared in draft form and released to the public for comment before a final EIS is written. Many state laws using NEPA as a model also require an EIS. Some people mistakenly view the EIS, in and of itself, as a device to protect the environment. While the NEPA forces consideration of environmental impacts and less environmentally damaging potential alternatives, it does not guarantee that projects will meet a certain environmental standard.

ENVIRONMENTAL JUSTICE   A relatively recent environmental issue brought to the U.S. public forefront in 1987 by the United Church of Christ's' Commission for Racial Justice, which charged that people who are poor, or of a minority group, are disproportionately affected by hazardous chemical production, waste, and disposal. The study also found that 3 out of 5 African and Hispanic Americans lived near one or more toxic dumps. Further, 3 to 4 million farm workers, mostly of Hispanic origin, are exposed to more toxics in pesticides than any other occupation in the country. Finally, the commission concluded that violating environmental laws in wealthier suburbs can bring about fines that are 5 times higher than those levied in minority communities. Because minorities are often excluded from the decision-making process, they have little say in policies that affect them and, thus, must rely on watchdog agencies to look out for their interests.

One example of alleged environmental racism occurred along a 100-mile strip between New Orleans and Baton Rouge, Louisiana, known as "Cancer Alley." This region has the highest rates of cancer, birth defects, and miscarriages in the country and 90 percent of the residents are black. It is also home to 28 percent of the nation's petrochemical production.

Environmental organizations throughout the United States are making environmental racism part of their agenda. They realize that the people who are destroying minority communities are wreaking havoc on the natural environment as well, and that by uniting causes, solutions to both problems are more likely.

ENVIRONMENTAL POLICY INSTITUTE (See **FRIENDS OF THE EARTH**)

ENVIRONMENTAL PROTECTION AGENCY (EPA) On December 2, 1970, President Richard Nixon signed an executive order that reorganized pollution regulation in the United States. Combining environmental and health responsibilities previously held by the National Air Pollution Control Administration, the Department of Health, the Federal Water Quality Administration, the Bureau of Solid Waste Management, pesticide regulation in the Department of Agriculture, and environmental research spread over numerous agencies, Nixon created the EPA. Its primary function is the setting of standards and administration of the country's major environmental laws, including the **Clean Air Act, Clean Water Act,** the **Safe Drinking Water Act,** the **Toxic Substances Control Act, Superfund,** and others. In addition to regulation, EPA conducts extensive scientific research. The agency operates 10 regional offices in addition to its headquarters in Washington, D.C.

Because of the high stakes of many EPA decisions— both economic and environmental—the EPA is often challenged in courts by both environmental groups and industry. Major divisions within the agency include the Office of General Counsel (to handle EPA enforcement actions as well as all the litigation in which the agency is consistently immersed); Air and Radiation; Water; Solid Waste; Emergency Response; Pesticides and Toxics; Enforcement and Compliance Monitoring; International Activities; Resource Management; Inspector General and Policy Planning.

ETHIOPIAN FAMINE   Once the breadbasket of the Roman Empire, the mid-1980s brought a horrendous famine to Ethiopia. Many factors contributed to this tragedy: a persistent drought, rapid population growth, an oppressive government, decades of domestic turmoil and war, and ethnic hostilities.

Nearly one million people died of starvation during a long drought from 1984 to 1985. In response, the Soviet-backed government moved farmers from the arid north to the fertile southern provinces. Ten to 20 percent of the one-half million people died along the way, while those who refused to move had their homes destroyed by fire. Critics have stated that the famine could have been avoided if the government spent $50 million per year planting trees and fighting soil erosion instead of pouring $275 million per year into a military arsenal.

Relief efforts from the world did not do much to improve the situation in Ethiopia. Foreign aid in the amount of $500 million and 560,907 tons of food was received, but the Ethiopian government stopped money and food from reaching the breakaway provinces where many of its starving citizens resided. The Mengistu government was overthrown in 1991 by several opposition groups that promised to hold multiparty elections. Since the overthrow, controversy has shrouded the government. While the country appears to be self-sufficient in food supply, it is plagued by government instability, ethnic fighting, and uncontrolled population growth. This famine, perhaps more than any other in history, focused world attention on the problem of Third World hunger.

Although hunger continues to be a worldwide problem, the world was greatly sensitized to this issue by the graphic television coverage of Ethiopia. This single issue began a tradition of large numbers of North American and European entertainers joining together to become involved in high profile fund-raising efforts for environmental causes.

EVERGLADES Located in southeast Florida, this subtropical wetland, which once covered 7 million acres, has been shrunk to tattered remnants of its native legacy. As was common in most American wilderness, early settlers viewed the Everglades as a wasteland that must be drained and developed before it could be valuable. This enormous wetland contains Lake Okeechobee on its north end (the third largest freshwater lake in the United States). It is also home to over 20 species of birds and many amphibians, reptiles and mammals. Significantly, the Florida panther, American crocodile, brown pelican, Everglades snail kite, and southern bald eagle are all endangered species that make their home in this ecosystem.

After human intrusion, the ecosystem was fragmented with a system of 2,000 miles of canals, 20-foot dikes on Lake Okeechobee, and the channelization of the Kissimee River. This was done to make the land habitable, provide water to residents, control flooding, and facilitate the water farmers needed. By 1970, half of the Everglades had been converted to land uses suitable to humanity, while one-fifth in the southern end was protected as Everglades National Park and now has the United Nations designation as a **biosphere reserve**.

In 1947 the Everglades National Park was created to protect the southern part of the ecosystem. However, even a fifth of the Everglades under protection as a park does not constitute ecosystem protection. The Everglades is still in danger from land uses on adjacent private lands. Dairy farms occupy 200,000 acres of former wetlands north of Lake Okeechobee and runoff seriously degrades water quality. Sugar cane farms occupy 700,000 acres south of the lake, and their fertilizers and pesticides likewise drain into Lake Okeechobee.

To compound runoff problems, canals and dams control the southwest flow of water. In the past, water was withdrawn to suit human demand. This did not match the needs of the biotic community—it is now wetter than normal in the wet season and drier than normal in the dry season. Populations of indigenous plants and animals have dropped significantly.

Florida adopted the "Save Our Everglades" initiative in 1983 to restore the quality of the Everglades to their pre-1900 condition by the year 2000. To assist this effort, the U.S. Congress now mandates more flow regulation to the park to restore higher flows in the dry season. By taking out human-engineered structures, attempts are now being made to restore this great ecosystem.

EXXON VALDEZ Just past midnight on March 24, 1989, as
the oil tanker *Exxon Valdez* was leaving its Alaskan
docks, the ship's captain, Joseph Hazlewood, turned over
the controls to a third mate. The tanker soon ran aground,
and the resulting spill was the largest in U.S. history. By
week's end, the oil had spread over a distance of 900
square miles.

The spill's ecological and human damage was enormous. The slick rapidly coated 1,000 miles of shoreline,
killing between 300,000 and 695,000 birds, 5,500 sea
otters, 30 seals, 23 whales, and countless fish. Exxon
responded to U.S. government and citizen pressure by
launching a $2.5-billion cleanup effort, and the state of
Alaska added another $500 million. Cleanup crews were
met with the thick, black oil that washed up on the
beaches and covered sea otters, birds, and fish.
Researchers of the spill noted that the most lethal
consequences were due to the oil that washed off the
beach and spread and sank to the sea floor. As it made
contact with the floor, it released deadly hydrocarbons,
which microorganisms consumed. In turn, the
microorganisms were consumed by organisms up the food
chain. Valdez residents, who depended on the fishing
industry for most of their livelihood, fear that it will be a
long time before the area is restored to a satisfactory
condition. Exxon spent over $2 billion in direct clean-up
costs. In 1991 it pled guilty to felony and misdemeanor
charges and paid the state of Alaska an additional $1
billion in fines.

This accident led to U.S. legislation requiring all new
tankers to be equipped with double hulls and all single-
hulled tankers to be phased out between 1995 and 2015.

F

FEDERAL ASSOCIATION FOR CITIZEN ACTION GROUPS FOR ENVIRONMENTAL PROTECTION (BUNDESVERBAND FÜR BÜRGERINITIATIVEN FÜR UMWELTSCHUTZ [BBU]) One of the first national umbrella environmental groups of the modern European environmental movement. Formed in 1971, this group united several hundred local German groups. A coalition of activist environmental groups, the BBU became a model of a new European organization, dedicated not to conservation of a species or the saving of one particular habitat, but rather to a more "ideological and political view of environmental policy and a group willing to use more assertive tactics in support of their cause" (Dalton 1994, p. 41).

FEDERAL INSECTICIDE, FUNGICIDE, AND RODENTICIDE ACT (FIFRA) (7 U.S.C. 136 ET SEQ.) This act, adopted in 1947, was designed to regulate pesticides in the United States. It mandated registration of insecticides, herbicides, rodenticides, fungicides—collectively termed pesticides—with the U.S. Department of Agriculture. It was significantly amended in 1972 and 1975. Before these amendments, pesticides were checked solely for their immediate toxic effect on some nontarget species. In sum, these amendments provided for the following: the reevaluation of old products that had to meet new standards; determination of risk for each pesticide; classification of particular uses of chemicals; capacity to suspend or cancel the use of both old and new pesticides that threaten human health or the environment; and the ability to enforce through inspections, labeling, notices, and state regulations.

Environmentalists have criticized the evaluation process set forth by FIFRA. They claim that few pesticides, mostly chlorinated hydrocarbons, have been removed from the market, while hazardous, persistent, and washoff-resistant chemicals are still used. In 1988, some of these concerns were relaxed, with further amendments to the law. The EPA has now created a reregistration process for pesticides currently on the market. An immediate effect of this amendment was that producers withdrew registrations for particular products that they knew would not pass the test or products whose profits would not warrant the costs of tests. Other 1988 amendments included better controls for enforcing compliance, higher registration fees, and increased criminal penalties for violation FIFRA requirements. Nonetheless, FIFRA allows the EPA to leave inadequately tested pesticides on the market without full health and safety data and gives the EPA unlimited time to remove a chemical even if the environmental risks outweigh environmental benefits.

FEDERAL WATER POLLUTION CONTROL ACT (See **CLEAN WATER ACT**)

FERNOW, BERNHARD (1851-1923)   German-born and trained forester who moved to the United States in 1876. His schooling shaped his belief in scientific forestry. After working for a mining company managing timber holdings in Pennsylvania, Fernow became interested in preservation and helped to organize the American Forestry Congress in 1882. Four years later, he became the Chief of Forestry, and held that position until 1898. Fernow left the Forestry Division to begin a silviculture program at Cornell University. **Gifford Pinchot**, who took over the division, began an aggressive campaign for forestry management and, in 1905, upgraded the division to the United States Forest Service within the Department of Agriculture.

During his tenure at Cornell, Fernow aggressively argued against keeping the Adirondack forest preserve "forever wild." He pointed to the recreational and resource benefits the area could support if guided by scientific principles and managed wisely.

FISH AND WILDLIFE CONSERVATION ACT (16 U.S.C. 2901) This act, passed by the U.S. Congress in 1980, provides financial and technical assistance to the states for the development, revision, and implementation of conservation plans for nongame species of fish and wildlife. These plans were to encourage states to conserve both species and the habitats of these species. The act recognized the importance of nongame species for their cultural, economic, recreational, and scientific value.

FISH AND WILDLIFE COORDINATION ACT (16 U.S.C. 661 ET SEQ.) This 1958 act requires the coordination of efforts to provide habitats for wildlife, through protection and/or stocking, in water resource development plans. This is accomplished by coordinating private development plans with federal and state governments.

The **Fish and Wildlife Service** is the lead agency that controls wildlife resources and conducts program activities. The act requires an evaluation of what positive and negative benefits a water development project will have on wildlife. Conservation plans on such lands are jointly approved by 3 parties: the Secretary of the Interior, the federal agency having primary administrative responsibility for the proposed project, and the administering state agency.

FISH AND WILDLIFE SERVICE (FWS) Created in 1940 (successor of the Bureau of Fisheries, created 1871), the

agency now is the lead agency in the protection of
endangered species as well as threatened fish and bird
species. The management of the National Wildlife Refuge
System is one of the chief responsibilities of the agency. It
oversees key provisions of the **Endangered Species Act,**
the **Migratory Bird Treaty Act,** and the **Marine Mam-**
mal Protection Act. Temporarily dissolved in 1970, the
FWS was redesignated by the U.S. Congress in 1974.
Environmentalists and the FWS have often been at
loggerheads with environmentalists charging that the
agency has been too concerned with the management of
game species and not concerned enough with nongame
species and habitat preservation. The FWS also develops
the endangered and threatened species lists, and
environmentalists have often been critical of the slow pace
of such listings. Indeed, the agency prides itself on its
cooperative role with the states in the conservation and
management of wildlife resources.

FOREMAN, DAVE (1921-) Former representative of the
Wilderness Society who left the group to help found
Earth First!, a radical environmental group with the
slogan "no compromise in defense of Mother Earth."
Foreman is a self-professed ecowarrior and celebrated
ecosaboteur who has become one of the most visible
proponents of wilderness preservation and restoration in
the United States.

Earth First! was founded with the recognition that the
piecemeal, diplomatic approaches of other environmental
groups were not working or were too slow in achieving
their objectives. Foreman favors direct action to defend
wildlands. He recognized that the professional environmentalist had adapted the same rules as the bureaucrats,
politicians, and industrialists they were trying to fight. He
opted, alternatively, to redefine the battle and ground
rules of action in defense of the earth. Foreman advocated

placing our bodies between the bulldozers and the rain forest.

Foreman explains his career as a spiral. In the 1970s, while working for the Wilderness Society, he thought that working in the system to force change was appropriate. After several years of disappointments, in 1980, he founded Earth First! feeling that direct action was the best way to express an alternative philosophy. By the 1990s, with his publication of *Confessions of an Eco-Warrior* (1991), he admitted going through a transition where he questioned the tactics of Earth First!

FORRESTER, JAY (See **LIMITS TO GROWTH**)

FRIENDS OF THE EARTH (FOE) This international organization, founded in 1969, now has chapters in 37 countries. **David Brower**, founder of FOE, went on to found the **League of Conservation Voters** (1970) and **Earth Island Institute** (1982). Although working on a broad range of environmental issues, if the organization has any focus, it would probably be resource conservation issues and threats to public health. FOE uses a variety of techniques to accomplish its goals, including lobbying and litigation, although its primary tool is public education. It works with smaller groups in many countries to foster its agenda of environmental quality over short-term economic benefits. Individual chapters work within the broad priorities of FOE to pursue their own projects. For example, FOE-UK and FOE-Malaysia are working together to reform tropical timber trade and protect native forest dwellers. In 1990, FOE merged with the Oceanic Society and the Environmental Policy Institute.

FULLER, BUCKMINSTER (1895-1983) Fuller was a man of many talents. An inventor, mathematician, architect, and designer, he believed that technology could solve most human problems. Although deep ecologists of today would claim he did not understand the real way to solve environmental problems, he used appropriate technology to help humans minimize adverse environmental effects. He is most known for his development of the geodesic dome, first constructed in 1949. His inventions, created to have man live more compatibly with the environment, included the design of a 1927 house that had a gray-water filtering and reuse system, solid-waste recycling for fertilizer, solar energy for heat, and low-flow shower heads. He was a technological optimist who believed proper planning and resource use could lead to abundant housing and food resources. His views might well be considered as the forerunner of the sustainable development theories of the technocratic optimism of the late 20th century. (See also **DEEP ECOLOGY**)

G

GAIA THEORY Named after the Greek goddess of the earth, the term was used in the 1970s by English chemist James Lovelock and American biologist Lynn Margulis. This theory states that the earth functions like a self-regulating living organism. All living organisms work with the nonliving chemical and geophysical processes in a symbiotic relationship to maintain the earth's environment. Lovelock argues that this interaction forms automatic processes that control climate and atmospheric composition, as well as ecological processes. He notes that, although the amount of energy coming from the sun is not constant, the earth's temperature has remained relatively unchanged since life appeared. Likewise, warm-blooded animals maintain a constant body temperature regardless of outside temperature.

Thus, Lovelock and his followers believe the earth is a superorganism that adjusts and regulates itself. Resulting from this is the ethic that all objects, living and nonliving, are equally important components of an indivisible whole and, thus, should be endowed with equal rights. He believed all ecosystem components are, thus, needed for the healthy functioning of the Earth's systems

GIBBS, LOIS (See **CITIZENS CLEARINGHOUSE FOR HAZARDOUS WASTE**)

GLOBAL WARMING Warning voiced by environmentalists and scientists who maintain that the use of fossil fuels will increase global temperatures and cause many significant secondary changes to the natural world. The scientific basis of global warming is the greenhouse effect. Under normal conditions, gases, including water vapor, carbon dioxide, ozone, methane, nitrous oxide, and chlorofluorocarbons (CFCs), are present in the earth's atmosphere in varying amounts. These gases form a blanket around the planet keeping temperatures warm at night by trapping heat in the atmosphere. While shorter incoming radiation can penetrate this layer, outgoing long-wave radiation is trapped by the greenhouse layer. Subsequently, the greenhouse layer around the earth's surface keeps temperatures warm (much like a greenhouse retains heat).

Proponents of the theory of global warming assert that due to excess burning of fossil fuels, greenhouse gases, especially carbon dioxide, have increased to the extent that a significant amount of heat is retained by greenhouse gases, causing an overall warming of the atmosphere. Water vapor, the most abundant gas, has remained stable over the years, but the other greenhouse gases, all produced in large amounts by industrial processes, have significantly increased throughout the 20th century.

Nations have implemented various laws to control these pollutants. The 1992 Climate Convention was an international effort organized to address global warming; however, due to the U.S. attitude of noncooperation, little was accomplished in the way of specific targets and deadlines for the reduction of greenhouse gases. The Bush administration committed the United States to a goal of a 12 to 15 percent reduction by 2000, while other nations proposed cutting emissions of greenhouse gases by as much as the needed 60 percent.

While scientists agreed that the temperature has risen by approximately one degree Celsius in the last 100 years, they disagree about whether these patterns are natural or are a result of human activities. If the mean temperature of the earth increases by 1.5 to 5.5 degrees Celsius by 2050, as predicted by various models, the following effects are anticipated: some areas of the world will get more rain, while others will get less, thus, food produc-tion patterns will change; storms and hurricanes will increase in intensity; areas farther north and south of the equator will become agriculturally productive, while some areas productive now will become too dry to cultivate; forests will be replaced by rangelands; sea levels will rise and cause a flooding of coastal communities, destruction of inland wetlands, floods in low-lying areas and destruction of coral reefs; and many secondary effects, such as movement of tropical insect pests north and south, will ensue. (See also **UNITED NATIONS FRAMEWORK CONVENTION ON CLIMATE CHANGE**)

GORE, ALBERT (1948-   ) Vice president of the United States, past senator of Tennessee, environmentalist, and author of the book *Earth in the Balance* (1992). During his political career, which began in 1978 in the U.S. Congress, Gore has devoted much time and energy to working toward a better environment on a national and global scale. He admits that his earliest exposure to environmentalism centered around soil erosion on his family farm. In college he became aware of the possibility of global warming, and in Vietnam he witnessed the effects of the herbicide, Agent Orange, and how it made jungles look like the surface of the moon.

Gore carried his environmental concerns to the U.S. Congress and soon organized the first congressional hearing on toxic waste. The two sites that were examined were located in Toon, Tennessee, and Niagara Falls, New York (**Love Canal**). Two years after these hearings, Gore (along with others such as Congressmen Jim Florio and Tom Downey) was integral in passing the **Superfund** Act, which aimed at cleaning up toxic waste sites throughout the country.

After these early accomplishments, Gore continued his investigation into the effect our civilization has on the natural world. He ran for president of the United States in 1987, and built his platform on such environmental concerns as banning CFC production. In 1990, he joined with other senators to create the Interparliamentarians Conference on the Global Environment. Parliamentarians from 42 nations entered into agreements on the full range of threats to the global environment.

In the late 1990s, as vice president under Bill Clinton, Gore continues to devote his efforts to environmental concerns. *Earth in the Balance* examined environmentalism on a global scale. He argued that the ecological perspective begins with viewing the world as a whole, integrated system, whose parts are all vital to the good of the planet.

GRAY, ELIZABETH DODSON (See **ECOFEMINISM**)

GREAT LAKES WATER QUALITY AGREEMENT First signed in 1972, this bilateral agreement between the

United States and Canada pledged each country to reduce pollutants entering the Great Lakes and to eliminate poisonous chemicals in toxic concentrations. As more scientific research demonstrated new problems in the lakes, new agreements were made. The Great Lakes Water Quality Agreement was renewed in 1978, and in 1987 a new protocol was developed to supplement the agreement. This protocol gave the **International Joint Commission** the responsibility to monitor progress in the cleanup of the lakes and to report to both governments on a biennial basis. Under this agreement significant progress has been made in the reduction of cultural eutrophication or nutrient enrichment, which causes blooms of algae and depletion of oxygen. While some progress has been made in reducing toxins, the countries have a long way to go to reach the goal of the virtual elimination of toxic substances in the Great Lakes.

GREELEY, HORACE (1811-1872) Radical editor and owner of the *New York Times* who promoted western settlement and championed the Homestead Act calling it "a magnificent national democratic triumph—a bold but noble promise" (Shabecoff 1993, p. 27). At the same time, after traveling through Europe, he warned eastern (Americans) to preserve some of their primitive forests. He warned of the difficulty in replacing native forests saying that "when these are cut away I apprehend they will not easily be replaced" (Nash 1982, p. 96). Similarly, speaking of the U.S. West, he called the Yosemite Valley "most unique and majestic, and unsurpassed by any other wonder like it 'on earth'" (Runte 1990, p. 14). He celebrated the scenic grandeur of scenes in the United States, which he felt were superior to European wilderness. (See also **YOSEMITE PARK**)

GREEN PARTY A political party whose main focus is on the preservation of environmental quality. Although not a majority in any country, the green parties of Germany, New Zealand, Belgium, and several other European countries are significant political forces. The green party of each country has its own political goals, but overarching principles such as opposition to nuclear power, grass-roots democracy, and reduced consumption of natural resources, are common to all. Unlike virtually all other political parties, green parties advocate policies in opposition to economic growth, especially growth that is consumptive of resources. The Greens have been less successful in gaining popular support in North America. The Greens in the United States find their greatest success by getting politicians to discuss environmental issues rather than electing their own candidates for office. In 1996, however, Alaska became the first state to officially recognize the Green Party. In the same year, Ralph Nader ran for the U.S. presidency as the Green Party candidate.

GREEN PLAN In 1990 the government of Canada issued a so-called Green Plan—committing the country to the concepts of sustainable development and protection of renewable resources, special areas and species, and the Arctic. In addition it discussed global issues such as **global warming,** changes needed in political and economic institutions, and emergency preparedness. Specific projects outlined included programs on drinking water safety, river cleanups, smog reduction, waste reduction, improvements in fisheries and agriculture, and additions to the National Park System. However, shortly after the program was initiated funds to implement it were drastically reduced. While environmentalists praised Canada's effort to include environmental considerations in all areas of government action, the program has not lived up to its promise.

GREEN REVOLUTION   A revolution in agriculture that began in the mid-1960s when scientists working in Mexico and the Philippines developed varieties of wheat and rice that were adapted to grow in tropical climates and could produce greater yields than other varieties. This technology was applied to several food crops and was responsible for preventing mass starvations on a global scale, which many had predicted. The new technologies developed required planting monocultures of genetically adapted plants and adding fertilizers, pesticides, and water to them. Between 1950 and 1970, impressive increases in crop yields were recorded. Despite its success, the new seeds required heavy doses of fertilizers and pesticides (inputs), which increased the cost of food production. Further, the success of specific strains of species has led to increased specialization and monoculture—single crop agriculture. Monocultures often result in pesticides becoming ineffective after a time period due to genetic resistance on the part of the invading weed, insect, rodent, or fungus. In response, many environmentalists have come out in support of alternative, organic agriculture, which relies on crop diversity, ecological integrity, and a reduction of inputs of chemicals and mechanization.

GREEN SCAMMING   The practice of giving environmentally friendly names to groups whose agendas have little to do with the welfare of the environment. Examples of green scamming include the National Wilderness Institute, a group working to roll back wetlands regulations in the **Endangered Species Act**, and the Environmental Conservation Organization, founded in 1990 as a front for real estate developers and other businesses opposed to wetlands regulation.

GREENHOUSE EFFECT (See **GLOBAL WARMING**)

GREENPEACE   Founded in 1971, Greenpeace is now the largest environmental group in the world, boasting over 2 million members. The group is best known for its daring activism to fulfill its goal of increasing public awareness of dangers to the marine environment and, more recently, hazardous waste pollution. The group's headline-grabbing actions included sending small rubber rafts between harpoons from whaling ships and the whales, sailing into waters where atomic testing was scheduled to occur, and unleashing banners from smokestacks, buildings, and bridges. The group captured world attention when the French government became so angered by the group's interruption of nuclear testing that they blew up the Greenpeace ship, *Rainbow Warrior.* Although viewed as "radical activists" by some, Greenpeace's investigation of pollution in the United States by a Ciba-Geigy plant in New Jersey resulted in over 30 criminal indictments of plant officials and fines of over $4 million. EPA has viewed their independent data on a hazardous waste incinerator in Ohio as among the most accurate available. (See also **SHEPARD, PAUL**)

GRINNELL, GEORGE BIRD (1849-1938) Grinnell had the fortune of growing up in a house in Audubon Park, New York, and earned both B.A. and Ph.D. degrees from Yale University. He was moved by the bird paintings of **John James Audubon,** which set a tone for his life's interests. He later accompanied General George Custer to do plant and animal identification in the U.S. West; he served as publisher of *Forest and Stream* magazine; and he was one of the first to argue for the preservation of the American bison and natural areas after he witnessed the declining numbers of each. He has been credited with being largely responsible for the establishment of Glacier National Park in Montana. His appreciation of birds led him to the idea of creating an organization specifically designed to preserve birds that were slaughtered without regard for their declining numbers. Others joined him in this pursuit, and they formed the **Audubon Society** in 1886.

Grinnell, along with **Theodore Roosevelt,** was also cofounder of the Boone and Crockett Club. This group was organized in 1888 with the purpose of encouraging the conservation of big-game animals. The group also encouraged its members to submerge themselves in the natural world to cultivate a greater appreciation of nature. By such immersion in this setting, the hunter would cultivate the characteristics that a culture of people depend on for greatness: sound body and mind, as well as the capacity for self-reliance.

H

HAECKEL, ERNST (1834-1919)   Haeckel, a German scientist, coined the term "ecology" to mean the study of interactions between organisms and their external world. Although he considered himself a Darwinian, he viewed the universe as a unified, holistic system. His ideas would later influence environmentalists who borrowed his belief that all living forms can be related into one single development sequence. Haeckel popularized the "recapitulation theory" which held that the growth of the embryo is analogous to the development of animals into increasingly complex forms that ended with human beings. Accordingly, "lower animals" could be identified with particular stages in the development of life. Similarly, he believed that each individual relives the history of the human race.

Haeckel was an avowed racist who thought that "lower races" were at earlier stages of human development. He thought that the urban lifestyle degenerated the higher

German race and argued for a harmonious existence in nature. Another of Haeckel's beliefs, which many say influenced right-wing policies like those adopted by Nazism, was that there was a spiritual element in the material universe. Known as the monist philosophy, it was adopted by those who distrusted the mechanical worldview of science. The "Monist League" was formed in early-20th-century Germany as an angry response to democratic values.

HARDIN, GARRETT (1915-   )   A controversial U.S. population biologist, ecologist, and microbiologist. He introduced the term "principle of competitive exclusion," which explains that no two species in an ecosystem can occupy the same niche. While two species may have similar feeding and/or sleeping habits, and thereby compete for the same resources, there are always at least subtle differences between them.

His 1968 essay, "Tragedy of the Commons," has been interpreted by some as a realization that the global commons must be equally shared and protected; others view it as promoting the environmental benefit of private property, while presenting an argument for limiting population growth and resource consumption. The essay presents a parable wherein several farmers share a commons area for the purpose of grazing their cattle. If each acts out of self-interest, he will graze as many cattle as possible on the land to increase his wealth. At the same time, if all farmers act according to this logic, the commons would be destroyed by overgrazing.

Hardin's interests led him to explore social, political, and ethical problems that our species confronts in terms of evolution and heredity. Some link him to social Darwinism because of his position that the developed world should not help to feed countries in poverty. In the controversial essay "Lifeboat Ethics," he presents the scenario that people are at sea on a sinking ship. Lifeboats are provided, but each accommodates only a few people. When the lifeboat has reached its maximum limit, the passengers must confront the dilemma of letting more people on the boat. Hardin's answer is that no more passengers should be permitted on the lifeboat after it has reached its carrying capacity. Thus, he concludes the freedom to breed will destroy the entire life-support system of the earth. His answer to this problem is mandatory population control as a requirement for food aid to overpopulated countries.

HAYES, DENIS (1944-   ) A Harvard Law School student who became the national coordinator of the first Earth Day on April 22, 1970. He attributed the success of the first Earth Day to discontented youth on American college campuses and elsewhere around the country. Hayes believed, "There was this broad, sort of all-encompassing sense that things were falling apart." He later described the event as "the largest organized demonstration in human history" (Shabecoff 1993, pp. 113-115).

Hayes also chaired the 1990 Earth Day. In looking back over the last 20 years, he questioned the irony of achievements made and asked how so many people could have fought so hard and achieved so much only to lose the war in fundamentally changing the course of a society headed toward destroying both itself and the natural world. He regretted the fact that all of the people who set out to change the world 20 years ago and "entered adulthood with dreams of global peace, racial justice, and a sustainable planet, are now on the threshold of failure" (ibid., p. 267). For the past 10 years Hayes has been an activist working on increasing the implementation of solar energy technology.

HEADLY, JOEL (1813-1897) Protestant minister, popular historian, journalist, and biographer who began venturing into the Adirondack Mountains of New York in the 1840s. His 1875 publication, *The Adirondacks; Or, Life in the Woods*, gained immediate popularity. It tells of two summers he spent in the forest as a result of "An attack on the brain" which drove him "from the haunts of men to seek mental repose and physical strength in the woods" (Headly 1875, p. 1). In its contribution to conservation, the book serves as an instruction manual for wilderness etiquette, explains how to prepare for camping and life in the woods, describes daily routines, and philosophizes on the meaning of life in the woods.

Headly was a writer in the romantic genre who encountered the wilderness experience as one of spiritual cleansing and physical and intellectual invigoration. However, his appreciation of wilderness was often qualified. He praised the beauty and spiritual nourishments, but noted that some landscapes were threatening and sublime. Descriptions of a "gloomy gorge and savage precipice," along with his belief that a beautiful landscape should be turned into a cultivated field to eliminate "useless wilderness," expressed the author's ambivalence toward the natural world.

Headly returned to the Adirondacks throughout the 1840s and 1850s in spite of his compromised attitudes. After the stresses of the civilized world had built up sufficiently, Headly would once again escape to the mountains because, "In the woods, the mask that society compels one to wear is cast aside, and the restraints which the thousand eyes and reckless tongues about him fasten on the heart, are thrown off, and the soul rejoices in its liberty and again becomes a child in action" (ibid., p. iii).

HENDERSON, HAZEL (1933-) Futurist economist of the late 20th century who urged that outmoded economic systems be modeled after nature. This involves appreciating growth and decay of outdated ideas or institutions and the gradual breaking down of some systems so that new ones may evolve. In *Creating Alternative Futures* (1978), she compared outdated economic systems to vegetation that breaks down into humus for spring growth.

Henderson coined the term "entropy state" to describe the economic condition where bureaucratic coordination and maintenance costs exceeds the productive capacities of society. This state demonstrates that economic and institutional structures have become antiquated and must be replaced.

Henderson argues for an interdisciplinary approach to meet the complexity of ecological, social, and economic challenges that confront us. She believes that this approach should replace the fragmented, linear character of the current economic system. Economists value economic gain but ignore environmental costs associated with wealth. For instance, when a new technology is considered, economic concerns should be broadened to environmental, sociological, and ethical ramifications. Included in this analysis should be the effect of a project on communities and cultural patterns, the use of non-renewable resources, and whether the project is centralizing or decentralizing.

HETCH HETCHY A glacier-carved valley that became part of **Yosemite National Park** in 1890. In the first years of the 19th century, ideas began to circulate about damming the valley to provide water for San Francisco. Following the 1906 earthquake, the necessity of the dam became more urgent. Like many Americans, President **Theodore Roosevelt**'s views on the dam were ambivalent. Later, President Woodrow Wilson's sympathies clearly supported development. In December 1913, a dam for the valley was authorized.

The controversy over damming the valley is one of the greatest in U.S. conservation history. This issue pitted two environmentalists—once allies with a common cause, albeit with divergent philosophies—one against the other. The preservationist **John Muir** required that the valley be left untouched by humans. Alternately, the conservationist **Gifford Pinchot** insisted that the valley and its resources should be used wisely. Muir described his opposition as "temple destroyers" who lifted their eyes only to the "almighty dollar." Pinchot believed that the benefits that would be reaped by civilization greatly outweighed those of the few that wanted the "swampy floor" of the valley preserved (Nash 1982, p. 161). Historian Roderick Nash commented on the clash, stating that the most notable thing about Hetch Hetchy is that there was a controversy at all. For the first time in U.S. history, feelings were ambivalent about whether the good of civilization necessarily exceeded the good of nature.

HOOKER CHEMICAL COMPANY (See **LOVE CANAL**)

HOUGH, FRANKLIN B. (1822-1885) U.S. forest manager who championed the European style of management in the United States in response to the overuse of resources by profiteers. Hough was a physician and surgeon during the Civil War who turned conservationist when, after serving as the superintendent of the census in 1870, he realized the destructiveness that results from the overuse of forest resources. Influenced by the writings of **George Perkins Marsh,** Hough claimed that lumber "management" techniques were illegal and resulted in land and watershed destruction. In 1873 he presented a paper to the American Association for the Advancement of Science on "The Duty of Governments in the Preservation of Forests." He went on to argue for forest preservation in the United States, basing his ideas on the European model.

In 1875, the U.S. Congress created the Division of Forestry under the Department of Agriculture, and Hough was appointed as its head. He was responsible for developing a report on U.S. forests. Utilizing Marsh's theoretical ideas, Hough made recommendations on how timber growing could be promoted while existing forests were conserved. Hough's work provided a significant impetus to Congress to provide for organized forestry under the Department of Agriculture, and in 1881, to create the Division of Forestry. The division was later upgraded to the United States Forest Service in 1905 under the leadership of **Gifford Pinchot.**

I

ICKES, HAROLD (1874-1952)   U.S. Secretary of Interior under President Franklin D. Roosevelt who convinced the U.S. Congress that his department, rather than the Department of Agriculture, should be entrusted with management responsibilities for wilderness areas in the United States and that these areas should be managed in a systemic fashion. His plan, based largely on Robert Marshall's ideas, was for a National Wilderness Preservation system. This system became a reality in 1964 under President Lyndon B. Johnson. Among Ickes's other accomplishments was appropriating $5 million for erosion control terracing projects, while he oversaw the Public Works Administration in the first 100 days of Roosevelt's New Deal program.

INFORM Founded in 1973 to work primarily on air pollution topics, this educational and research organization located in New York City now works on a wide range of environmental issues. Inform aims its educational activities toward business and government, and its thorough, detailed research reports, books, and articles have been widely regarded as furthering the environmental debate in many areas, including solid waste management, hazardous waste management, and urban air pollution. In addition to a thorough review of issues, the research published by Inform is noted for specific, constructive, and practical recommendations to improve environmental quality. The respect gained in both the industrial and environmental communities has led to the participation of Inform staff in many policy conferences and legislative hearings.

INSTITUTE FOR GLOBAL COMMUNICATIONS (See ECONET)

INTERNATIONAL JOINT COMMISSION (IJC) A Canadian-U.S. advisory council established in 1909 by the Boundary Waters Treaty; began work in 1912 out of a mutual concern over Great Lakes water quality. The commission resulted from the Boundary Waters Treaty of 1909, which addressed pollution crossing the international border between Canada and the United States. Thus, the goal of the IJC has been to maintain the boundary waters and waters flowing across boundaries so that health and property on each side would not be negatively impaired by the other nation's actions.

The body of the IJC consists of six members: three appointed by the president of the United States and three by the Canadian government. Additionally, numerous advisory boards and sub-committees carry out the principle functions of the IJC, which include regulation of water levels, investigations, and surveillance.

INTERNATIONAL UNION FOR CONSERVATION OF NATURE AND NATURAL RESOURCES (ICUN) (See **WORLD CONSERVATION UNION**)

INTERNATIONAL WHALING COMMISSION (IWC) In 1946, the International Whaling Commission replaced the International Whaling Convention in regulating the killing of whales. While it was initially organized in the interest of the whaling industry, it has become a device for protection. In 1982, 25 of 31 nations approved a 10-year moratorium on all whaling for nonscientific purposes. However, Japan, Norway, and the former Soviet Union continued whaling because of loopholes. In 1990, the moratorium was extended for one year, although Japan and Iceland refused to cooperate. While some nations have refused to cease whaling and have likely killed whales for nonscientific purposes, whale populations have somewhat recovered; however, air and water pollution continues to threaten them.

ISLAND BIOGEOGRAPHY A controversial theory introduced by R. H. MacArthur and E. O. Wilson that maintains that the number of species on an island represents a balance between immigration and extinction. Two components to this equilibrium theory is that larger islands contain more species than small islands (a tenfold decrease in area is accompanied by a 50 percent decline in number of species); secondly, islands closer to mainland experience higher rates of immigration, stability, and species diversity due to the so-called rescue effect: small populations can be augmented by immigrants of the same species.

This theory has been applied to reserves. Parks, wilderness areas, wildlife refuges, and other areas where biodiversity is protected can be viewed as islands. Clearly, these protection areas are discontinuous and fragmented. As unprotected lands are continually developed, protected islands of biodiversity can become more distant and shrink in size. Thus, preservation of biodiversity becomes jeopardized.

As a result of the knowledge of island biogeography, environmentalists have placed an emphasis on connecting reserves. Connectivity permits rescue effects to work more effectively and increases the likelihood that protected areas sustain maximum biodiversity.

IZAAK WALTON LEAGUE OF AMERICA In 1922, 54 sportsmen met in Chicago to discuss the deteriorating conditions of the streams where they fished due to municipal and industrial pollution. The result of this meeting was the formation of the Izaak Walton League, which took its name from the 17th-century angler and conservationist. Although originally focusing on water quality, the league has expanded its focus to the protection of air and land resources and habitat protection, as well. In 1995 membership was approximately 50,000.

J

JAMES BAY HYDROELECTRIC PROJECT One of the largest hydroelectric projects in the world, this massive system of dams in Quebec, Canada, was originally projected to include hundreds of dams, over 20 power stations and alteration of the flow of 19 rivers. It would have flooded approximately 68,000 square miles and destroyed much of the land inhabited by the Cree.

Three dams on the La Grande River have been completed, supplying 10,000 megawatts of power. In addition to the problems of habitat loss, leaching of mercury from rocks in the area has given rise to increased mercury contamination throughout the food chain. The completion of the later phases of the project, however, was affected when environmentalists from all over the world, but especially in the United States and Canada participated in massive protests. The Cree Indians, whose ancestral hunting lands would be flooded and whose fishing areas have already been polluted, also protested the second phase of the project, which would dam the Great Whale River. Environmental pressure and a reduced need for electricity in the 1990s caused both Vermont and New York State to cancel contracts to purchase electricity from the project's sponsor, Hydro Quebec. Without these contracts, Hydro Quebec, in 1994, delayed the later phases of the project indefinitely.

JOHNSON, ROBERT UNDERWOOD (1853-1937) On an 1889 visit to San Francisco, Johnson befriended **John Muir** and joined him on a camping expedition around the Yosemite Valley. During one of their campfire chats, Johnson listened to Muir's warnings that development posed threats to the natural beauty of the area, and that domesticated sheep also damaged the landscape. In response, Johnson initiated the idea of preserving **Yosemite** as a national park. Through publications of articles by both Muir and Johnson in *Century*, then the nation's leading literary monthly of which Johnson was editor, the two men promoted Yosemite's protection to the U.S. public. Besides writing editorials in *Century*, Johnson lobbied the U.S. House of Representatives for the cause. Later, he teamed with Muir in their fight to stop the **Hetch Hetchy** dam in the Yosemite Valley.

Unlike Muir, Johnson's desire to preserve wilderness rested more on philosophical ideals than a love for physical contact with the wild. That is, he believed that creating wilderness areas would enhance progress in the artistic creativity of the nation—that preservation for the sake of scenery was alone sufficient.

K

KRUTCH, JOSEPH WOOD (1893-1970)   Joseph Wood Krutch studied mathematics and humanities, and received a Ph.D. in literature in 1924. His future took another course after reading **Henry David Thoreau** one winter's night at his home in Redding, Connecticut. Soon after, he wrote his first book with an environmental theme: *The Twelve Seasons*, a collection of essays on nature, one poem for each month. Due to his newfound love for nature, he quit teaching and moved to Tucson, Arizona, in 1950. He continued to publish nature essays even he observed the environment under attack. Krutch soon became a promoter of preservation, and earned national recognition after his three NBC television specials in which he led a tour through the Grand Canyon and the Sonora and Baja, California deserts in Mexico. He differed from other preservationists in that he was somewhat low-key and preferred to celebrate the natural world instead of scorning developers.

He wrote his first book about the desert environment, *The Desert Year*, in 1952, and followed it with *The Voice of the Desert* in 1954. In them, he described the landscape and idiosyncrasies of creatures inhabiting the ecosystem; the works also expressed dismay toward society's unconscious yearning to destroy nature's beauty in order to surround itself with its own abundance. Krutch pointedly asked, "abundance of what?" While more cities, shopping centers, and housing developments are built, the abundance of nature's capital and beauty is necessarily diminished.

His 1956 book, *The Great Chain of Life*, expressed the joy of relating humanity's animal heritage to the laws of nature. Krutch speculated on a number of themes, such as the necessity for humans to explore their primitive relation to other animals, the joy expressed by other animals, and how humans can enhance their own existence and that of other animals simply through creative contact. Finally, in *The Forgotten Peninsula: A Naturalist in Baja California* (1961), Krutch described the sustainable lifestyles of the community of Baja California, Mexico, but also sees its end due to the demands of tourists that stream through the northern part of the state. He wrote that technological power, originally meant to serve humans, now controlled its creator and would ultimately lead to ecosystem and social destruction.

Krutch died leaving behind words of caution to a society continually sprawling over the last remnants of the desert: slow down, think of what technology and mastery is doing, what will be lost, and realize what ultimately will be gained by preservation.

L

LAND ETHIC (See **LEOPOLD, ALDO**)

LAPPE, FRANCES MOORE (1944-)   Twentieth-century spokesperson for alternative eating habits, whose books include *Food First: Beyond the Myth of Scarcity* (1978, with Joseph Collins) and *Diet for a Small Planet* (1975). The latter book is sometimes described as a counterculture cookbook, but her main contributions to environmentalism is as proponent of alternative nutrition and sustainable agriculture. She argued that once agriculture was mixed with the technologies of the **Green Revolution**, it ceased to produce nutritious food. Pesticides and manufactured fertilizers decreased its nutritional value and, in fact, contaminated our food. The present system of farming the land as if it were a factory is leading to desertification of once-fertile farmland as soil is stripped of its nutrients and polluted runoff infects aquatic ecosystems.

Lappe maintains that labor-intensive agriculture could make many developing countries once again self-sufficient for their food. Her vision is a world of small farmers producing sufficiently abundant harvests without the use of chemicals. By changing our food production system, she believes world hunger can be completely abolished.

LAW OF THE SEA (See UNITED NATIONS LAW OF THE SEA CONFERENCE)

LEAGUE OF CONSERVATION VOTERS Founded in 1970 by David R. Brower, the League of Conservation Voters is dedicated to informing the public about each U.S. senator's and representative's record on environmental legislation. It works toward the election of pro-environmental candidates and against those with especially poor environmental records. It accomplishes this via public information, cash contributions to campaigns, and the contribution of campaign staff to candidates it endorses. The league focuses its attention on candidates for office rather than on lobbying for any particular piece of legislation. Unlike most environmental organizations that seek tax-exempt status, the league shuns that status so it can actively participate in political campaigns. Its publication, *National Environmental Scorecard*, is the most definitive list of all environmental legislation, as well as the voting records of individuals concerning these issues.

LEOPOLD, ALDO (1886-1948)   Leopold is best known for his writing about the land and specifically about how humans might live compatibly on the land. Leopold's contributions lay in his combination of philosophy with ecology. He was educated at Yale University (B.S. 1908) and then began a career in forestry with the U.S. Forest Service. His efforts in this position resulted in the formation of the Gila Wilderness in New Mexico, the world's first designated wilderness. He was founder of the **Wilderness Society** in 1935. After leaving the Forest Service, he published his classic text, *Game Management*, which is today viewed as one of the foundation documents in the science of wildlife management. Leopold's interest in wilderness preservation grew into a philosophy of human responsibility for other species and their habitats. He termed "ecological conscience" as a genuine respect for all life.

By far, his best-known work is *A Sand County Almanac* (1948). It contains an essay titled, "A Land Ethic," which continues to enjoy popularity among academics, land managers, and the general reader. It calls for a broadening of ethics to embrace plants, animals, and the earth itself. The "land ethic," as Leopold described it, "simply enlarges the boundaries of the community to include soils, water plants, and animals. This requires a new relationship between humans and the natural environment. Leopold continued, "In short, a land ethic changes the role of *Homo Sapiens* from conqueror of the land-community to plain member and citizen of it. It implies respect of his fellow members, and also respect for the community as such" (Leopold 1966, p. 240).

Leopold's life ended suddenly when, in 1948, he died fighting a forest fire along the Wisconsin River. His land ethic boils down to a single statement that generations of environmentalists are intimate with: "A thing is right when it tends to preserve the integrity, stability, and

Fig. 1. Two members of the environmental group Earth First! hold a sign in front of the Lincoln Memorial to protest the destruction of the earth's rainforests. (UPI/Bettmann)

Fig. 2. A string of 48-inch-diameter pipe for the trans-Alaska pipeline is readied for burial in a hilly area about 10 miles north of the Yukon River. (UPI/Corbis-Bettmann)

Fig. 3. The geyser basins of Yellowstone Park, Wyoming. (UPI/Corbis-Bettmann)

Fig. 4. Associate Supreme Court Justice William O. Douglas (July 1973). (UPI/Corbis-Bettmann)

Fig. 5. Two scientists from a U.S. expedition studying the hole in the ozone layer overlook the vast Antarctic lansdcape. (Reuters/Corbis-Bettmann)

Fig. 6. The Exxon Valdez oil tanker that created the worst oil spill in U.S. history sits in drydock for repairs to its hull. The ship spilled 11 million gallons of crude oil into Prince William Sound in Alaska. (UPI/Corbis-Bettmann)

Fig. 7. A boarded-up home in Love Canal, Niagara Falls, New York. Over 200 homes contaminated with toxic waste from an old dumpsite had to be evacuated and torn down. (UPI/Corbis-Bettmann)

Fig. 8. Thoreau's hut in Walden, Massachusetts. (Corbis-Bettmann)

Fig. 9. Radiation-monitoring personnel at work in the Chernobyl Nuclear Power Plant after the worst civilian nuclear accident in history. (Corbis-Bettmann)

Fig. 10. R. Buckminster Fuller in front of a geodesic dome, an exhibit he designed for the Montreal Exposition (1967). (UPI/Corbis-Bettmann)

Fig. 11. Residents of Bhopal stand in front of the Union Carbide factory gate. In December 1984, deadly gas that was to be converted into a harmless pesticide leaked from the plant, causing widespread death and illness. (UPI/Corbis-Bettmann)

Fig. 12. Rachel Carson, American author and biologist. (The Bettmann Archive)

Fig. 13. Theodore Roosevelt with naturalist John Muir on Glacier Point above Yosemite Valley, California. (The Bettmann Archive)

beauty of the biotic community. It is wrong when it tends otherwise" (ibid. p. 262).

LIFEBOAT ETHICS (See **HARDIN, GARRETT**)

LIMITS TO GROWTH, THE In April 1972, *The Limits to Growth* hit the bookstores. Perhaps more than any other single book, *Limits* spawned more controversy, debate, and follow-up publications, than any environmental work of the 20th century. Under the direction of Dennis Meadows and **Jay Forrester** from MIT, a study of the implications of continued economic and industrial grow concluded that the world could not sustain continued growth for more than a century without catastrophic consequences. The study ran several models that all included population growth, agricultural production, nonrenewable resource depletion, industrial output, and pollution generation. The major conclusion of the various scenarios was that industrial capital and world population could not continue to grow if an equilibrium state was to be achieved and collapse of one or more of the variables studied was to be prevented. While admittedly an imperfect, oversimplified model, the goal of the study in sparking attention and debate was certainly realized.

LORENZ, KONRAD (1903-1986) Austrian ethologist and author of several books including *King Solomon's Ring* (translation 1952), which offers unique insights into the behavior of animals. His work, *On Aggression* (1966), drew parallels between animal and human behavior and concluded that humans are aggressive by nature. Unlike other animals, however, humans have not evolved surrender mechanisms, while modern technology has given them the capacity to significantly alter the environment for all creatures. The best condition for humans, Lorenz believed, is in appreciating their animal nature and adapting to the natural environment while recognizing differences between our species and others and using these specific talents to bring our species into a more sustainable relation with the earth.

LOVE CANAL An abandoned waste site in Niagara Falls, New York, which, in 1977, initiated concern over hazardous waste in the United States. Between 1942 and 1953, Hooker Chemicals and Plastics Corporation dumped 22,000 tons of toxic chemicals in steel drums into an old canal excavation. In 1953, the company covered the dump site with clay and topsoil and sold the property to the Niagara Falls school board for one dollar with the condition that the company would have no future liability for injury or property damage caused by the dump's contents. Later, an elementary school and housing project were built on the site. By 1976, residents began to complain of smells and sickness. **Lois Gibbs**, a homemaker, led a local grass-roots effort to demand answers to the illnesses affecting the community and in seeking retribution. In 1977, chemicals were detected leaking from the buried drums which prompted state officials to conduct health tests. In part, it was revealed that pregnant women around the site had miscarriages at 4 times the national average. In 1978, the school was closed, and 238 families were permanently relocated. Since then, most of the homes and the school have been torn down, and the dump has been covered with a clay cap and surrounded by a drain system that pumps leaking wastes to a new treatment plant. A 1988 survey revealed that 9 out of 10 houses next to the canal had at least one person in the family suffering from cancer.

LOVEJOY, THOMAS (See **DEBT-FOR-NATURE SWAPS**)

LOVELOCK, JAMES (See **GAIA THEORY**)

LOVINS, AMORY (1947-)   Popular spokesperson for energy conservation and articulator of a sustainable energy strategy for the United States. Trained as a physicist, Lovins has received several prizes and awards for his research on alternative energies and conservation. His studies at the Rocky Mountain Institute, which he founded in 1982 with his wife and fellow researcher, Hunter Lovins, are held in high regard. He serves as a consultant for utility companies, private industries, and all levels of government.

Lovins's approach is the "soft energy path." He argues that we must be more responsible in terms of the sources of energy that are used for different purposes. He points out that improving efficiency of industrial electric motor drive systems instead of fueling existing power plants to make electricity would save enough energy to replace the entire U.S. nuclear program. Further, using available technology to increase automobile fuel efficiency would allow many cars to get 62 to 138 miles per gallon. Finally, by building well-insulated and solar housing, people need little or no outside energy to maintain a comfortable home, even in extreme climates.

Thus, Lovins's approach discourages questions about how to find more sources of energy. Rather, he suggests that we get more work from the energy we already have. This would not only save money, but improve environmental quality and increase national security. Although projections he made in the 1970s and 1980s for energy use in the United States were ridiculed by government and industry leaders as impossibly low, his projections have proven to be very accurate.

LOW-INPUT SUSTAINABLE AGRICULTURE (LISA)   A system of crop production that combines the wisdom of traditional agricultural systems with new techniques that take advantage of local climates, soils, resources, and cultural systems. Programs for LISA have emerged from federal efforts with the objectives of reducing fertilizers, pesticides, and other inputs; the net result of this system is increased profits and agricultural output, conservation of energy and resources, reduction of soil loss and nutrient loss, and a greater degree of self-sufficiency by the farmer.

Among the concepts of LISA are crop rotation on a seasonal basis in order to reduce pest damage and increase outputs and soil fertility and regular addition of crop residues and animal manures to improve soil structure, fertility, and water storage capacity. LISA may rely on some pesticide use under an integrated pest management plan which includes cultural controls, biological controls, and some pesticide use. Cultural controls may consist of changing planting times each season and rotating crops on a seasonal basis. An additional cultural element involves consumer attitudes. When fungicides are eliminated, produce has a shortened shelf life and is often bruised. Consumers whose aesthetic criteria favors the ideal—untarnished produce—will only purchase food raised with preservatives. Thus, in order for organic produce to be purchased, consumer attitudes must change. Biological controls may involve importing natural predators and parasites of pests. Finally, some pesticides may be used, albeit only in the necessary amount, to control remaining pests.

M

MACKAYE, BENTON (1879-1975) A pioneer U.S. land planner. MacKaye's ideas rested on the philosophy of designing with nature. In 1921, he recommended that a belt of wilderness areas surround mountain ridges. He was responsible for leading the campaign for the creation of the Appalachian Trail running along mountain ridges from Maine to Georgia.

MacKaye believed that human beings had tendencies for both the gregarious and the solitary: all humans at times delight in the society of other humans, but at other times seek solitude. He explained this by the fact that human populations had once been more scattered across the landscape, but many now live in urban areas. His ideas toward regional planning were shaped from this notion; he believed that wilderness preserves were necessary to maintain on the edge of urban areas. This would provide people the opportunity to reinvigorate their energies in the tonic of wilderness, as needed, while living in a community of other humans.

MADRID PROTOCOL (See ANTARCTICA)

MALTHUS, THOMAS ROBERT (1766-1834) Malthus was a British clergyman and economist, who is most known for his writings on the relationship between humans and their food supply. His essay on the principle of population as it affects the future improvement of society was written in 1798, and was one of the first to bring home to individuals the notion that population, which was growing without limit and at a geometric rate, would outstrip the supply of food and resources, which were increasing at a linear rate. He argued that nothing could prevent ecological disaster, short of the poor voluntarily limiting their own family size. When Malthus expanded his 1798 work into a full-scale treatise in 1803, he softened his original position and noted that there were checks on human population beyond food supply (such as war, etc.), and that humans could intervene in their fates through such methods as abortion and infanticide, which would hold down the birthrate and postpone or alleviate human misery. He maintained, however, a pessimistic outlook on the ability of humans to regulate their populations. Despite his feelings about the problems of human population growth, he, like most figures of his day, regarded birth control devices as morally unacceptable, if not positively sinful. It wasn't until several decades after his death that the birth control movement used his theories in their platform. Although many details of the Malthusian theory, as it is now called, remain controversial, over-population in the Third World and its concurrent environmental problems, have led to a renewed interest in Malthus's work.

MAN AND BIOSPHERE PROGRAM (MAB) A United Nations program established in 1970 and devoted to developing a scientific basis, linking the natural and social sciences, for improving the relationship between humans and their environment. The focus of the program is on over 280 biosphere reserves in 70 countries.

MAN AND NATURE (See **GEORGE PERKINS MARSH**)

MAQUILADORA These factories that line the Mexico-American border were established in the 1960s to import raw materials from the United States and sell finished products back to the United States. Now they number over 2,000 and employ over 500,000 workers. It has been claimed that the growth in the number of these factories has been caused, at least in part, by the weaker environmental laws in Mexico and the lax enforcement of the environmental laws that do exist. Towns in which these factories are located have experienced population growth associated with greater employment opportunities, but this increase in population has exacerbated environmental problems like water pollution in these areas.

Many have argued that the **North American Free Trade Agreement** will strengthen Mexico's environmental laws and their enforcement. Others fear that the removal of trade barriers will serve only to increase pollution in these border areas.

MARGULIS, LYNN (See **GAIA THEORY**)

MARINE MAMMAL PROTECTION ACT (16 U.S.C. 1361 ET SEQ.) Passed in 1972 and amended in 1988, this law was created to protect marine mammals. Although the act prohibited the taking of marine mammals, it did allow for "incidental takes" associated with commercial fishing, especially the use of drift nets, and this provision continues to create controversy. This act may cover some of the same species as the **Endangered Species Act,** and when it does, the Marine Mammal Protection Act takes precedence. The jurisdiction for enforcing the act falls mainly to the **National Oceanographic and Atmospheric Administration** for whales, dolphins, and porpoises, and to the **Fish and Wildlife Service** for other marine mammals.

MARINE PROTECTION, RESEARCH, AND SANCTUARIES ACT (33 U.S.C. 1401 et seq.) This 1972 act considers the effects of all ocean dumping on the marine environment. Its long-term goal is to phase out ocean dumping. **The Environmental Protection Agency** (EPA) administers dumping permit applications and bases its decision on the following: the need for the proposed dumping; the effect it will produce on human health and welfare; the result of such action on the marine ecosystem; the persistence of dump contents; the effect of dumping particular volumes in specific concentrations; available alternative disposal methods; and alternative uses of the proposed dump site. The secretary of the army issues permits for transporting and disposing dredged material in ocean waters based on the same criteria used by the EPA. Permits issued by both regulatory agencies must designate the type and amount of material that will be dumped, location of the dump, the length of time the permits are valid, and any other special provisions to be included.

The other provision of the act is the Marine Sanctuaries program, in which states set aside marine sanctuaries to preserve or restore an ocean area's ecological, aesthetic, or recreational capacities.

MARSH, GEORGE PERKINS (1801-1882) Marsh obtained a law degree, was elected to the Vermont legislature, and also served in the U.S. House of Representatives. He also was a U.S. ambassador to Turkey and Italy. However, none of these achievements was related to his primary interest and the work that made him famous. In 1864, Marsh published *Man and Nature*, a classic treatise on the relationship between humans and their environment. He noted that "the earth is fast becoming an unfit home for its noblest inhabitants." He asked his readers to look at how they lived their lives and what their actions did to the environment. Marsh believed that humankind is supreme among all species, but it has a responsibility to maintain a healthy total environment. His arguments—made 140 years ago—favored the preservation of organisms and their habitats and echo the arguments environmentalists make today for the preservation of biodiversity. His writings influenced many conservationists who came after him, including **Gifford Pinchot, Theodore Roosevelt,** and John Meagher.

MARSHALL, ROBERT (1901-1939) Robert Marshall was born and raised in New York City. As a child, he spent summers with his family in the Adirondack Mountains. During these early years, he climbed the largest Adirondack mountains. As an adult, he continued to climb and explore the Adirondacks and other wilderness areas. Marshall earned a master's degree in forestry from Harvard, a doctorate in plant pathology from Johns Hopkins University, and became a professional forester and director of the U.S. Forest Service's Division of Recreation and Lands.

To Marshall, the wilderness experience offered two important benefits besides physical conditioning—aesthetic and mental. He stated, "wilderness perhaps furnishes the best opportunity for . . . pure aesthetic rapture" (Marshall 1930, pp. 144-145). Further, the city represses human expression, while the wilderness sanctuary both excites the imagination and offers a place of reflection and repose. Nowhere was this more true than in Alaska where Marshall dreamed of the possibility of protecting entire ecosystems as a permanent frontier that Americans could forever enjoy.

Although Marshall's life ended at the young age of 38, his accomplishments were numerous: in 1935 he formed the **Wilderness Society** "for the purpose of fighting off invasion of the wilderness and of stimulating . . . an appreciation of its multiform emotional, intellectual, and scientific values" (Nash 1982, p. 207). He pushed through the "U" regulations of the U.S. Forest Service. Adopted in 1939, these management tools extended the policy of wilderness preservation in the designated national forests by making wilderness recreation the dominant use for 14 million acres in the western national forests.

MATHER, STEVEN (1867-1930) Born in San Francisco, Mather was the first administrator of the national parks. He is often called the father of the **National Park Service**. An industrialist who made millions of dollars from 20 Mule Team Borax, he was also a dedicated outdoorsman. In 1914, on a trip through Sequoia and **Yosemite**, he was shocked at the poor conditions of the parks, and upon returning home wrote the secretary of Interior a highly critical report on park mismanagement. In response, Secretary Franklin K. Lane challenged Mather, writing, "Dear Steve: If you don't like the way the national parks are run, why don't you come down to Washington and run them yourself?" (Wild 1979, p. 61). That challenge prompted Mather to go to Washington and become assistant secretary of the Interior to oversee the parks.

To ensure the survival of parks, Mather led the charge for a single federal agency to protect and manage the **National Park Service** in the Department of the Interior. As the service's first director, he met several challenges unsuccessfully during his 14-year tenure. The most notable was opposing, along with **John Muir**, the **Hetch Hetchy** Dam of Yosemite Valley. Later, in 1920, he made a strong plea for absolute preservation of National Parks in his report to the U.S. Congress. A series of debilitating health problems forced Mather to retire in 1928, and he died soon after in Darien, Connecticut.

MAZUNTE, MEXICO A village in southern Mexico that had been one of the primary habitats of sea turtles because of the area's abundance of wetlands and shorelines. However, in the late 1960s turtle slaughterhouses moved into the area to benefit from cheap labor and a bountiful supply of resources. Through the 1980s, up to 2,000 turtles were slaughtered per day.

In 1990, after pressure from environmental groups, Mexican President Carlos Salinas de Gortari forbade the slaughter of turtles. With the help of environmental groups, the villagers of Mazunte took action: farmers promoted wetland protection, grew organic fruits and vegetables, and sold much of their products to local industries that supplied a local cooperative store; the village attracted tourists with its Marine Turtle Museum, and composed a "Declaration of Mazunte" that protected and restored turtle habitat. Mazunte has since become a model community for sustainable development and restoration.

MCPHEE, JOHN (1931-   )   McPhee was educated at Princeton University and did a postgraduate year at Cambridge University. He became a staff writer for *Time* in 1957, and then served as a staff writer for *The New Yorker*. His interests were diverse and varied, and his writings covered many topics. Environmentalists are most interested in McPhee's books that examine important people in the environmental movement, and the wild lands upon which he focused his concern. He has authored notable profiles of **David Brower** (*Encounters with the Archdruid*, 1971), and edible wild plant expert, Euell Gibbons. He has also written about wild lands, including the Pine Barrens and Alaska. Perhaps his most popular book, *Coming into the Country* (1977), focused on Alaska land battles of the late 1970s. In this book he also described the dangers of oil spills in Alaska's Prince William Sound. Although many consider him one of the best environmental writers of the second half of the 20th century, in reality his prolific writing covered sports, cooking, art, and a dozen other assorted topics as much as the environment.

MEADOWS, DENNIS (See **LIMITS TO GROWTH**)

MENDES, CHICO (1944-1988)   Francisco "Chico" Mendes followed his father in becoming a *serenguero* or rubber tapper in the Brazilian rain forests. He extracted the latex sap from trees twice per week and waited until the liquid dried to become natural rubber. This process does not harm the trees nor does other extractive activities like collecting Brazil nuts, wild fruits, and other resources.

In the 1970s, with help from the World Bank, Brazil built a highway immediately south of the province of Acre, where Mendes worked, in order to meet the demands of ranchers who converted forestland into rangeland for cattle. Because of the Amazon's infertile soils, rangelands were quickly depleted of their ability to support plants to feed cattle and more land was requested to support ranchers. In the 1980s, Brazil sought to extend the highway into Acre to meet these requests.

Mendes organized a resistance to the road development and proposed that the land be maintained for renewable extractive reserves. In 1986, he ran for legislator as a Worker's Party candidate to stop the road. He won the popular vote but lost the electoral count, although the legitimacy of the election was questioned.

In 1987, Mendes went to the United States to lobby against the Inter-American Development Bank—the agency that funded the highway. His effort resulted in the Senate Appropriations Committee funding only $58 million of the bank's requested $258 million due to the environmental destruction that would result from the project. He then met with Brazil's Interior Ministry, after which extractive reserves were established in most of Acre.

Ranchers promised retribution for Mendes's actions, and on December 22, 1988, he was shot dead at his home. Investigators convicted rancher Darli da Silva, da Silva's son, and a ranch hand. The rubber tappers union, founded by Mendes, became a powerful force in rain forest protection, and similar groups are forming in other rain forest countries.

MERCHANT, CAROLYN (1936-   ) A U.S. philosopher, environmental historian, and ecofeminist writer whose book *The Death of Nature* (1980) examined "the values associated with the images of women and nature as they relate to the formation of our modern world and their implications for our lives today" (Merchant 1980, p. xxi). It also illustrated how the scientific revolution was responsible for the subjugation of women in addition to the destruction of the natural world. The mechanistic philosophy of the "founding fathers" of modern science replaced the image of the earth as a living organism. She connected the situation of women with that of nature, arguing that our culture views women and nature as possessing similar qualities, which are subordinate to those possessed by men. The passive qualities assigned to both legitimated control and domination of them under society's socially constructed reality.

Merchant unites the purposes of the ecology and the women's movement—each seeks to overturn the dominant social paradigm, which views both women and the environment as culturally passive and subordinate. The feminist and ecology movements share an affiliation for an egalitarian perspective and embrace the goals of environmental integrity. They are both critical of the current economic system, which values pure competition, aggression, and domination.

Merchant prescribes the holistic scientific ecology approach as one that can liberate both women and nature and lead to environmental and social sustainability. In this approach, every part of the system (earth) is seen as a valuable interdependent component. The planetary system furnishes meaning upon each element as each part, in turn, enhances ecosystem or biospheric stability. (See also **ECOFEMINISM**)

MEXICAN FAMILY PLANNING Family planning programs have been widespread and somewhat successful in Mexico over the last 25 years. These programs, initiated by the government in 1973, reduced the fertility level from 6.7 births per woman in 1970 to 3.1 births per woman in 1996. However, the population of Mexico continues to grow extremely rapidly. The population growth rate of Mexico in 1996 was 2.2 percent which, if continued, would result in a doubling of the country's population in 32 years. This greatly increased population will add more stress to an already overstressed environment. (See also **MEXICO CITY'S AIR POLLUTION**)

MEXICO CITY'S AIR POLLUTION   With a 1994 population of 15.3 million, and 1,000 new immigrants each day, Mexico City suffers from a declining economy, increased urban violence, and deteriorating air quality. Over half of the city's residents have no sewer systems, and fresh, clean water must be purchased from vendors. The over 30,000 factories spew pollutants and employ much of the city's residents. More significant than the air pollution from factories, however, are the 3.5 million motor vehicles. In 1989, the city tried to reduce emissions by banning the use of 20 percent of automobiles each day. In response, residents began purchasing second cars. The effect of auto and other pollution is magnified by the fact that Mexico City lies in a basin surrounded by mountains, making it exceptionally susceptible to air pollution. Most days the air is declared unsafe to breathe, and between 1982 and 1992, contamination levels tripled.

Mexico City has intensified efforts to fight pollution by banning cars from a 50-block central zone, allowing only trucks that run on liquefied petroleum gas, and banning taxis built prior to 1985. Further, cars that burn leaded gasoline have been banned since 1991, and those built since 1993 are equipped with catalytic converters. Unfortunately because there are few newer cars in Mexico City, air quality has not yet shown significant improvement.

MICROLENDING   The concept of microlending was first used by the Grammeen Bank in Bangladesh. This system provides credit to the poorest of the poor who would not be able to secure loans from traditional banks. Microlending is now practiced in many countries in the developed and less developed world, often to support projects that lead to environmentally sustainable development. The Grammeen Bank provides very small loans to 400,000 borrowers. Most loans are under $100 and are used for purchasing things such as cows, bicycles, and low-cost necessities.

Most borrowers pay back their loans as required; the repayment rate is 98 percent. For those that do not pay, all other borrowers share the burden to repay the loan. This system is successful because it empowers individuals, encourages responsibility, and builds self-esteem and self-worth while improving local economies and community cohesion. This concept provides an opportunity for the United States, Canada, and other developed countries to share the burden of protecting global resources such as tropical rain forests.

MIGRATORY BIRD TREATY   In 1916, Canada and the United States signed a treaty for the protection of migratory birds. This treaty was in reality a federal government game law, which imposed closed seasons and limitations on commerce. Although this agreement was among the earliest attempts at international control of wildlife, it did not go into issues such as pollution or habitat protection nor commit either nation to the establishment of preserves or refuges within their borders. In 1934, the United States passed the Migratory Bird Hunting and Conservation Stamp Act, which required waterfowl hunters to purchase a duck stamp. The proceeds from these sales went to a fund to purchase land and easements for the benefit of waterfowl. (See also

AUDUBON   SOCIETY;   FISH   AND   WILDLIFE
SERVICE)

MILLS, ENOS ABIJAH (1870-1922)   Preservationist of the
Rocky Mountains who touted the region as nature's
wonderland. Leaving his Kansas home, Mills journeyed to
the U.S. West in 1884 when he was 14 years old. After
arriving, he built his own log cabin and did odd jobs for
the little money he needed, while he spent most of his
time climbing mountains and wandering wilderness areas.
At age 20 in 1889, he met **John Muir**. This relationship
resulted in Muir recruiting him as a strong crusader for
the preservation movement. Mills soon began writing for
magazines and teaching easterners about the natural areas
of the Rockies. He lectured to audiences in every state in
the union, as well as Europe and Mexico, on the
importance of preserving the remaining vestiges of
western nature for the grizzly bear, other animals, and for
the American people themselves.

Mills went on to write 16 books about his adventures
and interpretations of U.S. wilderness and the threat
miners, loggers, and cattlemen posed, especially to the
Rockies. Most books became immediately popular with
Americans. Mills's experiences led him to realize
fundamental ecological principles firsthand. For instance,
he realized, before most others, that periodic forest fires
were necessary to maintain a healthy and diverse
environment. Even before **Aldo Leopold** understood the
value of predators, Mills advocated restocking the grizzly
bear in areas where hunters and ranchers had nearly
exterminated the species.

His efforts at preservation were rewarded with the
establishment of Rocky Mountain National Park in 1915.
One year later, he assisted in creating the bills for a
unified **National Park Service**. However, after he saw

how the National Park Service mismanaged natural areas, he spoke out against it.

MONKEY WRENCH GANG (See **ABBEY, EDWARD**)

MONTREAL PROTOCOL   An international agreement, signed by 36 countries, to phase out ozone-depleting substances. The meeting convened in Montreal, Quebec, in 1987, in reaction to the discovery of a large ozone hole over the Antarctic region. Recognizing the need to avert disaster, the countries signed the Montreal Protocol, which committed the 36 countries to reducing by 1999 their use of chlorofluorocarbons to 50 percent of the amount used in 1986. After scientific evidence became more conclusive, 93 countries met in London in 1990 to amend the 1987 agreement and again in 1992 in Copenhagen to further strengthen the original protocol and speed up the phase-out of ozone depleting gases.

Not only did the protocol recognize the need to stop the depletion of the ozone, it marked a successful global initiative. Many countries are now aware that the warnings of environmentalists are not just doomsday prophecies, but represent real threats. It demonstrates that when international cooperation is needed, countries can come together to protect the global environment. The phaseout of CFCs in the world by their largest producers is ahead of schedule.

MORAN, THOMAS (1837-1926)   Born and raised in Philadelphia, Pennsylvania, Moran became an established painter in the Hudson River School by 1870. Unlike many of his contemporaries, Moran painted western landscapes rather than those in the East. He recorded the mountains of the West for a variety of reasons. First, he was commissioned by various magazines to record the scenes that would attract easterners to relocate west of the

Mississippi. Moran also painted the West as the official artist on several government expeditions. The prime motivating factor that established Moran as a Rocky Mountain painter was his commission to accompany a government exploration led by Dr. Ferdinand Haydn for the Department of the Interior in 1871 to the area around the **Yellowstone** River in Wyoming. This commission had a tremendous impact on Moran's artistic specialization and renown as well as on the future of national parks in the United States. Indeed, his paintings were influential in establishing Yellowstone as the first national park in 1872.

MOWAT, FARLEY (1921-) Writer of more than 25 books on the peoples and environment of Arctic cultures in Canada and Newfoundland, Farley Mowat was born in Belleville, Ontario. At a young age he was attracted to the abundant Saskatoon landscape. Although his early ambitions were to be a biologist, visits to the Arctic drove him to write about his experiences with native cultures and their environs in such early works as *People of the Deer* (1952) and *The Desperate People* (1959). His writings expressed a deep compassion for animals, such as the arctic wolf, caribou, and whale species, whose intrinsic worth, he believes, is completely disregarded by "modern" society, incessantly driven to exploit the resources of the north. Mowat's numerous writings describe diverse native cultures united by their commitment to living in harmony with their natural world. They are tied to the earth by a kinship with animals upon which they depend for survival and with whom they share the land.

MUIR, JOHN (1838-1914) Muir moved from his native Scotland to Wisconsin in 1849 at the age of 11. After spending two-and-a-half years at the University of

Wisconsin, he left on foot, walking from the Midwest to the Gulf of Mexico, recording his thoughts and observations in a journal, which he published in 1916. He made many other extended journeys throughout the United States noting scientific and aesthetically astounding impressions of nature. Muir went on to become a leader of the preservation movement in the late 19th and early 20th centuries.

Muir became an ardent defender of the preservation of wildland, and is today known as the "father of the preservation movement." He argued for the nontangible benefits of pure immersion into the wilderness. Subscribing to the transcendentalist philosophy of **Henry David Thoreau** and **Ralph Waldo Emerson**, his stance on wilderness protection became a religious conviction. In *My First Summer in the Sierra*, he commented:

> This I may say is the first time I have been at church in California, led here at last, every door graciously opened for the poor lonely worshipper. In our best times everything turns into religion, all the world seems a church and the mountains altars. (Muir 1987, p. 250)

He also appreciated wildlife and wildlands for their intrinsic value, stating that every life-form has its own good to pursue. His writing and zeal for maintaining wilderness convinced the U.S. federal government to adopt a forest conservation policy that resulted in the creation of Sequoia and **Yosemite National Parks**.

Although Muir had only a couple years of college, he impressed scientists with his knowledge of natural systems. In 1911, he stated, "When we try to pick anything out by itself, we find it hitched to everything else in the universe" (Muir 1987, p. 157). His capabilities in geology were equally as impressive, and he was among the first to recognize the role of glaciers in the creation of high sierra scenery. In 1892, he gathered 26 friends in a law office in San Francisco and founded the **Sierra Club** to "explore, enjoy, and render accessible the mountain regions of the Pacific Coast" and "to enlist the support of people of the government in preserving the forests and other features of the Sierra Nevada Mountains" (Shabecoff 1993, p. 72). He became the club's first president.

Muir became upset at the advance of sheep, or "hoofed locusts" as he called them, into the High Sierras. He was influenced by Henry George's ideas about the evils of private land ownership and argued for state action to preserve land. To preserve Yosemite as a National Park, he wrote popular essays describing the area and proposed a 1,500-square mile park. In 1890, Yosemite became the first park specifically designed to protect wilderness.

In his later years, Muir was embroiled in a battle with Chief of Forestry, **Gifford Pinchot**, over damming the Yosemite Valley. While he failed in this effort and died in the following year (1914), Muir's approach left a mythic power over future conservationists and numerous natural areas have been named to honor his legacy. (See also **HETCH HETCHY**)

MURIE, OLAUS (1889-1963) U.S. biologist, spokesperson for preservation, and 20th-century writer. Murie grew up in Moorhead, Minnesota, and experienced early the wonder of wild nature during canoe trips with his brother up the Red River. He went to Fargo College in North Dakota, Pacific University in Oregon, and earned an M.S. from the University of Michigan. He began his career as a field biologist, but found his real love two years later when he accepted the responsibility of collecting specimens and exploring Arctic Canada for the Carnegie Museum in Pittsburgh.

In 1920, the U.S. **Fish and Wildlife Service** sent him to Alaska to collect information on this unknown territory and its wildlife. His main task was to track the porcupine caribou—a very visible species and the primary food source for many native cultures. Murie's book *Alaska-Yukon Caribou* (1935) became a standard text for mammalogists. His wife, Margaret, accompanied him on Alaskan expeditions and produced her own book, *Two in the Far North* (1962). Finishing his work on the Alaskan caribou, Murie went to Jackson Hole, Wyoming, to study the elk whose numbers were diminishing as a result of the pressures of modern civilization.

Murie's work as a federal employee is significant for far more than his studies. He continually warned of the ecosystem danger of manipulating wildlife. He came to the defense of grizzly bear and wolves for their service of culling the weak-and-old-of-prey populations. In fact, he influenced **Aldo Leopold's** own revelation that predators are important to a well-functioning, holistic ecosystem. Murie's philosophy was to leave nature alone.

After retiring from the federal government at age 45, Murie moved his family to a log cabin on the Snake River. His home soon became a mecca for other like-minded preservationists. Among other accomplishments, Murie founded and later served as director and president of the **Wilderness Society.** He traveled around the world advising governments on habitat preservation and restoration; wrote several articles for various environmental publications, expressing his views on wildlife management; and warned of the disastrous consequences that could result from blind faith in technology and progress in the post-World War II United States. Given that he viewed the earth as a living organism, he scorned the technological prowess of U.S. culture as rivers were dammed, meadows paved, and forests destroyed. He vigorously lobbied for the **Wilderness Act** and wild areas of the western United States, and the **Arctic National Wildlife Refuge** in Alaska, which was established in 1960. Murie died the year before the passage of the Wilderness Act in 1964.

N

NAESS, ARNE (1912-) Norwegian philosopher, Nazi resister, and mountaineer. Naess coined the term *deep ecology* in 1972. The essence of **deep ecology** is to ask deeper questions. These questions encourage a consciousness shift in which every life-form is recognized to possess the right to compete and function in an ecosystem. Further, it holds that every life-form deserves the opportunity to blossom into its fullest potential or to become self-realized. Naess's brand of deep ecology emphasized the human realization of the intrinsic value of all life-forms, as opposed to shallow ecology, which reflects the dominant worldview in which people protect the environment out of self-interest (anthropocentrism). Deep ecology stresses the importance of protecting the environment for the good of each individual species inhabitant (biocentrism). When considering policy options, deep ecology encourages one to consider the good of other life-forms and ecosystems. As an ethical system, deep ecology values biological and cultural diversity, complexity, autonomy, decentralized power, egalitarianism, and symbiosis.

Naess later began to use the term *ecosophy* in addition to deep ecology, as the former indicates an affinity for the Greek term *sophia,* or wisdom, while, the latter, alternately, implies the science of ecology. Ecosophy then shifts the focus from science to wisdom and studies the interrelationship of society and wild nature. Naess believed that in order for the needed consciousness shift to occur, people must adopt the principles of deep ecology and interpret them in their own brand of ecosophy. Naess's ideas shaped environmental philosophy in North America. Deep ecology has become popularized in North America by **Bill Devall** and **George Sessions** in their book *Deep Ecology.*

NATIONAL COASTAL ZONE MANAGEMENT ACT (CZMA) (16.141 ET SEQ.) This 1972 act resulted from U.S. public concern over preserving coastal lands from development activities. The act established the **National Oceanographic and Atmospheric Administration (NOAA)** as well ˙as the Office of Coastal Zone Management. The act encouraged seacoast and Great Lakes states to submit coastal zone management programs to the federal government. These plans consider such factors as natural resources, coastal-dependent economic growth, and protection of life and property in critical areas. In assessing these factors, states often conduct inventories of coastal resources, establish protection measures, and designate critical areas as "nationally significant." Federal funds cover up to 80 percent of program administrative costs. Once a state program is approved, federal activities along coastal zones must assess the impact of an activity along the zones.

The law's amendment in 1980 extended the scope of coastal areas to include wetlands, floodplains, estuaries, beaches, dunes, barrier islands, coral reefs, and fish and wildlife habitats.

NATIONAL ENVIRONMENTAL POLICY ACT (NEPA) (42 U.S.C. 4341 ET SEQ.) The purpose of this 1969 act is "To declare a national policy which will encourage productive and enjoyable harmony between man and his environment"; and "to promote efforts which will prevent or eliminate damage to the environment and biosphere and stimulate the health and welfare of man." The act also created the **Council on Environmental Quality** with the responsibility to oversee compliance of federal agencies with provisions of this act. In 1978, the council set forth these provisions in 40 C.F.R. 1500-1508, and, since that time, has issued "guidelines" to agencies.

In sum, the act mandates that all federal agencies assess the environmental impact of undertaking a project. An environmental assessment is done in the preliminary project phase, and, if the project is likely to have a significant effect on the environment, the federal agency must write an **environmental impact statement (EIS)**. An EIS shall contain the following: purpose and need for action; probable positive and negative environmental impacts of action and project alternatives; unavoidable adverse environmental effects; short- and long-term environmental impacts; irreversible commitment of resources needed if activity is pursued; objections raised by reviewers of the preliminary impact statement; names and qualifications of people preparing the EIS; and references to support statements and conclusions.

Critics of the process argue that, overwhelmingly, impact statements merely justify projects rather than critically evaluate their impact and consider project alternatives. Further, vague descriptions are used to render the document and findings meaningless (e.g., loss of vegetation); inaccuracies in reporting are common, and often documents contain vast amounts of irrelevant or technical information to overwhelm reviewers.

NATIONAL HISTORIC PRESERVATION ACT (16 U.S.C. 470-470t) This act designates the Advisory Council on Historic Preservation to protect and restore cultural resources in the United States. Historic properties are protected by the National Register of Historic Places, which limits the activities that can occur on the property in exchange for federal renovation and maintenance assistance. The **National Park Service** was entrusted with the determination of eligibility for projects under act amendments, while state historic preservation officers have enforcement responsibilities within each state.

Under the act, regulations for eligibility on the National Register of Historic Places are provided for, as are the effects of any projects on the historic property. Further, the advisory council may comment on a federal project; federal agencies are entrusted with nominating properties for the Register and must maintain adopted sites; agencies must coordinate projects with the state historic preservation officer; and, finally, states can also qualify for federal monies to maintain and restore properties on the National Register.

NATIONAL MARINE FISHERIES SERVICE (NMFS) (See ENDANGERED SPECIES ACT)

NATIONAL OCEANOGRAPHIC AND ATMOSPHERIC ADMINISTRATION (NOAA) On October 3, 1970, President Richard Nixon created NOAA within the Department of Commerce. This agency was charged with coordinating most U.S. federal policy dealing with the ocean and concerns of the atmosphere, excluding air pollution (which only two months later was to become the domain of the **Environmental Protection Agency**). NOAAs responsibilities include the **Coastal Zone Management Act,** the **Marine Mammal Protection Act,** parts of the **Endangered Species Act**, and the Ocean Dumping Act. The public knows NOAA best as the agency that administers the National Weather Service and the National Satellite, Data, and Information Service. This agency also handles questions arising under numerous international laws and treaties including the 1959

Antarctic Treaty, the United Nations Law of the Sea Conventions, and the MARPOL convention governing pollution from vessels.

NATIONAL PARK SERVICE   The National Park Service was formed in 1916 for two primary reasons: to provide Americans with areas for recreation and to protect natural areas from development. The single incident that most influenced its creation was the authorization of the **Hetch Hetchy** dam. Congressional approval of the dam stimulated an ethic of nature preservation and the creation of an agency to manage and protect National Parks.

The duties of the Park Service consist of the administration of parks and national monuments, management of other landmarks of cultural and natural significance, and coordination of the **Wild and Scenic Rivers Act** and the National Trails System. It also administers federally funded research programs for environmental research in geology, ecology, and biology.

The Park Service has come under attack in the past due to its twofold purpose. Prior to 1960, the Park Service leaned toward recreation by providing hotels, extending roads, improving trails, stocking lakes with fish, and generally providing visitors with all the accoutrements of civilization. After 1960, due to increased visitation, the service stressed preservation of natural integrity. With visitation to National Parks increasing at an exponential rate, the service finds it difficult to maintain natural areas intact. Visitation is limited through such management measures as raising entrance fees and limiting length of stays during peak seasons of park use.

NATIONAL POLLUTANT DISCHARGE ELIMINATION SYSTEM (See CLEAN WATER ACT)

NATIONAL WILDLIFE FEDERATION With well over a million members (over 5 million if you count catalog shoppers and magazine subscribers), the National Wildlife Federation is the largest conservation education organization in the United States. Its methods of conservation education are diverse and include wildlife camps, Ranger Rick Clubs, and an Urban and Backyard Wildlife Habitat Program. It is perhaps best known for its wildlife magazines, *National Wildlife* and *International Wildlife*. The organization supports the preparation of wildlife policy studies by outside institutions and agencies, while it conducts its own investigations and lobbying. Most recently it has lobbied against the reconstruction of flooded out levies on the Mississippi River.

NATIVE AMERICAN ENVIRONMENTALISM While each culture had a different impact on the environment, Native Americans are recognized as being the nation's first environmentalists. Indigenous life-styles were not understood by European settlers–"Indians" lived a subsistence life-style, killing and taking from the earth only what was necessary to survive. Their cultures were well adapted to the seasonal demands of the environment.

Unlike the European settlers, the earliest Americans understood the balance existing in nature and their role in a healthy-functioning environment. Every aspect of their life-style prior to the arrival of settlers was focused on the maintenance of the ecological balance that sustained them. When they killed animals, they took the weak ones so that the stronger might improve their species. They learned to kill without disturbing the rest of the animals around their prey. They only killed what they needed, never depleting the population of an animal, for by doing so the natural balance would be disrupted and result in a disruption of their own society. Finally, many cultures gave thanks to the spirits of the plants and animals that willingly gave of themselves so that the humans had nourishment.

When the 1970s environmental movement began in the United States, many Americans held up the native American as a symbol for a sustainable culture. Their relationship with the land as sacred deeply influenced environmentalists who sought spiritual as well as pragmatic reasons why the fundamental assumptions of U.S. culture were ecologically dysfunctional.

NATURAL RESOURCES DEFENSE COUNCIL (NRDC)

A group of Yale law students founded the NRDC in 1970 to provide legal advice to environmental groups and to engage in litigation in important cases involving air quality, water quality, energy policy, and so on. With a 1995 membership of over 160,000, NRDC now ranks in the top 10 environmental groups. One of the group's most publicized campaigns was its 1989 battle against Alar sprayed on apples. In the recent past, NRDC has focused attention on rain forest preservation and has pressured the U.S. **Fish and Wildlife Service** to use the **Endangered Species Act** more effectively to preserve U.S. forests. Rather than working only on creation of new environmental laws, the NRDC is a watchdog of agency behavior and enforcement of existing environmental law as well. In addition to litigation, NRDC supports scientific research and public education programs. It has published dozens of books and articles on topics including nuclear weapons, urban environment, land resources, health effects of pollutants and coastal water pollution.

NATURE CONSERVANCY

Founded in 1951, the Nature Conservancy seeks out, identifies, and purchases important natural lands. Its large staff identifies and inventories land in need of protection, and then its army of fundraisers provides the needed capital. Where possible, the

Conservancy uses its nonprofit tax exempt status to solicit gifts of property and uses its own funds to purchase property when a donation is not a possibility. Although the Conservancy keeps and manages most of the land it acquires to ensure its conservation goals are met, some land is turned over to government or other private groups, which will provide adequate protection. In over 40 years, the Conservancy has helped preserve over 5 million acres and now manages more than 1,000 sanctuaries, several of which are home to endangered species. It is one of the largest environmental groups in the United States today with 1995 membership at over 600,000. Individuals who find many environmental groups, such as the **Sierra Club** and **Greenpeace**, too radical are attracted to the Nature Conservancy's "mainstream methods" of land acquisition. One conservancy official said "We're not in the business of confronting anybody." This is why the group has been dubbed the "industry's favorite environmental group." Its recent Last Great Places campaign aims to buy or protect 75 parcels and projects, raising a billion dollars to do so.

NEW YORK STATE FOREST PRESERVE Since 1885, state lands in northern New York (now over 2.5 million acres) and a smaller parcel in the Catskill Mountains north of New York City are protected by the New York State Constitution's "Forever Wild" clause. Article 14 of the New York State Constitution states:

> The lands of the state, now owned or hereafter acquired, constituting the forest preserve as fixed by law, shall be kept as forever wild forest lands. They shall not be leased, sold, or exchanged, or be taken by any corporation, public or private, nor shall timber thereon be sold, removed, or destroyed.

This historic preservation act in such a populous state was the result of abuses of large timber companies who stripped land of the timber and then let the state take them over for failure to pay taxes. The importance of this preservation act, which sets it apart from many others, is that it is a part of the state constitution, not merely legislation, and thus is not easily changeable by a given legislative or administrative body. This example of wilderness preservation helped to play a role in the creation of the Federal Wilderness Act of 1964.

NIXON, RICHARD M. (1913-1995) When Nixon entered the White House in 1969, environmental concerns were not among his priorities. Soon after, however, that changed. Under his leadership, the **Environmental Protection Agency** was formed and the **National Environmental Policy Act (NEPA)** was signed into law. Under NEPA, for the first time in U.S. history, environmental considerations would be considered in any federal action that could potentially harm the environment. In his 1970 State of the Union address, he acknowledged environmentalism, stating, "Clean air, clean water, open spaces—these should once again be the birthright of every American." In this speech, he designated April 18th through 24th, 1971, as Earth Week. He proposed a $10 billion clean water plan and suggested new air pollution regulations—the **Clean Air Act** of 1970 was a controversial but bold effort to preserve the nation's air quality.

NOISE CONTROL ACT (42 U.S.C. 4901 ET SEQ.) This act became necessary due to the effects of population growth, population density, increased mobility, and industrial activities. The Noise Control Act was adopted to (1) regulate noise emission from new products, especially those dealing with transportation and construction activities such as air compressors, trucks, earth-moving machinery, waste compactors, jackhammers, lawn mowers, and motorcycles; (2) control aviation, interstate motor carrier, and railroad noise; (3) ensure labeling of high-level noise products to protect against individual exposure; and (4) encourage development of state and local programs to control noise.

The 1987 Quiet Communities Act amended the Noise Control Act by giving states and localities authority to control noise by disseminating information on noise pollution and establishing regional technical assistance centers to help communities abate noise pollution.

NORTH AMERICAN FREE TRADE AGREEMENT (NAFTA)   A free trade agreement among Canada, Mexico, and the United States signed in 1993. Prior to its being signed, environmental groups, including the **Sierra Club** and **Friends of the Earth,** voiced opposition to it. These groups were concerned that free trade would result in lowering environmental protection laws

In response to these charges, the United States successfully negotiated with its member nations to produce the North American Agreement on Environmental Cooperation. This agreement established a commission to analyze the environmental ramification of the NAFTA and resolve contentious issues. This is the first time a trade agreement expressly addressed environmental issues.

O

OCEANIC SOCIETY (See FRIENDS OF THE EARTH)

OGALLALA AQUIFER   The world's largest freshwater aquifer lies below portions of 8 U.S. states, stretching from Texas to South Dakota. It was left by glaciers that melted 15,000 years ago. About 100 years ago, before exploited as an irrigation source for farmers and ranchers, it was estimated to contain approximately 16 times as much fresh water as all freshwater surfaces on earth, including lakes, rivers, and marshes. This single aquifer has been largely responsible for the productivity of U.S. agriculture, supplying large quantities of water to an otherwise arid region. Despite its benefits, today this aquifer is depleted at rates that far exceed recharge. In fact, water is pumped out at an estimated 8 times its recharge rate. Its destruction is promoted by tax incentives that allow farmers to deduct the cost for drilling wells. In many parts, the aquifer is already nearly depleted as water tables fall by up to 3 feet per year and water must now be pumped from depths that exceed 6,000 feet. Environmentalists often cite this aquifer as an example of the elimination or degradation of what should be a renewable resource.

OLMSTED, FREDERIC LAW (1822-1903) Preservationist, writer, gentleman farmer, and landscape architect. Besides writing about life in the southern United States, he designed New York City's Central Park in the 1850s. He first had to persuade the city's leaders that it was beneficial to preserve 770 acres in the center of Manhattan Island. His vision was for every sizable city to have a park in the city's center so that residents would have an escape from city life. Providing natural scenery in city centers would be a uniquely American invention.

Olmsted was also an enthusiastic supporter of preservation of unique wild places such as Niagara Falls. After working in New York, in 1863 Olmsted spent three years in California and became familiar with the **Yosemite** Valley. He soon became manager of the valley, which the federal government had granted to California for recreational uses. He urged the California government to adopt his management measures, which were aimed at preserving the natural integrity of the region while preventing the exploitation of its resources. He argued that scenic areas positively influenced health and intellect.

Olmsted also conceded that soon natural places would become overburdened with visitors and that tourists would overcrowd Yosemite and grow in exponential numbers over the decades. While his preservation plan did not initially find favor with politicians and entrepreneurs, his predictions came true with painful accuracy. Olmsted did return to Yosemite in the late 1880s, however, to assist **John Muir** in establishing it as a national park, thereby gaining it protection.

OLSON, SIGURD (1899-1982)   A 20th-century U.S. naturalist and wilderness preservationist whose writings described the unequaled beauties of the lakes and boreal forests of northern Minnesota in books such as *Listening Point* (1958) and *Reflections from the North Country* (1976). He fought to preserve the Quetico-Superior country in Minnesota against water power, lumber, and highway interests. Writing of the need for people to have a wilderness retreat to nourish both their mental and physical capacities, he wanted to preserve unspoiled areas as cultural relics and the "type of continent that our forefathers knew" (Olson 1948, p.4).

Along with the **Izaak Walton League** and others, Olson persuaded President Harry S Truman to issue an executive order to prohibit the flying of aircraft over the Quetico-Superior region below 4,000-feet altitude. In his fight against the **Echo Park Dam** in Dinosaur National Monument in 1955, Olson argued for the aesthetic values of wilderness in a speech before the U.S. Senate subcommittee. He warned that, by destroying natural

areas, we might destroy irreplaceable intangible qualities
that have evolved in an American wilderness philosophy.

OZONE DEPLETION   This environmental problem has
attracted the attention of almost every international
environmental group and has penetrated mainstream
society. Ozone gas, which is three parts oxygen (normal
oxygen is two parts), is a protective envelope that
surrounds the earth about 15 miles above the earth's
surface. This protective ozone layer in the stratosphere
should not be confused with increases in ozone in the
lower atmosphere or troposphere, which are detrimental to
human health. It filters out harmful short-wave radiation,
which otherwise has the potential to dramatically alter life
on the planet. Human effects include skins cancers and
eye cataracts, while various harmful effects on vegetation
include a reduction in photosynthesis in green plants.

In 1974, chemists Sherwood Rowland and Mario
Molina found that the ozone layer was thinning due to the
presence of a chlorofluorocarbons (CFCs). CFCs had been
manufactured since the 1930s. They were used as air
conditioner and refrigerator coolants, propellants in
aerosol spray cans, computer chip cleaners, and hospital
instrument cleaners. They were commonly used to make
styrofoam cups and bubbles in plastic foam for insulation
and packaging. When CFCs are released from these items,
they take decades to reach the ozone layer in the upper
atmosphere. When they arrive there, chlorine atoms are
released and they begin to break apart ozone molecules.
Each CFC atom destroys as many as 100,000 ozone
molecules during a 60- to 100-year lifetime. CFCs also
contribute to global warming.

While Rowland and Molina warned of this problem in
1974, it took 15 years before scientists and legislators
responded. In the meantime, a hole the size of the United
States formed over Antarctica; a hole over the Arctic later

formed and both holes are enlarging annually. Because CFC molecules are persistent and take decades to rise to the stratosphere, depletion of the ozone layer will get worse before it restores itself. There has been impressive global cooperation on this issue, and CFC use has now been banned. (See also **MONTREAL PROTOCOL**)

P

PANTHEISM This is a religious belief based on the abstract worship of nature. It rejected the worship of idols and books in favor of the natural world. In its crudest form, it never personifies "God" but holds the worship of nature as its highest form of praise. Pantheism understands God and nature as one united entity. Thus, mind and material has one unified aspect or presence. In pantheism, religion offered a naturalistic explanation for creation, the creator, and elevated the natural world to a spiritual plane.

PERMACULTURE Permaculture is the design and maintenance of agricultural systems which are diverse, stable, and resilient. "It is the harmonious integration of the landscape with people providing their food, energy, shelter and other material and non-material needs in a sustainable way" (Bell 1992, p. 15). The term was invented by Bill Mollison to imply permanent agriculture, although it has expanded to include sustainability, or a permanent culture. A permaculture design is an integrated system of information, plants, animals, energy, building materials, and other locally available resources into a self-sustaining living community patterned after the systems of nature.

Permaculture presumes that all of creation shares a common survival interest. In this sense, a system is permanent when, over time, it causes no harm to any other system. It recognizes that nature has no hierarchy, just different niches. Creation should be treasured and passed on, not used to exploit and exhaust. If we care for our immediate loved ones, we must care for the land. Everything we are and have comes from nature and will return to it.

PINCHOT, GIFFORD (1865-1946) Trained in the French Forest School in Europe after his graduation from Yale in 1889, Pinchot returned to the United States as the first American trained in forestry. He was hired in 1892 to design the first successful management plan in the United States for George W. Vanderbilt in the area around the Biltmore Estate in Asheville, North Carolina.

After working as a consultant for the federal government, he took the position of chief of forestry. His influence on the need for more management of federal forest lands led to the creation of the Bureau of Forestry in 1901. In 1905, when President **Theodore Roosevelt** created the U.S. Forest Service, Gifford Pinchot was appointed as its first chief. Pinchot pioneered the "wise-use" movement in resource preservation. This view, also referred to as the conservationist ethic (as opposed to the more pure preservationist ethic), demanded that resources be exploited at a sustainable rate so that tree harvests would not diminish the resource base. Additionally, he embraced the idea that forestlands should be guided by a multiple-use principle so that resources could be used for a variety of purposes; e.g., land for timbering, mining, grazing, recreation, and wildlife, soil, and water conservation. Pinchot was met with challenges from such preservationists as **John Muir** who argued that natural area preservation was not compatible with resource exploitation. These two men became embattled over the **Hetch Hetchy** dam controversy in the **Yosemite** Valley.

POLYCHLORINATED BIPHENYLS (PCBs) Organic molecules are comprised of 209 different toxic, oily, halogenated aromatic hydrocarbons. They have been used since 1966, and have caused widespread contamination. PCBs were commercially produced in plasticizers, lubricants, hydraulic fluids, paints, inks, adhesives, and paper coatings. Their major application, however, was as electrical capacitors and transformers used by electric utilities.

Once PCBs enter the environment, they are very stable and therefore persistent. They remain in the environment, are not water soluble, and bioaccumulate up the food chain. Exposure to PCBs causes nausea, dermatitis, dizziness, bronchitis, and eye irritation. Its chronic effects are that it is a known carcinogen and mutagen. Traces of these substances have been found all over the world in every environmental medium, bioregion, and most life-forms. Humans are exposed to them from birth as they are transmitted in breast milk and contaminate food.

In 1976, PCBs were banned in manufacture and most uses in the United States. They were, however, allowed in existing electrical transformers, capacitors, and other equipment. Due to fires in transformers exposing the public to the substances, the **Environmental Protection Agency** ordered that all PCBs be removed from transformers in apartment and office buildings, hospitals, and shopping malls by 1990. While they remain an environmental threat, they can be 99.9 percent detoxified by high-temperature burning, although this carries a hefty price tag and is not applicable for large quantities of contaminated soil or pure PCB oils. In the 1970s and '80s, PCBs became the symbol of the widespread contamination of the planet, which **DDT** was during the 1960s.

POPULATION BOMB, THE (See **EHRLICH, PAUL**)

POWELL, JOHN WESLEY (1834-1902) Promoter of careful development and settlement of the U.S. West in the late 19th century. In the "Report on the Lands of the Arid Region" (1878), Powell argued that the West's arid climate and limited capacity for farmland should limit the kind of dense settlement occurring in the eastern United States. Further, large mining, timber, and real estate interests were taking land away from the would-be small yeoman farmer. He argued that the government's survey system of square-mile parcels accorded in no way with watersheds. By parceling out 160-acre lots per family, the system made failure and hardship among settlers inevitable. Powell recommended that ranchers be allotted at least 2,560 acres around defined watershed boundaries. In fact, he proposed dividing the West into hundreds of watershed-defined communities, each of which would be a "commonwealth in itself," responsible for its own development and conservation. Clearly, if Powell's ideas had been accepted the Dust Bowl of the 1930s might have been avoided or would not have been so severe.

In 1869, Powell led a 100-day Grand Canyon expedition, which began at Green River, Wyoming and ended, after meeting the challenges of several waterfalls, at Green Wash Cliffs near the Utah-Nevada border. This brought national attention to this one-armed, self-educated college professor from the Midwest. He led 30 further adventures throughout several western states after the Canyon trip and befriended many Native American cultures along the way. His expeditions produced documentation of water and mineral resources, artifacts and information about indigenous cultures, and plants and animals of many undiscovered kinds.

Following these successes in 1879, Powell convinced the U.S. Congress to establish the Geological Survey. Afterward, he spent several years trying in vain to protect western lands from monopolistic exploiters. Powell's last years were spent writing history, philosophy, arguing for land reform, and exploring the material remains of Indian cultural artifacts.

PRIMITIVISM This is the philosophy that the happiness and well-being of humans decreases in proportion to their degree of civilization or, alternately, happiness increases in proportion to the degree of wilderness present. This is an important idea in Romantic philosophy. Also implied is the idealization of the "noble savage" who has both redeeming and repulsive characteristics. Spokespersons for this philosophy include Jean-Jacques Rousseau, William Byrd, **William Bartram**, and **John Bartram**.

R

RAINFOREST ACTION NETWORK (See **BIODIVERSITY CRISIS; BIOSPHERE RESERVES**)

RED LIST (See **INTERNATIONAL UNION FOR CONSERVATION OF NATURE AND NATURAL RESOURCES**)

RED TIDE An irruptive bloom of aquatic organisms, called dinoflagellates, caused by a specific mixture of water temperatures, salinities, and nutrient flows. Once these populations become abundant, a toxin is released, and a red deadly tinge permeates the water. Fish and other organisms will try fruitlessly to escape the poison by flapping out of the water. Soon, however, the fish succumb to the poison, and their dead bodies wash ashore for days. Most red tides last only a few days although, some are known to have persisted for several months. Red tides occurred infrequently until the 1950s and '60s when they nearly became an annual occurrence on the Gulf Coast and along other areas like the California and New Jersey coastlines. While the cause of the tides has not been clearly identified, scientists correlate them with agricultural runoff and poorly treated sewage runoff.

RESOURCE CONSERVATION AND RECOVERY ACT (RCRA) (42 U.S.C. 6901 ET SEQ.) This act began in 1965 as the Waste Disposal Act in an attempt to control solid waste disposal. In 1976, **RCRA** gave the **Environmental Protection Agency (EPA)** authority to: regulate hazardous waste disposal; encourage communities to develop waste management plans; prohibit open dumps; regulate underground storage tanks; and enable research, development, and demonstration plans to improve waste disposal methods and conservation techniques. The act separated hazardous waste into four classes (ignitability, reactivity, corrosivity, and toxicity) and required tracking of hazardous waste from the time of generation to disposal in a unique "cradle to grave" recordkeeping responsibility. Further, it required states to develop EPA-approved hazardous waste management plans.

In 1984, major amendments were enacted to address shortcomings of the act. These included: notification of data for underground tanks and regulating detection, prevention, and correction of releases; incorporation of a small quantity of hazardous waste generators into the regulatory scheme; condition disposal of several kinds of wastes upon EPA's approval; require corrective action by treatment, storage, and disposal facilities for all hazardous waste release regardless of when waste was disposed of; require annual EPA inspection of government-owned facilities and an every-other-year inspection of privately owned hazardous waste facilities; and regulate facilities that burn waste and oils in boilers and industrial furnaces.

RIFKIN, JEREMY (1945-) President of the Greenhouse Crisis Foundation and Foundation of Economic Trends, author, and environmental activist. In his written works, he offers an interdisciplinary mix on the study of science, technology, politics, and culture.

In *Biosphere Politics* (1991), Rifkin articulated a vision of the 21st century—a world where the biosphere is itself the framework for rethinking personality, politics, and culture. This future of human responsibility for the earth will replace our current notions of security through military might and high technology. Rifkin called for a greater participation of humanity with the planet as a process. This new understanding will revolutionize politics, economics, and social relationships in the next century.

Beyond Beef: The Rise and Fall of the Cattle Culture (1992) discussed the dependence that industrialized nations have on cattle and the problems such a dependence creates. Rifkin argued that the cattle population was much too large for the planet and required nearly one-quarter of the planet's landmass. As a result, cattle possess an unprecedented threat to the global environment, human health, and the economic stability of many nations. Finally, his 1995 book, *The End of Work*, forecasted the high levels of unemployment that will become increasingly realized as automation, computers, and robotics take the place of the global work force.

RIO DECLARATION   (See **UNITED NATIONS CONFERENCE ON ENVIRONMENT AND DEVELOPMENT**)

ROBBINS, JOHN (1914-) Activist and author of books and articles concerning animal rights issues and the interrelationships among environmental problems, ethical issues, and health effects of the U.S. meat production system. His book, *Diet for a New America* (1987), won national acclaim. It examines the problems with a meat-based diet and the inhumane and unhealthy conditions under which chickens, pigs, milk cows, and cattle are raised. In the book and film by the same name, Robbins awakened the consciousness of his audience as he took them on a journey through the U.S. meat production system, illuminating such health effects as the fat in animal products clogging arteries, which results in heart attacks and strokes and increases the likelihood for some types of cancer. At the same time, he claimed the majority of cropland in the United States is used to raise food for the animals we eat and this land could be used to raise crops for export to the world's hungry. Additionally, the waste from cattle feedlots pollutes waters with nitrates, which accelerate the natural eutrophication process. He noted that, while there are 5 times as many cattle as people in the United States, there is no sewage system for the animals. Further, the amount of water it takes to raise one head of cattle is equal to the amount needed to float a tanker. Atmospheric effects of cattle include increased methane levels, a greenhouse gas produced due to cattle flatulence. As president of the EarthSave Foundation, Robbins continues to work for the welfare of other species and the environment.

ROBERT, KARL-HENRIK   A leading Swedish cancer researcher who teaches others about the need for sustainability. Robert gathered professionals from science, music and art, politics, education, and even recruited Sweden's king, to develop a plan that would create national consensus on the need to attain sustainability. Rather than using antagonistic measures of debate and dispute, he looked for areas of agreement on basic issues and his working groups produced consensus reports. The ideas were implanted in booklets and audio cassettes and sent to all schools, households, and businesses in Sweden. Information was also sent to parliament, television stations, and magazines.

This concerted effort is credited with a transformation of thinking in Sweden. Although more work is called for, people recognized that a sustainable society was possible with existing technologies and governments. Many believe that Robert's ideas can serve as a useful model to help other nations make the transition to sustainability. **Denis Hayes** and others in the United States have promoted similar ideas. This type of massive outreach effort was Hayes's motivation for the first Earth Day as well as his more recent idea of the "Green Seal."

ROCKEFELLER, JOHN D., SR. (1839-1937) Oil speculator who early on stated that his goal in life was to serve as an exemplar to generations of Americans by becoming rich. He succeeded at this task through oil development and monopolies. Shortly after oil was discovered in Titusville, Pennsylvania, he invested in an oil refinery and established the Standard Oil Company in 1870. Within a short time afterward, he was refining most of the oil in the United States. He began taking over small oil refineries and monopolized the market. At the same time, Rockefeller's financial contributions to preservation were enormous, helping to secure territory in Acadia, Jackson Hole, and **Yosemite** for the **National Park Service.**

ROCKY MOUNTAIN INSTITUTE (See **LOVINS, AMORY**)

ROOSEVELT, THEODORE (1858-1919) Twenty-sixth president of the United States. His fascination with animals began in childhood, and he later wrote extensively on wildlife. He founded a museum, the Roosevelt

Museum of Natural History, which had over 100
specimens that he gathered from his travels.

Roosevelt attended Harvard from 1876 to 1880 and
devoted much of his time to the study of biology,
zoology, geology, and physiology. During his sophomore
year, he produced his first publication, "Summer Birds of
the Adirondacks." He went on to write extensively on the
subject of birds. His environmental knowledge grew on
his trips west into the Dakota Badlands. He also learned
many lessons as the first president of the **Boone and
Crockett Club**. His first experience with government was
as governor of New York.

Roosevelt was perhaps the first "environmentalist"
president of the United States. Serving as president from
1901 through 1909, he made the commitment to
conserving wildlands. His conservation achievements as
U.S. president were numerous. Between 1903 and 1909,
he created 50 wildlife refuges. The first was Florida's
Pelican Island in 1903, preserved as breeding grounds for
native birds. Other contributions were the reclamation of
arid lands and the reorganization of the Forest Service—
transferred from the authority of the Department of
Interior to the Department of Agriculture. This latter
action proved controversial as federal lands were leased
out to private timber companies due to a rider placed on
the Forest Reservation Act by Congress. At the end of his
tenure in office, Roosevelt had preserved 172 million
acres of national forests and protected 18 sites as national
monuments. In 1908, he hosted a conference of governors
at the White House on the subject of conservation. His
presidency has been termed the "Golden Age of
Conservation."

ROSZAK, THEODORE (1933-   ) Historian and interdisciplinary scholar who gained national notoriety during
the 1960s youth movement. His works include *The*

Making of a Counterculture (1969), *Where the Wasteland Ends* (1972), and *Person/Planet* (1978). Among his ideas were that the 1960s U.S. counterculture formed out of a rejection of technocracy in favor of a society that embraced the organic unity of human-earth relations. To reestablish this relationship, he urged a deurbanization of the United States to bring people back into physical contact with the natural world. According to Roszak, all aspects of modern society have brought us further from respect for and intimacy with the natural world.

He developed the ideas of a human-earth relationship in a more recent work, *The Voice of the Earth* (1992). Exploring the psychological underpinnings of the ecological crisis, he argued that our species is ecosystemically dysfunctional. The principles he suggested to reestablish a communion with the earth include permitting the ecological unconscious to guide us through cosmic evolution and reestablish ties with the planet (which technology alienates us from) and allowing the ecological ego to reestablish an ethical responsibility toward the earth. This includes reevaluation of masculine character traits and encourages an embrace of a feminist spirituality. Further, he advocated a recognition that small-scale social forms and "personal empowerment nourishes the ecological ego," and "the needs of the planet are the needs of the person, the rights of the person are the rights of the planet" (Roszak 1992, p. 321).

S

SAFE DRINKING WATER ACT (42 U.S.C. 300F ET SEQ.) This act, passed in 1974, has two main objectives: protect the nation's drinking water, and use proper water treatment methods to protect public health. Contaminant levels are set based on the **Environmental Protection Agency's (EPA)** regulations to protect underground drinking water supplies. Applicants who wish to inject wastewater into the ground must receive an EPA permit.

The act requires minimum safety standards for every community water supply (some of the contaminants regulated are arsenic, bacteria, barium, cadmium, chromium, fluoride, lead, mercury, nitrates, pesticides, and silver); the development of treatment techniques to meet said standards; regulation of radioactivity and turbidity; protection of groundwater aquifers; development of demonstration programs to protect aquifers, and state programs to protect wellhead areas from contaminants that threaten public health.

SAGEBRUSH REBELLION In the 1980s, as federal control of western public lands increased, many miners, cattlemen, and other range developers launched a crusade, The Sagebrush Rebellion, in order to wrest the authority of land management from the U.S. federal government and to put it back into the control of western states. This was one of the first "antienvironmental" movements of the modern era. (See also **WISE-USE MOVEMENT**)

SALE, KIRKPATRICK (1937-) Late 20th-century popularizer of the concept of "bioregion." In *Dwellers in the Land* (1985) he defined a bioregion as: part of the earth's surface whose rough boundaries are determined by natural characteristics rather than human dictates. They are distinguishable from other areas by particular attributes of flora, fauna, water, climate, soils, and landforms.

Sale is a critic of industrial society, which he claims is responsible for abusing the natural world along with social, political, and economic environments. In his bioregional approach, he argues that society should be structured according to community biological and physical carrying capacity and natural limits.

The economy of society should thus respect limits of the local bioregion and use resources only from that area. Such an economy will cooperate and recognize its interdependence with nature; society's power structure will be decentralized and will evolve toward peace rather than grow in violence. He believes that this society will come about and will be embraced by both the politically left and right because its values are shared by each.

SAND COUNTY ALMANAC (See **LEOPOLD, ALDO**)

SAVE-THE-REDWOOD LEAGUE The league was founded in 1918 to protect redwood lands for public parks. It has, over the decades, purchased over a quarter of a million acres of redwood lands located in 32 California Redwood State Parks, Muir Woods National Monument, Redwood National Park and Sequoia National Park. In addition to purchases, the league has also worked with other environmental groups to prohibit or limit the commercial logging of redwoods.

SAVE THE WHALES Founded in 1971, Save the Whales is one of several groups that focuses on whale preservation. It sponsors public service announcements on television and radio and provides advertisements in print media to garner public support for its goals. Unlike some whale preservation groups, Save the Whales is not opposed to subsistence whaling carried on by indigenous people. The group also sends a representative to annual International Whaling Commission meetings.

SCHUMACHER, E. F. (1911-1977) A Rhodes scholar in economics, Schumacher has been president of the Soil Association (one of Britain's oldest organic farming

organizations), and founder and chair of the Intermediate
Technology Development Group (specializing in tailoring
tools, small-scale machines, and production methods to
the needs of developing countries).

Schumacher is a follower of Gandhi's philosophy,
which advocates small-scale economies and nonviolence.
He believes that small-scale, decentralized economies are
sustainable and can run by themselves with little need for
government. They would rely on local materials to make
products for local consumption.

Schumacher also emphasized that economies should be
run on appropriate technology. The advantages appropriate technology offers are that it employs many more
people than present economies, and, because it is on a
small scale, it is efficient and can be tailored to fit the
needs of the local economy; it uses locally available
resources and has less impact on the environment because
of low energy inputs and little pollution. His views are
best expressed in his 1973 book, *Small is Beautiful*.

SCHURZ, CARL (1829-1906) U.S. Secretary of the Interior
under Rutherford Hayes from 1877 to 1881, Schurz was a
German immigrant educated and concerned about scientific management of forests. Although his pleas for
preservation made little impression on the U.S. federal
government, he introduced the idea for a National Forest
System in his 1877 annual report. In 1891, the U.S.
Congress eventually passed an act permitting the president
to create forest reserves by withdrawing land from the
public domain.

His report called attention to the enormous amount of
timber that had been withdrawn from the public domain
by commercial interests and sold to foreign countries.
Further, he claimed that the exhaustion of U.S. timber
would necessitate the decline of the country's prosperity
in coming decades. Schurz also addressed the ecological

ramifications of stripping mountainsides of their timber covering, writing:

> When these mountain sides are once stripped bare, the rain will soon wash all the earth necessary for the growth of trees from the slopes down into the valleys, and the renewal of the forests will be rendered impossible forever. (Nash 1976, p. 26)

To avoid such catastrophes, he suggested that:

> All timber-lands still belonging to the United States should be withdrawn from the operation of the preemption and homestead laws. (Ibid., p. 27)

SEA TURTLES A group of tropical and subtropical land nesting turtles, including Green turtles, Hawksbills, Loggerheads, Leatherbacks, and Kemp's Ridleys, are all threatened by humans. Of the 270 known turtle species, 42 percent are rare or threatened with extinction. Attempts to preserve the turtles are hindered by the fact that turtle eggs must be incubated on land. Thus, when thousands of turtles come ashore to lay millions of eggs, poachers often wait for their arrival, collect eggs, and kill the grown turtles. Collectors take the eggs for food and kill turtles for their succulent meat (soft cartilage under the shell which is used for soup). Their shells are made into combs, lamps, and many tourist souvenirs. People in Third World countries often depend on these endangered turtles as a main protein source.

Indirect threats to sea turtles are equally troubling. Baby turtles lucky enough to return to the sea often ingest styrofoam pellets from drift lines, and beach development destroys nesting grounds. Turtles that hatch at night mistake the light emitted by seaside development from the glow of moonlight over that ocean and move the wrong way. Animals domesticated in a human environment also threaten turtles. Raccoons, rats, dogs, and cats eat the beached eggs and baby turtles, while crows and gulls grab the hatchlings as they scramble toward the sea.

Breeding programs protect eggs and hatchlings. After one year's time, turtles are rereleased from beaches where eggs are laid. Researchers have much to learn about turtle habits. For instance, it is not known how and why turtles return to specific beaches or where hatchlings go once they return to the sea. Other efforts to protect turtles include a 1990 decree by the president of Mexico making it illegal to kill the turtles.

SESSIONS, GEORGE (1938-   ) Professor of philosophy, consultant to the National Endowment for the Humanities, and editor of the *International Ecophilosophy Newsletter*. While Sessions's contributions to environmentalism are numerous, his explication of **deep ecology** is perhaps most significant. *Deep Ecology*, coauthored with **Bill Devall** (1985), developed a philosophy originally presented by Norwegian philosopher **Arne Naess**. Deep ecology:

> goes beyond a limited piecemeal shallow approach to environmental problems and attempts to articulate a comprehensive . . . philosophical worldview. . . . (Its) basic insight . . . of biocentric equality is that all things in the biosphere have an equal right to live and blossom and to reach their own individual forms of . . . self-realization. (Devall and Sessions 1985, p. 65)

Reissuing the message of **John Muir**, Sessions argued that respect for the natural world should be independent of its usefulness to humans.

Sessions is among the environmental philosophers who carved out a niche in the 1970s to address the philosophical considerations of the environmental crisis.

Devall and Sessions recognize two fundamental norms embraced by deep ecology: biocentric egalitarianism and self-realization. Biocentric egalitarianism maintains that all living things including rivers, mountains, and ecosystems have equal intrinsic value. Self-realization is defined in wider circles than the individual self or ego. In their context, the term refers to an identification of the individual with the rest of the human and nonhuman world. It transcends cultural definitions of self and integrates the individual with the universe.

SHEPARD, PAUL (1925-) An ecotopian visionary who explicated many of his ideas in *Man in the Landscape: A Historic View of the Esthetics of Nature* (1967) and *Nature and Madness* (1982). In explaining the reason for contemporary society's hostility toward the environment, Shepard contends that humans broke a psychic and spiritual relationship with the earth with the dawn of agricultural societies. During the hunting and gathering stages of existence (and still in existence today in some primitive societies), the natural world was psychologically internal. Children were born and established a lifelong kinship with the world. When agriculture began around 10,000 years ago, humans experienced an "ontogenetic crippling," as they broke a deep-seated bond with nature. This resulted in "chronic madness," which continues to affect our species. Renewing our kinship with the natural world can only be accomplished by obeying our latent need for reestablishing an original ecological harmony with the nonhuman world.

Shepard's brand of primitivism encourages an end to all genetic engineering and most kinds of agriculture. In its place, he envisions a return to hunter-gatherer lifestyles and cultures, where possible, and a superconcentration of people into coastal communities. For this to be feasible, population must also stabilize at 8 billion by the year 2050. This plan for reinhabiting the planet and rehabilitating the land necessitates that societies live in 5-mile ribbon communities on the edges of continents. The interior regions could then be preserved as wilderness and stand as a permanent frontier.

SIERRA CLUB Founded in 1892 by naturalist **John Muir**, the Sierra Club now boasts over 600,000 members. The club, formed for the purpose of helping to preserve land, claims to have had a role in the preservation of over 130 million acres. Today the Sierra Club is known as an effective lobbying group for not only land and park preservation, but a wide range of environmental protection causes. The club still keeps with its roots in promoting the exploration and enjoyment of wild areas by conducting an extensive outing program to protected areas all over the globe.

SIERRA CLUB LEGAL DEFENSE FUND Founded in 1971, the Legal Defense Fund works closely with the Sierra Club, but it is an independent organization. Its role is to provide legal services to the environmental movement; primarily, they sue. Some of the most notable lawsuits in which the Legal Defense Fund has participated include Mineral King Valley where a ski area was halted until the valley was added to Sequoia National Park; Kaiparowits Plateau, Utah, where construction of the world's largest coal plant was halted; and Little Granite Creek, Wyoming, where proposals by then-Interior Secretary **James Watt** to allow oil and gas drilling were delayed until the area was designated as wilderness.

SILENT SPRING (See **CARSON, RACHEL**)

SIMON, JULIAN (1932-   ) Professor of economics and business administration and well-known U.S. critic of environmentalism and champion of modern society's focus on progress and technological know-how. His controversial views have pitted him against environmentalists as when he argued that, in the face of environmental damage or overpopulation, it becomes more important to rely on technology and industrial development. He points out that each generation in the United States lives better than the preceding one, in spite of the warning of ecological catastrophe. His books *The Ultimate Resource* (1981) and *The Resourceful Earth* (1984, with Herman Kahn) encouraged expansion of industrialism and further control of the earth, its resources, and socioeconomic desideratum of consumption.

As a critic of population control, Simon argues that we have been successfully manipulating the earth over the past several hundred years to allow more people to use and share its resources and live longer and healthier lives in each successive generation. He credits this progress to triumphs in agriculture, sanitation, and medicine. With respect to resource consumption, he maintains that it is precisely at those times when resources become scarce, that human ingenuity and technological prowess adopts technologies to improve conditions for survival.

Simon concedes that conditions for humans are not improving everywhere or that better futures are guaranteed. Rather, humanity is confronted with constant challenges from the environment but that well-functioning political, economic, and social systems can meet the demands of the earth.

SINGER, PETER (1946-   ) A writer for animal liberation who believes that animals should be endowed with the same rights as humans. Every individual animal as well as species deserve equal consideration. While each of their capacities may not be equal, each individual has its own interests and, if they have interests, they have the capacity to suffer.

He contends that people who oppose abortion and euthanasia usually do not oppose the killing of nonhumans. Thus these people do not truly believe in the sanctity of life, but merely the sanctity of human life.

Singer and other animal liberationists like Thomas Regan have helped the environmental movement by extending rights to the nonhuman world. In addition, by respecting the rights of animals, we must protect their habitats and ecosystems. By protecting these, we preserve access to animal rights so they can live to their fullest expression.

SMALL IS BEAUTIFUL (See SCHUMACHER, E. F.)

SMELTERS--SUDBURY, ONTARIO Sudbury, Ontario, in Canada is home to one of the world's largest copper and nickel ore operations. It has large quantities of ore along with mines, smelters, and refineries all within a few square miles. Smokestacks spewed out particulates of heavy metals and the largest quantities of sulfur dioxide in North America. Since 1969, emissions have been reduced by 40 percent, although 2,000 metric tons per day are still released into the atmosphere. To minimize pollution, several years back, smokestacks were increased in height; however, this just spread emissions to farther distances.

The sulfur dioxide pollutants create acid rain, which, along with heavy metals, destroy ecosystems for nearly 250 square kilometers (100 square miles). Vegetation is destroyed, rivers and lakes acidify to the point that virtually all life-forms are choked to death. Secondary effects of removing vegetation include an increase in soil erosion and alteration of soil chemistry.

SNYDER, GARY (1930-   )   Snyder's family moved to Washington from his birthplace in San Francisco where he learned an appreciation for the outdoors. He attended Reed College, where he developed sympathies for anarchist ideas and radical politics. After college, he worked for the U.S. Forest Service and did graduate work in linguistics at Indiana University. Later Snyder studied Asian languages at Berkeley, where he met Allen Ginsberg and Jack Kerouac with whom he shared similar values. In 1956, Snyder went to Japan on a scholarship from the First Zen Institute of America. He lived in a monastery in Kyoto, Japan, and became a disciple of Zen Buddhism.

After returning to the United States, Snyder began to develop an ethic that combined Buddhist and Native American principles with an American natural rights ideology. He argued that nature was an oppressed minority whose rights were violated.

Perhaps his greatest literary contribution to environmentalism was *Turtle Island*, which won the Pulitzer Prize in 1975. After winning this award, he often spoke for the rights of nature. As a Buddhist, he used Asian religions as a guide to improving human relationships with the natural world.

SOFT ENERGY PATH (See **LOVINS, AMORY**)

SPACESHIP EARTH (See **BOULDING, KENNETH**)

STEGNER, WALLACE (1909-1993) Novelist, historian, and motivating force for the U.S. conservation movement. In his efforts to gain national protection for wilderness, he wrote about the importance of wild country in the modern United States. His 1960 essay, "The Meaning of Wilderness in American Culture," was originally written in the report of the Wildland Research Center to the Outdoor Recreation and Resources Review Commission; later it was published in both **David R. Brower's** *Wilderness: America's Living Heritage* (1961) and Roderick Nash's *The American Environment* (1976).

While recognizing the recreational and scenic benefits of nature, this essay spoke for wilderness. Stegner wrote that the wilderness has shaped the American character and has been intrinsic to cultural development. Thus, he argued, the national character will be diminished should Americans let wilderness be destroyed or degraded by pollution, overuse, and complacency. He recommended to the Outdoor Recreation and Resources Review Commission that land be put in a "wilderness bank" to preserve the American collective experience in a type of outdoor historical museum where generations could share the experience of the frontier culture.

In his efforts to preserve Dinosaur National Monument from the **Echo Park Dam**, Stegner used essays and photographs to demonstrate that dinosaurs should be preserved for the American spirit.

Stegner warned of the future of the United States should it allow its wilderness to be destroyed. In his essay "The Wilderness Index" (1961) he wrote:

> We need wilderness preserved—as much of it as is still left, and as many kinds—because it was the challenge against which our character as a people was formed. The reminder and the reassurance that it is still there is good for our spiritual health even if we never once in ten years set foot in it. (Stegner 1961, p. 97)

STOCKHOLM DECLARATION (DECLARATION OF THE CONFERENCE ON THE HUMAN ENVIRON-MENT) The document released at the conclusion of the

1972 United Nations Conference on the Human Environment. It set forth principles and guidelines that were to be a guide for worldwide environmental protection. Although raising many important goals related to the preservation of key ecosystems, the declaration created no legally binding obligations.

Although the conference is often viewed as the beginning of modern global cooperation on environmental issues, no specific actions resulted. Many environmentalists believe binding agreements, such as CITES **(Convention on International Trade in Endangered Species)**, are the only truly successful outcomes of international meetings.

STUDENT ENVIRONMENTAL ACTION COALITION (SEAC) An organization of student environmentalists that began at the University of North Carolina at Chapel Hill in 1989. Since it began, hundreds of other universities have formed SEAC groups. National and regional conferences bring members together to discuss issues and strategies and to work on issues of environmental protection and social justice. It has become the largest student organization in the country and now includes high school groups as well.

SEAC's monthly newsletter, *Threshold*, informs readers on current environmental campaigns and provides advice on organizing grass-roots movements around specific issues. Further, a team of field organizers travel to campuses to educate groups through workshops. A structure of 17 regional networks and 50 state networks strengthens group solidarity and makes the organization a more powerful force. SEAC accepts individual and group memberships. Those unable to pay for membership and a subscription to *Threshold* can have these fees waived.

SUPERFUND   (See **COMPREHENSIVE ENVIRON-MENTAL RESPONSE, COMPENSATION AND LIABILITY ACT**)

SUPERFUND AMENDMENTS AND REAUTHORIZA-TION ACT (SARA) (42 U.S.C. 1101 ET SEQ.) SARA serves to revise the **Comprehensive Environmental Response, Compensation and Liability Act (CERCLA)** (Superfund) by adding new authorities known as the Emergency Planning and Community Right-to-Know Act of 1986 (Title III of SARA). The revision enabled "emergency planning and preparedness, community right-to-know reporting, and toxic chemical release reporting." SARA also established a program to restore contaminated lands, similar to the Superfund under CERCLA. The U.S. Department of Defense is entrusted with this latter responsibility.

This act requires that hazardous waste facilities keep a record, available to state and federal authorities as well as the public, of information on any regulated substance on the premises. Three types of information are required. First, material data sheets are prepared by the chemical manufacturer and retained by the facility operator containing general information on the hazardous chemical. Second, emergency and hazardous chemical inventory forms are submitted to state and local authorities annually and are available to the public. Information includes the location of and the maximum amount of a hazardous chemical that may be present on site during the year and that was present in the previous year, and detailed information on the chemicals. This data must be made available to an emergency entity upon request. Finally, a process is in place for toxic chemical release reporting.

SUSTAINABLE AGRICULTURE   (See **LOW-INPUT SUSTAINABLE AGRICULTURE**)

SUSTAINABLE DEVELOPMENT A term first brought into common use by the World Commission on Environment and Development in its publication *Our Common Future* (1987). Recognizing that protection of the environment could not be realized by a cap on all growth and development, many environmentalists began to embrace the concept of sustainable development. Sustainability is the notion that a society can continue generation after generation without depleting its resource base of renewable or nonrenewable resources or without exceeding the capacity of the air, water, and land to accept waste products. Although the meaning of this term is clear in agricultural or forestry activities, it has been so widely used in the 1990s, that its real meaning for industrial societies is hotly debated and not well articulated. (See also **LOW-INPUT SUSTAINABLE AGRICULTURE; MICROLENDING; ROBERT, KARL-HENRICK).**

T

TEILHARD DE CHARDIN, PIERRE (1881-1955) This French-born priest and geologist views humans as the center of the universe (metaphysically). However, his hope is that one day our species will recognize itself as a leader, without assuming a position of dominance with the right to do as it wishes with other species.

Chardin referred to the scheme of things as a "tree of life." Over billions of years, life has bloomed into what we witness today. Humans are merely a branch on that tree, and, even though humans occupied the top branch, without the branches and trunk to support us, humans could not survive.

Chardin asked the question whether or not evolution is directed or whether it is a random process. He explained that it is possible to see an order developing, but, among that order, there is little organization. He stated that there is a hierarchy of organisms, but that alone does not suggest that evolution is working toward a goal and that humans are that goal. In fact, Chardin noted that the only thing that separates humans from other animals is the ability to reflect (It is unclear whether other animals have this capacity).

His book *The Phenomenon of Man* ended with a discussion of the end of the earth. He believes that we will deplete the resources, ravage the land, and make the planet unlivable for many, if not most, species. Chardin stated that humanity holds the destiny of the earth in its hands and that humans must act responsibly because they are not at the center of the universe, only a branch in its tree. Chardin's writings, especially *The Phenomenon of Man*, have been very influential in North American sociological, cultural, and environmental circles.

TELLICO DAM   A dam in Tennessee that was started in 1967, only to be stopped six years later after the **Endangered Species Act** was passed. A zoologist discovered a small species of snail-eating fish, which he called the snail darter, which was believed to be found only in the water behind the Tellico Dam. Completing construction would destroy the habitat of the fish and the species would become extinct.

The dam project was halted. As the court stated, "The plain intent of Congress in enacting this statute (The Endangered Species Act) was to halt and reverse the trend toward species extinction, whatever the cost." In 1978, the Endangered Species Act was amended to allow the following exceptions: federal disaster areas, areas involving national defense, and cases permitted by special review committee. This committee of federal cabinet heads is often called the God Committee, because they can, like God, eliminate a species by their decisions. These amendments allowed continuation of the dam as the snail darters were removed to other adjacent streams and other populations of the species were found nearby.

TENNESSEE VALLEY AUTHORITY (TVA) Created under President Franklin D. Roosevelt's "New Deal." The TVA was to provide the region of Appalachia with a cheap source of energy, while providing jobs to residents of this depressed region. The timber, gas, and petroleum resources of the Tennessee basin had been stripped with little regard for ecosystemic viability. **Stewart Udall** noted that "By 1933, this region of thin soils had become one of the most depressed and most depressing areas in all the United States." The TVA began a massive dam building effort soon after being formed, and in the next 10 years, over 700 miles of streams were made navigable, while 200 million trees were planted, and energy was provided at low cost. The TVA also provided flood control protection, irrigation water, and water through the dams built in the Tennessee River watersheds.

In later years the TVA was criticized as acting as any private utility, ignoring environmental values and contributing to the environmental degradation of the region. Rather than being a model for environmental improvement, the agency became a superutility with a narrow focus on energy production. In the 1970s, the agency once again changed its role and tried to become a leader in environmental compliance.

THAILAND'S POPULATION PROGRAM In 1971, Thailand's growth rate stood at 3.2 percent as government leaders worried how to reduce the resource and pollution stress of the coming year. By 1986, the growth rate was reduced to 1.6 percent and to 1.2 percent by 1992. This unprecedented decline resulted from four principal reasons.

First, 95 percent of Thai people are Buddhists who frown on large families and thus embrace family planning. Second, Thai culture is known to actively respond to change when needed. Third, the government encouraged the desirability of small families by promoting such activities as making contraceptives readily accessible via a program jointly sponsored by the Population and Community Development Association of Thailand. Lastly, the government sponsored a loan program that favored communities that encouraged family planning, and loans were apportioned based on a community's use of contraceptives.

Thailand's success in decreasing its population growth rate has been coupled with economic growth and a significant increase in per capita income since 1971. This program has been hailed by North American governments as a model of linking economic development and population growth rate reductions.

THOREAU, HENRY DAVID (1817-1862)   Nineteenth-century poet, philosopher, and conservationist, Thoreau was perhaps the first U.S. "environmentalist." One of his oft-quoted statements taken from a speech on April 23, 1851, before the Concord Lyceum recognizes the importance of ecological values of wilderness. He stated that "in wildness is the preservation of the World." Thoreau spent much of his life living in and around the woods, most notably around Walden Pond near Concord, Massachusetts.

He juxtaposed the wilderness with the city and reasoned that nature was a symbol for the Divine. Along with **Ralph Waldo Emerson**, Thoreau promoted the transcendentalist philosophy, which explained that there was a "higher reality," or divinity, behind physical objects. For Thoreau, the city represented what was evil in civilization and he delighted in the uncultivated landscape. Like many others, however, his praise of the wilderness was not without its hesitations. When he climbed Mt. Katadin in the Maine woods, his descriptions were of a "savage and dreary" wilderness. This experience led to an appreciation of both civilization and wilderness.

In 1845 Thoreau moved into a one-room cabin he built near the shore of the sixty-acre Walden Pond. While residing there, he wrote his first book: *A Week on the Concord and Merimack Rivers*. This was about the two-week rowboat and walking adventure with his older brother John. While he was there, he also wrote down reflections and passages he would later incorporate into *Walden*. He was critical of the dehumanizing effect of industrial society, especially as he foresaw the destruction of wildlands, for the benefit of the capitalist who viewed the woods as trees for profit. In *Walden*, he stated, "Thank God, men cannot yet fly and lay waste the sky as well as the earth." For the most part, *Walden* is a diatribe against materialism.

Thoreau was also a spokesman for the value of the individual against governmental powers and once went to jail instead of paying government taxes to support the war with Mexico. His essay "Civil Disobedience" was read and influenced the crusades of Mahatma Gandhi and Martin Luther King Jr., as well as contemporary militant environmental activists.

THREE MILE ISLAND   On March 29, 1979, a nuclear accident occurred at the Three Mile Island nuclear facility in Harrisburg, Pennsylvania. The accident resulted from a partial meltdown in one of the reactors due to a combination of human and mechanical error. A reactor lost its cooling water due to these accidents, the core of the reactor became partially uncovered, and a partial meltdown resulted. Approximately 70 percent of the core was damaged, and 50 percent of it melted.

As a result of the accident, 50,000 people were evacuated, while another 50,000 left on their own accord. Preschool children and pregnant women within a 5-mile radius were advised to evacuate the area. While no deaths resulted, plant workers were exposed to high radiation levels, and some radiation was released into the environment. Although the actual damage from this accident was minimal, the view that the situation was out of control and that the potential consequences could have been devastating, resulted in a meltdown in public confidence in nuclear power that has not to this day been restored.

TOXIC SUBSTANCES CONTROL ACT (TOSCA) (15 U.S.C. 2601 ET SEQ.) This act requires the premarket testing of toxic substances. When a chemical substance is planned to be manufactured, the producer must notify the **Environmental Protection Agency (EPA),** and, if the data presented is determined to be inadequate to approve its use, the EPA will require the manufacturer to conduct further tests. Or, if it is later determined that a chemical is present at a level that presents an unreasonable public or environmental risk, or if there is insufficient data to know the chemical's effects, manufacturers have the burden of evaluating the chemical's characteristics and risks. If testing does not convince the EPA of the chemical's safety, the chemical's manufacturing, sale, or use can be limited or prohibited.

The act also regulates the labeling and disposal of **polychlorinated biphenyls** and has prohibited their production and distribution since July 1979. The act attracted media coverage through its inspection and removal of asbestos products in public schools; it studies the danger of asbestos in public and commercial buildings.

TRAGEDY OF THE COMMONS (See **HARDIN, GARRETT**)

TROUT UNLIMITED A sportsmen's organization, founded in 1959, the group seeks to preserve and enhance cold-water habitat of trout, salmon, and other cold-water fish. It maintains programs to inform the public about water quality issues and provides input to government agencies, such as the U.S. **Fish and Wildlife Service**, to foster its goals. It also provides expertise for action-oriented projects such as stream restoration and enhancement.

U

UDALL, STEWART L. (1920-   )   An Arizona-born Congressman who represented that state in the 1950s, Udall became President John F. Kennedy's Secretary of the Interior in 1961, and served both Presidents Kennedy and Lyndon B. Johnson. His book *The Quiet Crisis* (1964) brought him into the arena of U.S. environ-mentalism. His efforts helped to preserve both national parks and wilderness areas. Udall demonstrated a commitment to environmentalism in his personal life while holding office. He heated his Washington, D.C. home with firewood, maintaining temperatures of 55 (Fahrenheit) degrees in winter and also led members of Congress on hikes of potential national parks. His commitment to preservation added 59 additional lands to the **National Park Service**.

His frequent writings and speeches in defense of wild lands preached that, without careful stewardship, the United States cannot regard itself as a success in spite of its material or economic wealth. As a promoter of **Aldo Leopold's** philosophy, Udall believes that humans have an ethical responsibility to the land and that only if these ethical principles are upheld, can civilization become sustainable. He also followed **John Muir's** lead in advocating a new society attuned to the rhythms of the total environment. His *1976: Agenda for Tomorrow*, written in 1968, addressed the need to link environmental goals to broad social changes.

In *The Quiet Crisis*, he traced the country's development back to the Native Americans who demonstrated respect toward the earth. He noted that modern society has wantonly disregarded the wisdom of natives and is now on the brink of destroying our life-support system. He also, noted, however, that many individuals and groups have spoken out in defense of the natural environment. After Thomas Jefferson recognized the importance of maintaining the condition of the land for successful and sustainable husbandry, generations of Americans had wilderness spokespersons such as **Henry David Thoreau, George Perkins Marsh, John Muir**, and both **Teddy** and **Franklin Roosevelt** who spoke for the value of conservation.

Udall continues to encourage environmental change, working for environmental groups, offering his legal skills for the cause of preservation, and writing on the continual need for environmental change.

UNITED FARM WORKERS (UFW)   The United Farm Workers is a trade union for agricultural migrant workers who follow the cycle of ripening fruit and vegetable crops. The geographic area of the UFW is primarily the U.S. West and Southwest. The group has worked to remove chemical pesticides from agriculture since the 1960s. It charges that fruit and vegetable growers, especially within the grape industry, view migrants as expendable and knowingly expose workers to dangerous chemicals.

In its 1986 film, *Wrath of Grapes*, the UFW documented accounts of workers collapsing and dying after entering recently sprayed fields. The film claimed that one-third of all pesticides used on grapes are known carcinogens and are inhaled by workers as well as absorbed through their skin. Twenty years before the production of this film, the UFW launched a campaign to remove **DDT**, DDE, Aldrin, Dieldrin, and Endrin from agricultural use. This campaign educated consumers, and soon after, these chemicals were banned.

In addition to films, the UFW uses the journal, *Food and Justice*, published free of charge, to educate the public. Since group leader Cesar Chavez died in 1993, the group continues to fight for fair and clean working conditions, safe food for the U.S. public, and their own safety.

UNITED NATIONS CONFERENCE ON ENVIRONMENT AND DEVELOPMENT (UNCED) Held in 1992, the Rio Summit, or Earth Summit as it has been called, was the largest meeting of world leaders focusing on environmental questions in history. Over 175 countries were represented and discussions on global problems such as biodiversity, forestry, climate change (see United Nations Framework Convention of Climate Change), and ozone depletion were central. Simultaneous to the formal UNCED Conference a large number of nongovernmental organizations held a global forum to network and call attention to environmental issues. The UNCED Conference yielded several major documents including: The Rio Declaration, a statement of broad principles; treaties on climate and biodiversity; a statement of forest principles; and Agenda 21, a working plan for sustainable development.

A general consensus emerged following the conference that, although such a gathering focusing on environmental questions was an excellent beginning, the treaties signed were too vague and merely a recognition of the need for a concrete plan of action. Perhaps the most important outcome of the conference was the heightened awareness of a myriad of environmental problems and the lack of any concerted or coordinated effort to reverse current trends of environmental degradation.

UNITED NATIONS ENVIRONMENT PROGRAMME (UNEP) Headquartered in Nairobi, Kenya, UNEP is the primary United Nations agency to promote and coordinate environmental protection programs, assistance for environmentally compatible development, and environmental information exchange throughout the world. Founded in 1972, the agency's chief focus is developmental programs that lead to sustainability including protection and enhancement of soil, water, and biological resources. In addition to technical assistance and demonstration programs, UNEP also works to increase environmental education around the world. To this end, UNEP has designated June 5 as World Environment Day. UNEP's programs are complemented by efforts such as those led by the Peace Corps in the United States. Such programs recognize the importance in assisting developing countries to become sustainable in light of the Third World's built-in momentum for tremendous growth and the shrinking global resource base.

UNITED NATIONS FRAMEWORK CONVENTION ON CLIMATE CHANGE (CONFERENCE OF THE PARTIES) More than 120 nations convened between March 28 and April 7, 1993, in Berlin, Germany, to discuss global warming. A compromise plan was approved that established a two-year negotiation process aimed at setting specific targets and timetables for reducing carbon dioxide and other greenhouse gases. This conference was a follow-up to the Rio Earth Summit at which the United States pushed for a weak document on climate change that contained no specific mandates, targets, or timetables. The Berlin Mandate, as the agreement coming from this meeting was called, officially deemed the agreement signed at the Rio Summit as inadequate and called for the establishment of specific targets and timetables for greenhouse gas reductions to be completed by 1997. Thus far commitments have not gone beyond cutting emission levels of greenhouse gases to 1990 levels by the 2020. Progress on even this modest goal has been minimal, with the exception of chlorofluorocarbons (See also **UNITED NATIONS CONFERENCE ON ENVIRONMENT AND DEVELOPMENT**)

UNITED NATIONS LAW OF THE SEA CONFERENCE The United Nations has sponsored three conferences (1958, 1960, 1973-1982) to discuss issues relating to laws of the common area of the open ocean, outside territorial waters of specific countries. Important environmental issues that were debated at these conferences included pollution and the resources of deep sea beds. In December of 1982, 189 countries signed a Law of the Sea Convention. Unfortunately, the largest industrial nations, including the United States, Great Britain, France, Germany, and Japan, did not sign because of a provision that have made the resources of the deep sea beds "the common heritage of mankind." A major outcome of this document, agreed to by even nonsignature countries, is that all coastal countries have the legal right to control fishing within 200 nautical miles of their coasts. (See also **NATIONAL OCEANOGRAPHIC AND ATMOS-PHERIC ADMINISTRATION**).

UNITED NATIONS, MAN, AND THE BIOSPHERE PROGRAM (See BIOSPHERE RESERVES)

UTILITARIAN ETHIC   As an environmental ethic, utilitarianism defines a good act as that which promotes the greatest good, or utility, for the greatest number of people. An example of this philosophy is humans viewing the best use of the natural environment to be that which most fulfills humankind's needs, e.g., valuing trees highest for the lumber they produce; prairies for their fertile farmland; and canyons or valleys for their potential for hydroelectric power. Utilitarianism guided the early 20th-century conservation movement. **Gifford Pinchot,** the chief of the U.S. Forest Service, stated that conservation did not mean protecting or preserving nature, rather it represented wise, efficient, and sustained use of natural resources. Historian Roderick Nash avers that the first national parks were preserved for utilitarian reasons. Parks like **Yellowstone** (1872), the **Adirondacks** (1885), and **Yosemite** (1890) protected people's pleasure experiences, while maintaining water resources and game supply.

More recently, the **deep ecologists** have charged that the U.S. conservation movement was built on utilitarian foundations. For instance, wilderness areas and national parks were preserved for human recreation and aesthetic needs rather than for the good of natural inhabitants; that is, out of anthropocentric rather than biocentric motives.

W

WASTE DISPOSAL ACT (See **RESOURCE, CONSERVATION, AND RECOVERY ACT**)

WATT, JAMES (1938-) Secretary of the Interior under U.S. President Ronald Reagan, James Watt tried to reverse decades of environmental progress by greatly increasing the leasing of federal mineral rights, opening up large areas of the coast for offshore oil drilling, weakening the **Endangered Species Act,** and selling federal lands. Congress thwarted virtually all of Watt's proposals, and he was forced to resign in controversy before the end of Reagan's first term. (See also **SIERRA CLUB; LEGAL DEFENSE FUND**)

WHITE, GILBERT (1720-1793) Gilbert White's major contribution to environmentalism was *The Natural History of Selborne*, a book about his Hampshire hometown. Published in 1789, this work expresses his perception of nature in his parish in the south of England. He observed the natural harmony among all species, each of which have their own function in the larger natural community. He praises all creatures, however large or small. For instance, he identified the important role of the earthworm in sustaining the natural community. He realized that the study of natural systems allowed the naturalist to establish a communion with nature. White looked at how humans were a part of the harmony of Selborne in what is known as the Arcadian image. After he died in 1793, his followers became a quasi-cult, writing about and visiting Selborne.

White is often looked upon as an early forerunner to environmentalism and environmental science. Environmental historian Donald Worster wrote *"Natural History* is one of the most important early contributions to field ecology in English Science" (Worster 1994, p. 7). Indeed, the ethic that Gilbert White promoted became part of the U.S. environmental movement's philosophy in the 1960s and '70s.

WILD AND SCENIC RIVERS ACT (16 U.S.C. 1271 ET SEQ.) This 1968 act established the Wild and Scenic Rivers System to protect rivers and segments of rivers that are determined to have wild and scenic values from activities that threaten those qualities. Designated rivers are to be kept forever free of development or alteration of any kind. In fact, the only activities permitted are camping, swimming, nonmotorized boating, sporthunting, and fishing. Development is barred because freeflowing rivers offer aesthetic opportunities unmatched by dammed and developed rivers. Unobstructed waterways are also more suitable homes for most fish and other wildlife forms.

By 1993, 151 rivers and river segments ranging over 17,000 km (10,000 miles) had been protected under the act, and conservationists were then promoting 1,500 more segments for designation. A three-tiered classification is used to designate rivers: "wild" rivers are inaccessible and undisturbed; "scenic rivers" are mostly undeveloped and offer tremendous scenic access; and "recreational rivers" are mostly developed yet still offer recreational potential.

WILDERNESS ACT (16 U.S.C. 1131 ET SEQ.) Established in 1964, this act provided for the permanent protection of millions of acres of unspoiled natural areas. Lands set aside under the wilderness designation cannot have permanent structures, roads, or mechanized transport. Obviously, timber harvesting is also banned. These areas were established to recognize that the best way to protect species is to protect their habitat and that large undisturbed tracts of land are needed to maintain naturally functioning ecosystems. Today approximately 100 million acres, or 5 percent of the country, is set aside as wilderness, the vast majority of which is in Alaska and the western states. (See also **MURIE, OLAUS; NEW YORK STATE FOREST PRESERVE; WILDERNESS SOCIETY).**

WILDERNESS SOCIETY   Founded by **Aldo Leopold** in 1935, the Wilderness Society with its 400,000 members works toward protection of wilderness and wise use of our ecological resources. Unlike many other environmental organizations that have broadened their functions, the Wilderness Society devotes itself exclusively to issues related to public lands. The society's programs to this end are primarily lobbying and education. It is most active in congressional decisions regarding the creation of federal wilderness areas, and it played a key role in the passage of the Wilderness Act of 1964 and the 1990 **Alaska National Interest Lands Conservation Act**. The focus of the group in the 1990s has been the preservation of ancient forests. In 1996 the Wilderness Society concluded a campaign for forest preservation in Australia which culminated in 12 new wilderness area and 9 new national parks.

WILSON, EDWARD O. (1929-) A biologist and naturalist and proponent of biodiversity, Wilson is Pellegrino University Professor and curator in entomology at the Museum of Comparative Zoology at Harvard University and the winner of two Pulitzer prizes. He became intrigued with the natural world at a young age while walking the Gulf Coast of Alabama and Florida. Wilson is perhaps best known for establishing many of the central principles of evolutionary biology.

Among his accomplishments, Wilson developed a model, along with Dr. Robert MacArthur, to project species loss; they predicted that, in these last decades of the 20th century, between 4,000 and 6,000 species per year are becoming extinct. Wilson maintains that global biological preservation should be a top priority for the United States. He recommended spending a small portion of U.S. support for foreign military to fund this transition to sustainability.

WISE-USE MOVEMENT   Originally used by many as another term for the conservation movement, in recent years this term has gained a new meaning. It refers to the group founded by Ron Arnold, which has become a major influence in the antienvironmental campaign. Arnold states the goal of this movement is to "destroy, to eradicate, the environmental movement." The battles are often on the western front. The Wise-Use Movement thwarted efforts to unite the polices of Wyoming, Montana, and Idaho and many federal agencies that govern the **Yellowstone National Park**. Arnold's group published letters telling local citizens that they would lose their property rights under a plan to create a 19-million acre de facto wilderness areas around the park.

Other goals of this group include cutting old-growth forests and replacing them with tree plantations, making economic decisions the primary guiding factor for the **Endangered Species Act,** opening all public lands to mineral and energy production, and recognizing private rights to mineral claims, water, grazing permits, and timber contracts on public lands.

WORLD CONSERVATION UNION   The IUCN is an organization of governments and agencies that works with the United Nations in carrying out programs related to biological conservation. Its mission is to influence and assist societies throughout the world to conserve the integrity and diversity of nature. Founded in 1949, IUCN members include 69 state governments, 101 government agencies, and over 600 nongovernmental organizations. The primary role of the organization is research and demonstration projects that preserve biodiversity. Its research is very well respected and has influenced government policies on curtailing wildlife trade and habitat protection through the creation of national parks. In 1980, the IUCN published its *World Conservation Strategy: Living Resource Conservation for Sustainable Development*, which provides a rationale for, and methods to, protect biodiversity around the world. The update of this document, *Caring for the Earth: A Strategy for Sustainable Living*, was published in 1991. The Species Survival Commission of the IUCN produces the *UCN Red List* of endangered and threatened species throughout the world.

WORLD ENVIRONMENT DAY (See **UNITED NATIONS ENVIRONMENT PROGRAMME**)

WORLD WIDE FUND FOR NATURE (See **WORLD WILDLIFE FUND**)

WORLD WILDLIFE FUND (WWF) Founded in 1961, the fund merged with the Conservation Foundation in 1985, making it one of the largest environmental groups in the world. Its mission is the preservation of habitat and biodiversity, primarily in tropical forests of Latin America, Asia, and Africa. Its promotion of ecologically sound development, assistance to local groups to take the lead in conservation projects, and its support of scientific investigations, have been credited with the designation of almost 500 national parks and nature preserves. Recently, however, this renowned group has been criticized for not paying enough attention to the needs of indigenous people while protecting African wildlife. The WWF has recently announced new efforts to make specific preservation economically beneficial to local people. The group has also been instrumental in working for trade sanctions against countries that consume endangered species, e.g., China for its lack of curbing tiger bone products. More broadly, it opposed the North American Free Trade Agreement, which it feared would weaken the ability of the United States to curb wildlife trade. This organization uses the name World Wide Fund for Nature outside the United States and Canada.

WORLDWATCH INSTITUTE (See **BROWN, LESTER**)

Y

YARD, ROBERT STERLING (1861-1945) President of the **Wilderness Society**, spokesperson for national parks, and preservationist. In the early 1900s, Yard joined forces with **John Muir, Stephen Mather,** and others in the fight against the **Hetch Hetchy** Dam in **Yosemite**. After working for the Geological Survey, he helped Mather by serving as publicity chief for the **National Park Service**, organizing conferences and soliciting support from the literary community to promote U.S. parks to the public. Yard later formed the National Parks Association as a voice for parklands.

YELLOWSTONE NATIONAL PARK Yellowstone, comprising over 2 million acres, became the first national park in the United States in 1872. It was established by Congress and President Ulysses S. Grant to be "set apart as a public park or pleasuring ground for the benefit and enjoyment of the people." With its designation came a ban on hunting. In 1892, the American bison was relocated in Yellowstone to try to repopulate this species, which declined by 2.5 million between 1870 and 1875.

Yellowstone's establishment is surrounded with controversy. First, some contend that the Northern Pacific Railroad was behind its creation as the company saw a great potential to transport the eastern public to the parklands in most of northwestern Wyoming. Historian Alfred Runte claimed that Yellowstone was preserved because of its monumentalism and uselessness in terms of resources. Its topographic features, such as "Old Faithful," and mountain landscapes made it attractive to visitors and, due to its rugged terrain, it was difficult to harvest resources.

Controversy still exists in the management of Yellowstone today. Despite opposition from ranchers and hunters, the U.S. **Fish and Wildlife Service** began reintroducing the grey wolf into Yellowstone National Park in 1995. The introduction of this large predator continues the effort to reestablish the 19th-century Yellowstone ecosystem.

YOSEMITE NATIONAL PARK   In 1864, President Abraham Lincoln signed an act that set aside the Yosemite Valley "for public use, resort, and recreation." **John Muir** led the fight and first convinced the state and the federal government to preserve the land. Muir's proposal was for a 1,500-square mile park. In 1890, Yosemite got the designation that many felt it deserved, and it became the first national park designed to protect wilderness. Nonetheless, most visitors have come to Yosemite for its spectacular scenery.

Since its establishment, however, the park has been plagued with development pressures. The most notable one began just after its designation. **Gifford Pinchot** and the **"wise-use school"** of conservation wanted to dam the Yosemite Valley to provide water to San Francisco. **John Muir** argued for the value of preserving the valley intact. In 1913, the proponents of the dam won their battle. Since this event, the battle between conservation and preservation has been a point of contention within the environmental movement (See also **HETCH HETCHY**).

Today, Yosemite ranks with **Yellowstone** as the most visited and endangered national park. Visitors stress the ecological fabric of the ecosystem and development pressures around Yosemite threaten its stability. Historian Alfred Runte ended his book *Yosemite: The Embattled Wilderness* (1990), stating:

> Yosemite is too important to be just another place. Civilization has many undeniable advantages, yet even the most inventive civilization has never built a Yosemite. Yosemite by every imaginable standard is one of a kind. In that perception, and no other, lie the only tried and true principles for guiding the future of the park's natural heritage.

Z

ZAHNISER, HOWARD (1906-1964) Director, lobbyist and spokesperson for the **Wilderness Society** who revived the ideas of **Robert Marshall** and **Aldo Leopold** by successfully arguing the need for establishing permanent wilderness lands under the **Wilderness Act** of 1964. Beginning in 1951, he worked with various conservation groups and prepared a bill for such purposes. He convinced Senator Hubert H. Humphrey and Representative John P. Saylor to sponsor the bill. In part, the bill was to "secure for the American people of present and future generations the benefits of an enduring reservoir of wilderness."

Zahniser's philosophy was built around the notion that wilderness enhanced civilization rather than retarding progress. Further, that we needed wilderness in order to humble ourselves and see the human race as a member of the planet rather than a ruler as our technological prowess would have us believe. Wilderness reminds us of our interdependence with the rest of the natural world. He called attention to the fact that unspoiled lands were disappearing rapidly and, thus, the urgency of forever protecting some pristine lands from development pressures of any kind was critical.

His earlier preservation accomplishments included defending the **Adirondacks** in the 1940s and working along with **David R. Brower** and others to prevent the **Echo Park Dam** in Dinosaur National Monument in the 1950s. Zahniser died in 1964, while speaking in favor of the wilderness bill and attending each congressional hearing on the matter.

BIBLIOGRAPHY

By its nature, a reference work on environmentalism must draw from a variety of sources from many diverse disciplines. We have broken down the bibiliography into several classifications that unite a rich collection of literature on the topic. While many of the sources have been used for the content of this project, the following books offer the reader an introduction to a broader array of scholarship available on this topic. That is, titles in this section provide a more complete guide to the body of material dealing with environmentalism than just the sources we relied on for entries could provide.

The works cited here have been chosen for various reasons. Some were used for the content of this work; many are classics in their field; others are excellent sources of up-to-date material on specific topics; finally, many were chosen because they represent works familiar to the authors.

For anyone searching for texts on the history of environmentalism, preservation, or environmental science, there are a few authors and works that stand out. Roderick Nash has published books on the history of American attitudes toward the natural world and the history of environmental ethics. These include *Wilderness and the American Mind*, *The Rights of Nature*, and *The American Environment*. Donald Worster has written books on single topics (*Dust Bowl* and *Rivers of Empire)*, a history of the ecological sciences (*Nature's Economy*), and essays on environmental history (*The Wealth of Nature*). Philip Shabecoff's book on the history of American environmentalism (*A Fierce Green Fire*) also provides an excellent summary in this regard.

Finally, other writers who have captured specific aspects of environmentalism and/or environmental history include: Thomas Arrandale, Wendell Berry, Peter J. Bowler, Michael Cohen, William Cronon, Alfred Crosby, Mario Diani, Thomas Dunlap, Dave Foremen, Samuel P. Hays, J. Donald Hughes,

George Perkins Marsh, Lee Clark Mitchell, Carolyn Merchant, Joseph M. Petulla, Jeremy Rifkin, Max Oelschlaeger, Alfred Runte, Philip Terrie, Stewart L. Udall, and Howie Wolke.

1. NOVELS AND NATURE WRITING

Abbey, Edward. *Desert Solitaire: A Season in the Wilderness.* New York: McGraw Hill, 1968.

Abbey, Edward. *Confessions of a Barbarian.* Toronto: Little, Brown & Company, 1994.

Carson, Rachel. *The Sea Around Us.* New York: Oxford University Press, 1951.

McPhee, John. *Coming Into the Country.* New York: Bantam Books, 1977.

Mowat, Farley. *The Desperate People.* Boston: Little, Brown, 1950.

Mowat, Farley. *People of the Deer.* Boston: Little, Brown, 1952.

Olson, Sigurd. *Listening Point.* New York: Knopf, 1958.

Olson, Sigurd. *Reflection from the North Country.* New York: Knopf, 1976.

Snyder, Gary. *Turtle Island.* New York: New Direction, 1974.

Thoreau, Henry David. *A Week on the Concord and Merrimac Rivers.* London: Walter Scott Ltd., 1889.

Thoreau, Henry David. *The Maine Woods.* New York: Thomas Y. Crowell, 1909.

Thoreau, Henry David. *Walden.* London: J. M. Dent & Sons, 1930.

2. GENERAL TEXTS AND REFERENCES

Arms, Karen. *Environmental Science.* Philadelphia: Saunders College Publishing, 1990.

Ashworth, William. *The Encyclopedia of Environmental Studies.* New York: Facts on File, 1991.

Baer-Brown, Leslie. *Earth Keepers: A Sourcebook for Environmental Issues and Action.* San Francisco: Mercury House, 1995.

Bamaby, Frank, ed. *The Gaia Peace Atlas: Survival into the Third Millennium.* New York: Doubleday, 1988.

Basta, Nicholas. *The Environmental Career Guide: Job Opportunities with the Earth in Mind.* New York: John Wiley & Sons Inc., 1991.

Botkin, Daniel B., and Edward A. Keller. *Environmental Science: Earth as a Living Planet.* New York: John Wiley & Sons, Inc., 1995.

Briggs, Shirley A. "Silent Spring: The View from 1990." In *Taking Sides: Clashing Views on Controversial Environmental Issues,* edited by Theodore D. Goldfarb. 4th ed. Guilford, Conn.: Duskin/McGraw-Hill, 1991.

Burroughs, John. *Accepting the Universe.* Boston: Houghton Mifflin, 1920.

Chiras, Daniel D. *Environmental Science: A Framework for Decision Making.* 2nd ed. Menlo Park, Calif.: The Benjamin/Cummings Publishing Company Inc., 1988.

Chiras, Daniel D. *Environmental Science: Action for a Sustainable Future.* 4th ed. Redwood City, Calif.: 1994.

Club of Rome. *The Limits to Growth.* New York: University Books, 1972.

Cunningham, William P. *Understanding Our Environment: An Introduction.* Dubuque, Iowa: William C. Brown Publishers, 1994.

Cunningham, William P., and Barbara Woodworth Saigo. *Environmental Science: A Global Concern.* 2d ed. Dubuque, Iowa: William C. Brown Publishers, 1992.

Cunningham, William P., Gary S. Phillips, and Barbara Woodworth Saigo. *Environmental Science: A Global Concern—Environmental Issues and Analysis Workbook.* 2d ed. Dubuque, Iowa: William C. Brown Publishers, 1992.

Dobson, Andrew. *The Green Reader: Essays toward a Sustainable Society.* San Francisco: Mercury House, 1991.

Franck, Irene, and David Brownstone. *The Green Encyclopedia.* New York: Prentice Hall, 1992.

Goudie, Andrew. *The Human Impact on the Natural Environment.* 3rd ed. Cambridge, Mass.: MIT Press, 1990.

Greenpeace. *The Greenpeace Guide to Anti-Environmental Organizations.* Berkeley, Calif.: Odonian Press, 1993.

Harms, Valerie. *The National Audubon Society Almanac of the Environment: The Ecology of Everyday Life.* New York: G. P. Putnam's Sons, 1994.

Kaufman, Donald G., and Cecilia M. Franz. *Biosphere 2000: Protecting Our Global Environment.* New York: HarperCollins College Publishers, 1993.

Love, Sam, ed. *Earth Tool Kit: A Field Manual for Citizen Activists.* New York: Pocket Books, 1971.

Meadows, Donella, Dennis Meadows, and Jorgen Randers. *Beyond the Limits.* Post Mills, Vt.: Chelsea Green Publishing, 1992.

Miller, G. Tyler. *Living in the Environment: An Introduction to Environmental Science.* 9th ed. Belmont, Calif.: Wadsworth Publishing Company, 1996.

Mitchell, John G., with Constance L. Stallings. *Ecotactics: The Sierra Club Handbook for Environment Activists.* New York: Pocket Books, 1970.

National Academy of Sciences. *Global Environmental Change: Understanding the Human Dimensions.* Washington, D.C.: National Academy Press, 1992.

Nebel, Bernard J., and Richard T. Wright. *Environmental Science: The Way the World Works.* 4th ed. Englewood Cliffs, N.J.: Prentice Hall, 1993.

Paehlke, Robert, ed. *Conservation and Environmentalism: An Encyclopedia.* New York: Garland, 1995.

Rifkin, Jeremy, and Carol G. Rifkin. *Voting Green: Your Complete Guide to Making Political Choices in the 90s.* New York: Doubleday, 1992.

Rittner, Don. *Ecolinking: Everyone's Guide to Online Environmental Information.* Berkeley, Calif.: Peachpit Press, 1992.

Seredich, John, ed. *Your Resource Guide to Environmental Organizations.* Irvine, Calif.: Smiling Dolphin Press, 1991.

Shanks, Bernard. *This Land Is Your Land.* San Francisco: Sierra Club Books, 1982.

Shedenhelm, Richard. *Critics of Environmentalism: A Comprehensive Bibliography Covering Philosophy, Economics, and Science.* Athens, Ga.: University of Georgia Libraries, 1993.

Turner, B. L. II, ed. *The Earth as Transformed by Human Actions.* New York: Cambridge University Press, 1990.

Watt, K. E. F. *Understanding the Environment.* Boston: Allyn & Bacon, 1982.

Wilson, Edward O. *Naturalist.* Washington, D.C.: Island Press, 1994.

Worldwatch. *State of the World.* New York: W. W. Norton, yearly 1984-1997.

3. ENVIRONMENTAL HISTORY/BIBLIOGRAPHY

Albright, Horace M., as told to Robert Cahn. *The Birth of the National Park Service.* Salt Lake City, Utah: Howe Brothers, 1985.

Arrandale, Thomas. *The Battle for Natural Resources.* Washington, D.C.: Congressional Quarterly Books, 1983.

Audubon, John James. *The Quadrupeds of North America.* New York: V. G. Audubon, 1854.

Audubon, John James. *The Birds of America.* New York: Macmillan, 1937.

Baigell, Matthew. *Albert Bierstadt*. New York: Watson Guptill, 1981.

Bartram, William. *Travels*. New Haven, Conn.: Yale University Press, 1958.

Beinart, William. *Environment and History: The Taming of Nature in the USA and South Africa*. New York: Routledge, 1995.

Bowler, Peter J. *The Norton History of the Environmental Science*. New York: W. W. Norton, 1993.

Brown, Michael, and John May. *The Greenpeace Story*. New York: Dorling Kindersley, Inc., 1991.

Carty, Winthrop P., and Elizabeth Lee. *The Rhino Man and Other Uncommon Environmentalists*. Washington, D.C.: Seven Locks Press, 1992.

Catlin, George. *North American Indians: Being Letters and Notes on Their Manners, Customs, and Conditions, Written During Eight Years' Travel amongst the Wildest Tribes of Indians in North America*. Philadelphia: Stuart and Company, 1913.

Clark, Carol. *Thomas Moran: Watercolors of the American West*. Austin: University of Texas Press, 1980.

Cohen, Michael P. *The Pathless Way: John Muir and American Wilderness*. Madison: University of Wisconsin Press, 1984.

Cohen, Michael P. *The History of the Sierra Club*. San Francisco: Sierra Club Books, 1988.

Cronon, William. *Changes in the Land*. New York: Hill and Wang, 1983.

Crosby, Alfred W. *Ecological Imperialism: The Biological Expansion of Europe, 900-1900*. New York: Cambridge University Press, 1986.

Dunlap, Riley E., and Angela G. Mertig, ed. *American Environmentalism: The U.S. Environmental Movement, 1970-1990*. Philadelphia: Taylor and Francis, 1992.

Dunlap, Thomas. *Saving America's Wildlife*. Princeton, N.J.: Princeton University Press, 1988.

Engberg, Robert, and Donald Westing, ed. *John Muir: To Yosemite and Beyond: Writings from the Years 1863 to 1875.* Madison: University of Wisconsin Press, 1980.

Flader, Susan L. *Thinking Like a Mountain: Aldo Leopold and the Evolution of an Ecological Attitude toward Deer, Wolves, and Forests.* Columbia: University of Missouri Press, 1974.

Fleming, Donald. "Roots of the New Conservation Movement." *Perspectives in American History* 6 (1972):7-96.

Fox, Stephen. *John Muir and His Legacy: The American Conservation Movement.* Boston: Little, Brown, 1981.

Glover, James M. *A Wilderness Original: The Life of Bob Marshall.* Seattle, Wash.: The Mountaineers, 1986.

Graham, Frank. *Man's Dominion: The Story of Conservation in America.* New York: M. Evans, 1971.

Hartzog, George B., Jr. *Battling for the National Parks.* Mt. Kisco, N.Y.: Moyer Bell, 1988.

Hays, Samuel P. *Conservation and the Gospel of Efficiency: The Progressive Conservation Movement, 1890-1920.* Cambridge, Mass.: Harvard University Press, 1959.

Hays, Samuel P. *Beauty, Health, and Permanence: Environmental Politics in the United States: 1955-1985.* New York: Cambridge University Press, 1987.

Headley, J. T. *The Adirondack: Or Life in the Woods.* New York: Scribner, Armstrong, and Company, 1875.

Hepworth, James, and Gregory McNamee. *Resist Much, Obey Little: Some Notes on Edward Abbey.* 2d ed. Tucson, Ariz.: Harbinger House, Inc., 1989.

Homan, Tim. ed. *A Yearning toward Wildness: Environmental Quotations from the Writings of Henry David Thoreau.* Atlanta, Ga.: Peachtree Publishers Ltd., 1991.

Hughes, J. Donald. *American Indian Ecology.* El Paso: Texas Western Press, 1983.

Hull, David. *Darwin and His Critics.* Cambridge, Mass.: Harvard University Press, 1973.

Jacobsen, Judith, and John Firor, ed. *Human Impact on the Environment: Ancient Roots, Current Challenges.* Boulder, Colo.: Westview Press, 1992.

Krutch, Joseph Wood. *The Twelve Seasons.* New York: William Sloane Associates, 1949.

Krutch, Joseph Wood. *The Desert Year.* New York: William Sloane Associates, 1952.

Krutch, Joseph Wood. *The Voice of the Desert.* New York: William Sloane Associates, 1955.

Krutch, Joseph Wood. *The Great Chair of Life.* Boston: Houghton Mifflin, 1956.

Krutch, Joseph Wood. *The Forgotten Peninsula: A Naturalist in Baja California.* New York: William Sloane Associates, 1961.

Malthus, Thomas. "A Summary View of the Principle of Population" In *Three Essays on Population.* New York: Mentor Books, 1960.

Marsh, George Perkins. *Man and Nature.* New York: Charles Scribner, 1864.

Marsh, George Perkins. *Man and Nature.* Edited by David Lowenthal. Cambridge, Mass.: Harvard University Press, 1965.

Marshall, Robert. "The Problem of the Wilderness," Scientific Monthly 30 (February 1930):141-148.

McHenry, Robert, and Charles Van Doren, ed. *A Documentary History of Conservation in America.* New York: Praeger Publishers, 1972.

McLaughlin, Charles Capen, ed. *The Papers of Frederick Law Olmsted.* Vol. 1. Baltimore, Md.: Johns Hopkins University Press, 1977.

Meine, Curt. *Aldo Leopold: His Life and Work.* Madison: University of Wisconsin Press, 1988.

Mitchell, Lee Clark. *Witness to a Vanishing America: The 19th Century Response.* Princeton, N.J.: Princeton University Press, 1981.

Morris, Edmund. *The Rise of Theodore Roosevelt.* New York: Coward, McCann & Geogheghan, 1979.

Muir, John. *My First Summer in the Sierra.* New York: Penguin Books, 1987.

Murie, Olaus. *Two in the Far North.* New York: Knopf, 1962.

Murie, Olaus. *Alaska-Yukon Caribou.* Washington, D.C.: United States Government Printing Office, 1935.

Nash, Roderick. *Wilderness and the American Mind.* 3rd ed. New Haven, Conn.: Yale University Press, 1982.

Nash, Roderick. *The Rights of Nature: A History of Environmental Ethics.* Madison: University of Wisconsin Press, 1988.

Nash, Roderick Frazier, ed. *American Environmentalism: Readings in Conservation History.* 3rd ed. New York: McGraw-Hill, 1990.

Pepper, David. *The Roots of Modern Environmentalism.* London: Routledge, 1989.

Petulla, Joseph M. *American Environmental History.* 2d ed. Columbus, Ohio: Charles E. Merrill, 1988.

Piel, Gerard, and Osborn Segerberg Jr., ed. *The World of Rene Dubos.* New York: Henry Holt & Co., 1990.

Pinchot, Gifford. *The Fight for Conservation.* Seattle: University of Washington Press, 1910.

Ponting, Clive. *A Green History of the World: The Environment and the Collapse of Great Civilizations.* New York: St. Martin's Press, 1992.

Roe, Frank G. *The North American Buffalo.* Toronto: University of Toronto Press, 1970.

Rubin, Charles T. *The Green Crusade: Rethinking the Roots of Environmentalism.* New York: Free Press, 1994.

Rudig, Wolfgang. *Green Blues: The Rise and Decline of the British Green Party.* Glasgow: Dept. of Government, University of Strathclyde, 1993.

Runte, Alfred. *National Parks: The American Experience.* 2d ed. Lincoln: University of Nebraska Press, 1987.

Runte, Alfred. *Yosemite: The Embattled Wilderness.* Lincoln: University of Nebraska Press, 1990.

Shabecoff, Philip, and Thurman Wilkins. *Thomas Moran: Artist of the Mountains.* Norman: University of Oklahoma Press, 1966.

Short, C. Brant. *Ronald Reagan and the Public Lands: America's Conservation Debate: 1979-1984.* College Station: Texas A&M University Press, 1989.

Squire, C. B. *Heroes of Conservation.* New York: Fleet Press Corporation, 1974.

Steffoff, Rebecca. *The American Environmental Movement.* New York: Facts on File, 1995.

Tanner, Thomas, ed. *Aldo Leopold: The Man and His Legacy.* Ankeny, Iowa: Soil Conservation Society of America, 1987.

Thoreau, Henry David. *The Maine Woods.* New York: Thomas Y. Crowell, 1909.

Thoreau, Henry David. *Walden.* 28th print. New York: Signet, 1960.

U.S. Department of Agriculture, Forest Service. *Highlights in the History of Forest Conservation.* Washington, D.C.: Government Printing Office, 1976.

Udall, Stewart L. *The Quiet Crisis.* San Francisco: Holt, Rinehart and Winston, 1963.

Udall, Stewart L. *1976: Agenda for Tomorrow.* New York: Harcourt, Brace and World, 1968.

Wallace, Aubrey. *Eco-Heroes.* San Francisco: Mercury House, 1993.

Watson, Paul, and Warren Rogers. *Sea Shepherd: My Fight for Whales and Seals.* New York: W. W. Norton, 1982.

White, Gilbert. *Natural History of Selborne and Observations on Nature.* New York: Oxford University Press, 1994.

Wild, Peter. *Pioneer Conservationists of Western America.* Missoula, Mont.: Mountain Press Publishing Company, 1979.

Williams, Michael. *Americans and Their Forests: A Historical Account.* New York: Cambridge University Press, 1989.

Worster, Donald. *American Environmentalism: The Formative Period, 1860-1915.* New York: John Wiley & Sons, Inc., 1973.

Worster, Donald. *Under Western Skies: Nature and History in the American West.* New York: Oxford University Press, 1992.

Worster, Donald. *The Wealth of Nature: Environmental History and the Ecological Imagination.* New York: Oxford University Press, 1993.

Worster, Donald. *Nature's Economy: A History of Ecological Ideas.* 3rd. ed. New York: Cambridge University Press, 1994.

Worster, Donald, ed. *The Ends of the Earth: Perspectives on Modern Environmental History.* New York: Cambridge University Press, 1988.

4. ENVIRONMENTAL ETHICS

Armstrong, Susan J., and Richard G. Botzler, ed. *Environmental Ethics: Divergence and Convergence.* New York: McGraw-Hill, 1992.

Attfield, Robin. The *Ethics of Environmental Concern.* 2d ed. Athens: The University of Georgia Press, 1991.

Barbour, Ian. *Technology, Environment, and Human Values.* New York: Praeger, 1980.

Bookchin, Murray. *The Philosophy of Social Ecology: Essays on Dialectical Naturalism.* 2d ed. Toronto: Black Rose Books, 1995.

Bradford, George. *How Deep Is Deep Ecology? A Challenge to Radical Environmentalists.* Ojai, Calif.: Times Change Press, 1989.

Brennan, Andrew. *Thinking about Nature: An Investigation of Nature, Value and Ecology.* Athens: University of Georgia Press, 1988.

Callicott, J. Baird. "American Indian Land Wisdom? Sorting Out the Issues." *Journal of Forest History* 33, no.1 (1989): 35-42.

Callicott, J. Baird. *In Defense of the Land Ethic.* Albany: State University of New York Press, 1989.

Callicott, J. Baird, ed. *Companion to a Sand County Almanac: Interpretive and Critical Essays.* Madison: University of Wisconsin Press, 1987.

Capra, Fritjof. *The Turning Point.* New York: Simon and Schuster, 1982.

Capra, Fritjof. *Belonging to the Universe.* San Francisco: Harper, 1991.

Carson, Rachel. *Silent Spring.* Boston: Houghton Mifflin, 1962.

DesJardins, Joseph R. *Environmental Ethics: An Introduction to Environmental Philosophy.* Belmont, Calif.: Wadsworth, 1993.

Devall, Bill. *Simple in Means, Rich in Ends: Practicing Deep Ecology.* Salt Lake City, Utah: Peregrine Smith Books, 1988.

Devall, Bill, and George Sessions. *Deep Ecology: Living as if Nature Mattered.* Salt Lake City, Utah: Peregrine Smith Books, 1985.

Douglas, William O. *A Wilderness Bill of Rights.* Boston: Little, Brown, 1965.

Douglas, William O. *Farewell to Texas: A Vanishing Wilderness.* New York: McGraw Hill, 1967.

Dyson, Freeman. *From Eros to Gaia.* New York: Pantheon Books, 1992.

The Earth Beneath: A Critical Guide to Green Theology. London: SPCK, 1992.

Eckersley, Robyn. *Environmentalism and Political Theory: Toward an Ecocentric Approach.* Albany: State University of New York Press, 1992.

Elhot, Robert, and Arran Gare, ed. *Environmental Philosophy: A Collection of Readings.* University Park: Pennsylvania State University Press, 1983.

Finsen, Lawrence. *The Animal Rights Movement in America: From Compassion to Respect.* New York: Twayne, 1994.

Gore, Albert. *Earth in the Balance: Ecology and the Human Spirit.* Boston: Houghton Mifflin, 1992.

Gunn, Alastair S., and Aame Vesifind, ed. *Environmental Ethics for Engineers.* Chelsea, Mich.: Lewis Publishers, 1986.

Hardin, Garrett. "The Tragedy of the Commons. " *Science* 162 (1968):1243-1248.

Hardin, Garrett, "Lifeboat Ethics." *Psychology Today* 8, no. 4 (September 1974):38-43, 123-126.

Hanson, Philip P., ed. *Environmental Ethics: Philosophical and Policy Perspective.* Vol. 1. Burnaby, British Columbia: Simon Fraser University, 1986.

Hart, Richard E., ed. *Ethics and the Environment.* Lanham, Md.: University Press of America, 1992.

The Intrinsic Value of Nature. *The Monist* 75, no. 2 (April 1992).

Johnson, Lawrence E. *A Morally Deep World: An Essay on Moral Significance and Environmental Ethics.* New York: Cambridge University Press, 1991.

LaChapelle, Delores. *Earth Wisdom.* Silverton, Colo.: Way of the Mountain Center, 1978.

Leopold, Aldo. *Game Management.* New York: Charles Scribner's Sons, 1933.

Leopold, Aldo. *A Sand County Almanac.* New York: Oxford University Press, 1948.

Leopold, Aldo. *A Sand County Almanac.* New York: Oxford University Press, 1966.

Lovelock, James. *Gaia: A New Look at Life on Earth.* New York: Oxford University Press, 1981.

McCloskey, H. J. *Ecological Ethics and Politics.* Totowa, N.J.: Rowman and Littlefield, 1983.

McDaniel, Jay B. *Earth, Sky, Gods and Mortals.* Mystic, Conn.: Twenty-Third Publications, 1990.

McKibben, Bill. *The End of Nature.* New York: Random House, 1989.

Oelschlager, Max. *The Idea of Wilderness from Prehistory to the Age of Ecology.* New Haven, Conn.: Yale University Press, 1991.

Olson, Sigurd. "Why Wilderness?" *American Forests* 44, 1938.

Passmore, John. *Man's Responsibility for Nature: Ecological Problems and Western Traditions.* New York: Charles Scribner's Sons, 1974.

Potter, Van Rensselaer. *Global Bioethics: Building on the Leopold Legacy.* Lansing: Michigan State University Press, 1989.

Regan, Tom, ed. *Earthbound: New Introductory Essays in Environmental Ethics.* New York: Random House, 1984.

Rolston, Holmes, IV. *Environmental Ethics.* Philadelphia: Temple University Press, 1988.

Roszak, Theodore, Mary E. Gomes, and Allen D. Kanner, ed. *Ecopsychology: Restoring the Earth, Healing the Mind.* San Francisco: Sierra Club Books, 1995.

Ryder, Richard D. *Painism: Ethics, Animal Rights and Environmentalism.* Cardiff: Centre for Applied Ethics, University of Wales College of Cardiff, 1992.

Scherer, Donald. *Upstream/Downstream: Issues in Environmental Ethics.* Philadelphia: Temple University Press, 1990.

Scherer, Donald, and Thomas Attig, ed. *Ethics and the Environment.* Englewood Cliffs, N.J.: Prentice Hall, 1983.

Seed, John, Joanna Macy, Pat Fleming, and Arne Naess. *Thinking Like a Mountain: Towards a Council of All Beings.* Philadelphia: New Society Publishers, 1988.

Shepard, Paul. *Man in the Landscape: A Historic View of the Esthetics of Nature.* New York: Knopf, 1967.

Shepard, Paul. *Nature and Madness.* San Francisco: Sierra Club Books, 1982.

Shrader-Frechette, K. S. *Environmental Ethics.* Pacific Grove, Calif.: The Boxwood Press, 1981.

Stone, Christopher D. *Should Trees Have Standing?* Los Altos, Calif.: William Kaufmann, 1974.

Stone, Christopher D. *Earth and Other Ethics: The Case for Moral Pluralism.* New York: Harper and Row, 1987.

Teilhard de Chardin, Pierre. *The Phenomenon of Man.* New York: Harper and Row, 1959.

VanDeVeer, Donald, and Christine Pierce. *People, Penguins and Plastic Trees: Basic Issues in Environmental Ethics.* Belmont, Calif.: Wadsworth Publishing Co., 1986.

Weston, Anthony. *Toward Better Problems: New Perspectives on Abortion, Animal Rights, the Environment, and Justice.* Philadelphia: Temple University Press, 1992.

Wilson, Edward O. *Biophilia.* Cambridge, Mass.: Harvard University Press, 1984.

Worldviews and Ecology: Religion, Philosophy, and the Environment. Maryknoll, N.Y.: Orbis Books, 1994.

Zimmerman, Michael, J. Baird Callicott, George Sessions, Karen J. Warren, and John P. Clark, ed. *Environmental Philosophy: From Animal Rights to Radical Ecology.* Englewood Cliffs, N.J.: Prentice Hall, 1993.

5. ENVIRONMENTAL MOVEMENT

Abbey, Edward. *The Monkey Wrench Gang.* New York: Avon Books, 1976.

Abbey, Edward. *Abbey's Road.* New York: E. P. Dutton, 1979.

Arnold, Ron. *Ecology Wars: Environmentalism as if People Mattered.* Bellevue, Wash.: The Free Enterprise Press, 1987.

Bahro, Rudolf. *Building the Green Movement.* London: Heretic Books, 1986.

Bell, Graham. *The Permaculture Way.* London: Thorsons, 1992.

Bookchin, Murray. *Our Synthetic Environment.* New York: Colophon, 1962.

Bookchin, Murray. *The Ecology of Freedom: The Emergence and Dissolution of Hierarchy.* Palo Alto, Calif.: Cheshire Books, 1982.

Bookchin, Murray. *Which Way for the Ecology Movement?* San Francisco: AK Press, 1994.

Borrelli, Peter. "Environmentalism at a Crossroads: Reflections on the Old Old, New Old, Old New, and New New Movements." *Amicus Journal* 9, no.3 (Summer 1987): 24-37.

Borrelli, Peter, ed. *Crossroads: Environmental Priorities for the Future.* Covelo, Calif.: Island Press, 1988.

Brower, David, with Steve Chapple. *Let the Mountains Talk, Let the Rivers Run: A Call to Those Who Would Save the Earth.* New York: HarperCollins West, 1995.

Brown, Michael, and John May. *The Greenpeace Story.* New York: Dorling Kindersley, Inc., 1991.

Caldicott, Helen. *Missile Envy: The Arms Race and Nuclear War.* Toronto: Bantam Books, 1986.

Caldicott, Helen. *If You Love the Planet: A Plan to Heal the Earth.* New York: W. W. Norton, 1992.

Caldicott, Helen. *Nuclear Madness: What You Can Do.* New York: Norton, 1994.

Chase, Steve, ed. *Defending the Earth: A Dialogue between Murray Bookchin and Dave Foreman.* Boston: South End Press, 1991.

Clark, John, ed. *Renewing the Earth: The Promise of Social Ecology. A Celebration of the Work of Murray Bookchin.* London: Green Planet, 1990.

Cohen, Michael P. *The History of the Sierra Club.* San Francisco: Sierra Club Books, 1988.

Cohn, Susan. *Green at Work: Finding a Business Career That Works for the Environment.* Covelo, Calif.: Island Press, 1992.

Commoner, Barry. *The Closing Circle.* New York: Alfred A. Knopf, 1971.

Commoner, Barry. *Making Peace with the Planet.* New York: Pantheon Books, 1990.

Comp, T. Allan, ed. *Blueprint for the Environment.* Salt Lake City, Utah: Howe Brothers, 1989.

Coyle, David Cushman. *Conservation.* New Brunswick, N.J.: Rutgers University Press, 1956.

Dalton, Russell, J. *The Green Rainbow: Environmental Groups in Western Europe.* New Haven, Conn.: Yale University Press, 1994.

Davis, John, and Dave Foreman, ed. *The Earth First! Reader: Ten Years of Radical Environmentalism.* Salt Lake City, Utah: Peregrine Smith Books, 1991.

Day, David. *The Environmental Wars: Reports from the First Line.* New York: St. Martin's Press, 1990.

Diani, Mario. *Green Networks: A Structural Analysis of the Italian Environmental Movement.* Edinburgh: Edinburgh University Press, 1995.

Dowie, Mark. *Losing Ground: American Environmentalism at the Close of the Twentieth Century.* Cambridge, Mass.: MIT Press, 1995.

Drengson, Alan R. *Beyond Environmental Crisis: From Technocrat to Planetary Person.* New York: Peter Lang Publishing Co., 1989.

Dunlap, Riley E., and Angela G. Mertig, ed. *American Environmentalism: The U.S. Environmental Movement, 1970-1990.* Philadelphia: Taylor and Francis, 1992.

Durning, Alan B. *Action at the Grassroots: Fighting Poverty and Environmental Decline.* Washington, D.C.: Worldwatch Institute, 1989.

Ehrlich, Paul R., and Anne H. Ehrlich. *Healing the Planet.* Reading, Mass.: Addison-Wesley Publishing, 1991.

Elkins, Paul, and Jakob von Uexhuil. *Grassroots Movements for Global Change.* New York: Routledge, 1992.

Empfield, Jeffrey Morgan. "Wilderness Rivers: Environmentalism, the Wilderness Movement, and River Preservation during the 1960s." M.A. thesis, Virginia Polytechnic Institute and State University, 1994.

Environmentalism. Peterborough, N.H.: Cobblestone, 1989.

Environmentalism and Americans: A Guide to the Foremost Trend of Our Time. Long Island City, N.Y.: Research Alert, 1990.

Erickson, Brad, ed. *Call to Action: Handbook for Ecology, Peace, and Justice.* San Francisco: Sierra Club Books, 1990.

Foreman, Dave. *Confessions of an Eco-Warrior.* New York: Crown, 1991.

Foreman, Dave, and Bill Haywood, ed. *Ecodefense: A Field Guide to Monkeywrenching.* 2d ed. Tucson, Ariz.: Ned Ludd Books, 1985.

Fox, Warwick. *Toward a Transpersonal Ecology: Developing New Foundations for Environmentalism.* Boston: Shambhala, 1990.

Henning, Daniel H., and William R. Manguin. *Managing the Environmental Crisis.* Durham, N.C.: Duke University Press, 1989.

Hunter, Robert. *Warriors of the Rainbow: A Chronicle of the Greenpeace Movement.* New York: Holt, Rinehart and Winston, 1979.

Kelly, Petra. *Thinking Green: Essays on Environmentalism, Feminism, and Nonviolence.* Berkeley, Calif.: Parallax Press, 1994.

Korten, David C. 1990. *Getting to the 21st Century: Voluntary Action and the Global Arena.* West Hartford, Conn.: Kumarian Press, 1990.

League of Conservation Voters. *National Environment Scorecard.* Washington, D.C. (Published yearly).

Lewis, Martin W. *Green Delusions: An Environmentalist Critique of Radical Environmentalism.* Durham, N.C.: Duke University Press, 1994.

Lipietz, Alain. *Green Hopes: The Future of Political Ecology.* Cambridge, Mass.: Polity Press, 1995.

List, Peter C. *Radical Environmentalism: Philosophy and Tactics.* Belmont, Calif.: Wadsworth Publishing Company, 1993.

Love, Sam, and David Obst, ed. *Ecotage!* New York: Pocket Books, 1972.

Manes, Christopher. *Green Rage: Radical Environmentalism and the Unmaking of Civilization.* Boston: Little, Brown, 1990.

Marietta, Don, Jr., and Lester Embree. *Environmental Philosophy and Environmental Activism.* Lanham, Md.: Rowman and Littlefield, 1995.

McCormick, John. *Reclaiming Paradise: The Global Environmental Movement.* Bloomington: Indiana University Press, 1989.

McPhee, John. *Encounters with the Archdruid.* New York: Farrar, Straus, and Giroux, 1971.

Morine, David E. *Good Dirt: Confessions of a Conservationist.* New York: Ballantine, 1990.

Nicholson, Max. *The Environmental Revolution.* London: Hodder & Stoughton, 1970.

Nicholson, Max. *The New Environmental Age.* New York: Cambridge University Press, 1987.

Norton, Bryan G. *Toward Unity among Environmentalists.* New York: Oxford University Press, 1991.

Odell, Rice. *Environmental Awakening: The New Revolution to Protect the Earth.* Cambridge, Mass.: Ballinger, 1980.

O'Riordan, Timothy. *Environmentalism.* London: Pion, 1981.

Parkin, S. *Green Parties.* London: Heretic Books/GMP, 1989.

Pearce, Fred. *Green Warriors: The People and Politics behind the Environmental Revolution.* London: Bodley Head, 1991.

Petulla, Joseph M. *American Environmentalism: Values, Tactics, Priorities.* College Station: Texas A&M University Press, 1980.

Rohrschneider, Robert. "The Greening of Party Politics in Western Europe: Environmentalism, Economics and Partisan Orientations in Four Nations." Ph.D. thesis, Florida State University, 1989.

Scarce, Rik. *Eco-Warriors: Understanding the Radical Environmental Movement.* Chicago: The Noble Press, Inc., 1990.

Scheffer, Victor B. *The Shaping of Environmentalism in America.* Seattle: University of Washington Press, 1991.

Schultz, Robert C., and J. Donald Hughes, ed. *Ecological Consciousness: Essays from the Earthday X Colloquium.* Washington, D.C.: University Press of America, 1981.

Schwab, James. *Deeper Shades of Green: The Rise of Blue-Collar and Minority Environmentalism in America.* San Francisco: Sierra Club Books, 1994.

Shabecoff, Philip. *A Fierce Green Fire: The American Environmental Movement.* New York: Hill & Wang, 1992.

Snow, Donald. *Inside the Environmental Movement: Meeting the Leadership Challenge.* Covelo, Calif.: Island Press, 1992.

Snow, Donald, ed. *Voices from the Environmental Movement.* Covelo, Calif.: Island Press, 1992.

Spiller, Robert E., ed. *Selected Essays, Lectures, and Poems of Ralph Waldo Emerson.* 5th ed. New York: Washington Square Press, 1975.

Strong, Douglas H. *Dreamers and Defenders: American Conservationists.* Lincoln: University of Nebraska Press, 1971.

Tayler, Bron Raymond, ed. *Ecological Resistance Movements: The Global Emergence of Radical and Popular Environmentalism.* Albany: State University of New York Press, 1995.

Tokar, Brian. *The Green Alternative: Creating an Ecological Future*. San Pedro, Calif.: R. & E. Miles, 1987.

Watson, Paul, and Warren Rogers. *Sea Shepherd: My Fight for Whales and Seals*. New York: W. W. Norton, 1982.

Watts, Nicholas S. J. *Environmentalism in Europe: Social Change and the New Politics*. Berlin: N. S. J. Watts, 1987.

Wenz, Peter S. *Environmental Justice*. Albany: State University of New York Press, 1988.

Young, John. *Sustaining the Earth: The Past, Present and Future of the Green Revolution*. Kensington: New South Wales University Press, 1991.

6. ENVIRONMENT AND CULTURE

Austin, Mary Hunter. *Land of Little Rain*. Boston: Houghton Mifflin Company, 1903.

Benjamin, Medea, and Andrea Freeman. *Bridging the Global Gap: A Handbook to Linking Citizens of the First and Third Worlds*. Baltimore, Md.: Seven Locks Press, 1989.

Berry, Thomas. *The Dream of the Earth*. San Francisco: Sierra Club Books, 1988.

Berry, Wendell. *The Unsettling of America: Culture and Agriculture*. San Francisco: Sierra Club Books, 1977.

Berry, Wendell. *The Gift of Good Land*. San Francisco: North Point Press, 1981.

Bookchin, Murray. *Our Synthetic Environment*. New York: Colophon, 1974.

Bookchin, Murray. *Toward an Ecological Society*. Montreal: Black Rose Books, 1980.

Bookchin, Murray. *The Ecology of Freedom: The Emergence and Dissolution of Hierarchy*. Palo Alto, Calif.: Cheshire Books, 1982.

Bookchin, Murray. *Which Way for the Ecology Movement?* San Francisco: AK Press, 1994.

Bronowski, Jacob, Jr. *The Ascent of Man.* Boston: Little, Brown, 1974.

Capra, Fritjof. *The Turning Point.* London: Fontana, 1983.

Capra, Fritjof. *The Tao of Physics.* Sydney: ABC, 1988.

Capra, Fritjof. *Belonging to the Universe.* New York: Penguin, 1992.

Chisholm, Mariellen. *Nature and Community toward a Marcusean-Informed Environmentalism.* Ottawa: National Library of Canada, 1993.

Clark, John, ed. *The Anarchist Moment: Reflections on Culture, Nature, and Power.* Toronto: Black Rose Books, 1984.

Clark, John, ed. *Renewing the Earth: The Promise of Social Ecology. A Celebration of the Work of Murray Bookchin.* London: Green Planet, 1990.

Dubos, Rene. "Symbiosis between Earth and Humankind." *Science* 193, no. 4252 (6 August 1976):459-462.

Eiseley, Loren. *The Immense Journey.* New York: Random House, 1957.

Eiseley, Loren. *The Firmament of Time.* New York: Atheneum, 1966.

Eiseley, Loren. *The Unexpected Universe.* New York: Harcourt, Brace, and World, 1969.

Galbraith, J. K. *The Affluent Society.* Boston: Houghton Mifflin Company, 1958.

Gray, Elizabeth Dodson. *Patriarchy as a Conceptual Trap.* Wellesley, Mass.: Roundtable Press, 1982.

Gray, Elizabeth Dodson. *Why the Green Nigger: Green Paradise Lost.* Wellesley, Mass.: Roundtable Press, 1982.

Haifa, Yrjo, and Richard Levins. *Humanity and Nature: Ecology, Science, and Society.* Boulder, Colo.: Westview Press, 1993.

Jacobs, Donald Trent. *The Bum's Rush: The Selling of Environmental Backlash: Phrases and Fallacies of Rush Limbaugh.* Boise, Idaho: Legendary Pub., 1994.

Jacobsen, Judith, and John Firor, ed. *Human Impact on the Environment: Ancient Roots, Current Challenges.* Boulder, Colo.: Westview Press, 1992.

Kazis, Richard, and Richard L Grossman. *Fear at Work: Job Blackmail, Labor, and the Environment.* Philadelphia: New Society, 1991.

Kelly, Petra. *Thinking Green: Essays on Environmentalism, Feminism, and Nonviolence.* Berkeley, Calif.: Parallax Press, 1994.

Lamay, Craig L., and Everette E. Dennis, ed. *Media and the Environment.* Covelo, Calif.: Island Press, 1991.

Mander, Jerry. *In the Absence of the Sacred: The Failure of Technology and the Rise of Indian Nations.* San Francisco: Sierra Club Books, 1991.

Marsh, George Perkins. *Man and Nature.* New York: Charles Scribner, 1864.

Marsh, George Perkins. *Man and Nature.* Edited by David Lowenthal. Cambridge: Harvard University Press, 1965.

Martin, Calvin Luther. *In the Spirit of the Earth: Rethinking History and Time.* Baltimore, Md.: Johns Hopkins University Press, 1992.

McDaniel, Jay B. *Earth, Sky, Gods and Mortals.* Mystic, Conn.: Twenty-Third Publications, 1990.

McLuhan, T. C. *The Way of the Earth.* New York: Simon and Schuster, 1994.

Merchant, Carolyn. *The Death of Nature.* San Francisco: Harper and Row, 1983.

Merchant, Carolyn. *Earthcare: Women and the Environment.* New York: Routledge, 1995.

Mikin, Colleen Ann. *Ecofeminist Theories: A Socio-Historical Analysis of Contemporary Environmental Movements,* 1994.

Miller, Alan S. *Gaia Connections: An Introduction to Ecology, Ecoethics, and Economics.* Totowa, N.J.: Rowman and Littlefield, 1991.

Mowat, Farley. *The World of Farley Mowat: A Selection from His Works*. Edited by Peter Davison. Boston: Little, Brown and Company, 1980.

Naess, Arne. *Ecology, Community, and Lifestyle*. New York: Cambridge University Press, 1989.

Nash, Roderick. *The American Environment*. 2nd ed. New York: Alfred A. Knopf, 1976.

Petulla, Joseph M. *American Environmentalism: Values, Tactics, Priorities*. College Station: Texas A&M University Press, 1980.

Rifkin, Jeremy. *Beyond Beef: The Rise and Fall of the Cattle Culture*. New York: Dutton, 1992.

Rifkin, Jeremy. *The End of Work*. New York: G. P. Putnam and Sons, 1995.

Rohrschneider, Robert. "The Greening of Party Politics in Western Europe: Environmentalism, Economics and Partisan Orientations in Four Nations." Ph.D. thesis, Florida State University, 1989.

Roszak, Theodore. *Where the Wasteland Ends: Politics and Transcendence in a Post-Industrial Society*. Garden City, N.Y.: Anchor Press/Doubleday, 1972.

Roszak, Theodore. *Person/Planet: The Creative Disintegration of Industrial Society*. Garden City, N.Y.: Anchor Press/Doubleday, 1978.

Roszak, Theodore. *The Making of a Counterculture: Reflections on True Technocratic Society and its Youthful Opposition*. Garden City, N.Y.: Anchor Press/Doubleday, 1989.

Roszak, Theodore. *The Voice of the Earth*. New York: Simon and Schuster, 1992.

Seed, John, Joanna Macy, Pat Fleming, and Arne Naess. *Thinking Like a Mountain: Towards a Council of All Beings*. Philadelphia: New Society Publishers, 1988.

Shephard, Paul. *Nature and Madness*. San Francisco: Sierra Club Books, 1982.

Shephard, Paul. *Man in the Landscape: A Historic View of the Esthetics of Nature.* 2d ed. College Station: Texas A&M University Press, 1991.

Simmons, I. G. *Changing the Face of the Earth: Culture, Environment, and History.* London: Basil Blackwell, 1989.

Simmons, I. G. *Interpreting Nature: Cultural Constructions of the Environment.* New York: Routledge, 1993.

Spiller, Robert E., ed. *Selected Essays, Lectures, and Poems of Ralph Waldo Emerson.* 5th ed. New York: Washington Square Press, 1975.

Stegner, Wallace. "The Wilderness Idea." In *Wilderness: America's Living Heritage.* Edited by David Brower. San Francisco: Sierra Club Books, 1961.

Telba, M. K. *Saving our Planet: Challenges and Hopes.* New York: Chapman & Hail, 1992.

Thomas, Keith. *Man and the Natural World.* New York: Pantheon Books, 1983.

Vecsey, Christopher T., and Robert W. Venables, ed. *American Indian Environments: Ecological Issues in Native American History.* Syracuse, N.Y.: University of Syracuse Press, 1980.

Wallach, Bret. *At Odds with Progress: Americans and Conservation.* Tucson: University of Arizona Press, 1991.

Watts, Nicholas S. J. *Environmentalism in Europe: Social Change and the New Politics.* Berlin: N. S. J. Watts, 1987.

White, Lynn, Jr. "The Historical Roots of Our Ecological Crisis." *Science* 155 (March 10, 1967):1203-1207.

7. ENVIRONMENTAL LAW, POLITICS, AND POLICY

Atkinson, Adrian. *Principles of Political Ecology.* London: Belhaven Press, 1991.

Boulding, Kenneth E. *Three Faces of Power*. Beverly Hills, Calif.: Sage Publications, 1989.

Brown, Janet W., ed. *In the U.S. Interest: Resources, Growth, and Security in the Developing World*. Washington, D.C.: World Resources Institute, 1990.

Buck, Susan J. *Understanding Environmental Administration and Law*. Covelo, Calif.: Island Press, 1991.

Cahn, Robert, ed. *An Environmental Agenda for the Future*. Washington, D.C.: Agenda Press, 1985.

Caldwell, Lynton K. *Between Two Worlds: Science, the Environmental Movement, and Policy Choice*. New York: Cambridge University Press, 1990.

Caldwell, Lynton K. *International Environmental Policy*. 2d ed. Durham, N.C.: Duke University Press, 1990.

Capra, Fritjof, and Charlene Spretnak. *Green Politics*. New York: E. P. Dutton, 1984.

Chiras, Daniel D. *Beyond the Fray: Reshaping America's Environmental Response*. Boulder, Colo.: Johnson Books, 1990.

Clawson, Marion. *The Federal Lands Revisited*. Washington, D.C.: Resources for the Future, 1983.

Cooper, David E., and Joy A. Palmer, ed. *The Environment in Question*. London: Routledge, 1992.

Costanza, Robert. "Social Traps and Environmental Policy." *BioScience* 37, no. 6 (1987): 407-412.

Culhane, Paul J. *Public Land Politics: Interest Group Influences on the Forest Service and the Bureau of Land Management*. Washington, D.C.: Resources for the Future, 1981.

Dahlberg, Kenneth A., ed. *Environment and the Global Arena*. Durham, N.C.: Duke University Press, 1985.

Dobson, Andrew. *Green Political Thought: An Introduction*. New York: Routledge, 1990.

Dubos, Rene. *Only One Earth*. New York: W.W. Norton and Company, 1972.

Eckersley, Robyn. *Environmentalism and Political Theory: Toward an Ecocentric Approach.* Albany: State University of New York Press, 1992.

Ehrlich, Paul R., Anne H. Ehrlich, and J. P. Holdren. *Ecoscience: Population, Resources, Environment.* San Francisco: W. H. Freeman, 1977.

Ferguson, Denzel, and Nancy Ferguson. *Sacred Cows at the Public Trough.* Bend, Oreg.: Maverick, 1983.

Firestone, David B., and Frank C. Reed. *Environmental Law for Non-Lawyers.* Salem, N.H.: Butterworths, 1983.

Fitzgerald, Sarah. *International Wildlife Trade: Whose Business Is It?* Washington, D.C.: World Wildlife Fund, 1989.

French, Hilary E. *After the Earth Summit: The Future of Environmental Governance.* Washington, D.C.: Worldwatch Institute, 1992.

Gardner, Richard N. *Negotiating Survival: Four Priorities after Rio.* Washington, D.C.: Council on Foreign Relations, 1993.

Gore, Albert. *Earth in the Balance: Ecology and the Human Spirit.* Boston: Houghton Mifflin, 1992.

Gorz, Andre. *Ecology as Politics.* Boston: South End Press, 1989.

Hall, Bob. *Environmental Politics: Lessons from the Grassroots.* Durham, N.C.: Institute for Southern Studies, 1990.

Hurrell, Andrew, and Benedict Kingsbury, ed. *The International Politics of the Environment.* New York: Oxford University Press, 1992.

International Union for Conservation of Nature and Natural Resources. *World Conservation Strategy.* Gland, Switzerland, 1980.

International Union for Conservation of Nature and Natural Resources. *IUCN Red List of Threatened Animals.* Gland, Switzerland: IUCN, 1986.

International Union for Conservation of Nature and Natural Resources. *Caring for the Earth: A Strategy for Sustainable Living.* Gland, Switzerland, 1991.

Jacobs, Donald Trent. *The Bum's Rush: The Selling of Environmental Backlash. Phrases and Fallacies of Rush Limbaugh.* Boise, Idaho: Legendary Pub., 1994.

Killingsworth, M. J., and Jacqueline S. Palmer. *Ecospeak: Rhetoric and Environmental Politics in America.* Carbondale: Southern Illinois University Press, 1992.

Landy, Marc K., Marc J. Roberts, and Stephen R. Thomas. *The Environmental Protection Agency: Asking the Wrong Questions.* New York: Oxford University Press, 1990.

Leamer, Steve. *Beyond the Earth Summit: Conversations with Advocates of Sustainable Development.* New York: Common Knowledge Press, 1992.

Lipietz, Alain. *Green Hopes: The Future of Political Ecology.* Cambridge, Mass.: Polity Press, 1995.

Mathews, Jessica Tuchman, ed. *Preserving the Global Environment: The Challenge of Shared Leadership.* Washington, D.C.: World Resources Institute, 1990.

McCloskey, H. J. *Ecological Ethics and Politics.* Totowa, N.J.: Rowman and Littlefield, 1983.

Meadows, Donella H. *Global Citizen.* Covelo, Calif.: Island Press, 1991.

Meadows, Donella H., Dennis L. Meadows, Jorgen Randers, and William W. Behrens III. *The Limits to Growth.* New York: Universe Books, 1972.

Milbrath, Lester W. *Environmentalists: Vanguard for a New Society.* Albany: State University of New York Press, 1984.

Morales, Leslie Anderson. *The Impact of Radical Environmentalism on Policy and Practice: A Bibliography.* Monticello, Ill.: Vance Bibliographies, 1991.

Myers, Norman. "Environment and Security." *Foreign Policy* 74 (1988): 23-41.

Ophuls, William, and A. Stephen Boyan Jr. *Ecology and the Politics of Scarcity Revisited: The Unraveling of the American Dream.* New York: W. H. Freeman, 1992.

Paehlke, Robert C. *Environmentalism and the Future of Progressive Politics.* New Haven, Conn.: Yale University Press, 1989.

Peskin, Henry M., Paul R. Portney, and Allen V. Kneese, ed. *Environmental Regulation and the U.S. Economy.* Baltimore, Md.: Published for Resources for the Future by Johns Hopkins University Press, 1981.

Petulla, Joseph M. *Environmental Protection in the United States: Industry, Agencies, Environmentalists.* San Francisco: San Francisco Study Center, 1987.

Pinchot, Gifford. *The Fight for Conservation.* Seattle: University of Washington Press, 1910.

Porritt, Jonathan. *Seeing Green: The Politics of Ecology Explained.* Oxford: Blackwell, 1984.

Porter, Gareth, and Janet Welsh Brown. *Global Environmental Politics.* Boulder, Colo.: Westview Press, 1991.

Renner, Michael. *National Security: The Economic and Environmental Dimensions.* Washington, D.C.: World-watch Institute, 1989.

Repetto, Robert, ed. *The Global Possible: Resources, Development and the New Century.* New Haven, Conn.: Yale University Press, 1986.

Rosenbaum, Walter A. *Environment, Politics, and Policy.* 2d ed. Washington, D.C.: Congressional Quarterly, 1990.

Roussopoulos, Dimitrios I. *Political Ecology: Beyond Environmentalism.* Montreal: Black Rose Books, 1993.

Sanjor, William. *Why the EPA Is Like It Is and What Can Be Done about It.* Washington, D.C.: Environmental Research Foundation, 1992.

Simon, Julian. *The Ultimate Resource.* Princeton, N.J.: Princeton University Press, 1981.

Simon, Julian, and Herman Kahn. *The Resourceful Earth.* New York: Basil Blackwell, 1984.

Spretnak, Charlene, and Fritjof Capra. *Green Politics: The Green Promise.* Santa Fe, N.M.: Bear, 1986.

Stroup, Richard L., and John A. Baden. *Natural Resources: Bureaucratic Myths and Environmental Management.* San Francisco: Institute for Public Policy Research, 1986.

Taylor, Ann. *A Practical Politics of the Environment.* New York: Routledge, 1992.

Vig, Norman J., and Michael E. Kraft, ed. *Environmental Policy in the 1980s: Reagan's New Agenda.* Washington, D.C.: Congressional Quarterly Press, 1984.

Vig, Norman J., and Michael E. Kraft, ed. *Environmental Policy in the 1990's: Toward a New Agenda.* Washington, D.C.: Congressional Quarterly Press, 1990.

World Commission on Environment and Development. *Our Common Future.* New York: Oxford University Press, 1987.

World Resources Institute. *The Crucial Decade. The 1990s and the Global Environmental Challenge.* Washington, D.C.: World Resources Institute, 1989.

8. ENVIRONMENTAL EVENTS AND SPECIFIC TOPICS

Carson, Rachel. *Silent Spring.* Boston: Houghton Mifflin, 1962.

Church, George A. "The Big Spill." *Time* (April 10,1989): 35-41.

Dunlap, Thomas. *Saving America's Wildlife.* Princeton, N.J.: Princeton University Press, 1988.

Ehrlich, Paul R. *The Population Bomb.* Rivercity, Mass.: Rivercity Press, 1975.

Fagan, Brian M. *The Journey from Eden: The Peopling of Our World.* London: Thames & Hudson, 1990.

Finsen, Lawrence. *The Animal Rights Movement in America: From Compassion to Respect.* New York: Twayne, 1994.

Foreman, Dave, and Bill Haywood, ed. *Ecodefense: A Field Guide to Monkeywrenching.* 2d ed. Tucson, Ariz.: Ned Ludd Books, 1988.

Lappe, Frances Moore. *Diet for a Small Planet.* New York: Ballantine Books, 1985.

Lappe, Frances Moore, and Joseph Collins. *Food First: Beyond the Myth of Scarcity.* New York: Ballantine Books, 1978.

Mander, Jerry. *In the Absence of the Sacred: The Failure of Technology and the Rise of Indian Nations.* San Francisco: Sierra Club Books, 1991.

Noss, Reed, and Allen Cooperrider. *Saving Nature's Legacy.* Washington, D.C.: Island Press, 1994.

Regenstein, Lewis. *America the Poisoned.* Washington, D.C.: Acropolis Books, 1982.

Rifkin, Jeremy. "Beyond Beef." *Utne Reader* 50 (March/April 1992): 96-109.

Sears, Paul B. *Deserts on the March.* Norman: University of Oklahoma Press, 1980.

Wilson, Edward O. *The Diversity of Life.* Cambridge, Mass.: Harvard University Press, 1992.

Zaslowsky, Dyan, and Wilderness Society. *These American Lands.* New York: Henry Holt, 1986.

9. ENVIRONMENTAL ECONOMICS

Daly, Herman E., and John B. Cobb Jr. *For the Common Good: Redirecting the Economy toward Community, the Environment, and a Sustainable Future.* 2d ed. Boston: Beacon Press, 1994.

Galbraith, J. K. *The Affluent Society.* Boston: Houghton Mifflin Company, 1958.

Schumacher, E. F. *Small Is Beautiful.* New York: Perennial Library/Harper & Row, 1975.

10. ENVIRONMENTAL SCIENCE

Bramwell, Anna. *Ecology in the 20th Century*. New Haven, Conn.: Yale University Press, 1989.
Colborn, Theo, Dianne Dumanoski, and John Peterson Myers. *Our Stolen Future*. New York: Dutton, 1996.
Ehrlich, P. R., and J. Roughgarden. *The Science of Ecology*. New York: Macmillan, 1987.
Elton, Charles S. *Animal Ecology*. New York: Macmillan, 1927.
Hull, David. *Darwin and His Critics*. Cambridge, Mass.: Harvard University Press, 1973.
Wilson, Edward O., ed. *Biodiversity*. Washington, D.C.: National Academy Press, 1988.

11. SUSTAINABILITY

Brown, Lester R. *Building a Sustainable Society*. New York: W. W. Norton & Company, 1981.
Brown, Lester R., Christopher Flavin, and Sandra Postel. *Saving the Planet: How to Shape an Environmentally Sustainable Global Economy*. New York: W.W. Norton, 1991.
Buenfil, Alberto Ruz. *Rainbows Without Borders: toward an Ecotopian Millennium*. Santa Fe, N.M.: Bear & Company, 1991.
Caldecott, Leonie, and Stephanie Leland. *Reclaim the Earth: Women Speak out for Life on Earth*. London: Women's Press, 1983.
Henderson, Hazel. *Creating Alternative Futures: The End of Economics*. New York: Berkley Corp., 1978.
Leamer, Steve. *Beyond the Earth Summit: Conversations with Advocates of Sustainable Development*. New York: Common Knowledge Press, 1992.

Meadows, Donella H., Dennis L. Meadows, Jorgen Randers, and William W. Behrens III. *The Limits to Growth.* New York: Universe Books, 1972.

Sale, Kirkpatrick. *Dwellers in the Land: The Bioregional Vision.* San Francisco: Sierra Club Books, 1985.

12. GENERAL ENVIRONMENTAL ISSUES

Cahn, Robert. *Footprints on the Planet.* New York: Universe Books, 1978.

Caldicott, Helen. *If You Love This Planet: A Plan to Heal the Earth.* New York: W.W. Norton, 1992.

Coalition of Environmental Groups. *Blueprint for the Environment.* Salt Lake City, Utah: Howe Brothers Press, 1989.

Cornish, Edward, ed. *Global Solutions: Innovative Approaches to World Problems.* Bethesda, Md.: World Future Society, 1984.

DiSilvestro, Roger L. *The Endangered Kingdom.* New York: John Wiley & Sons, Inc., 1989.

DiSilvestro, Roger L. *Fight for Survival.* New York: John Wiley & Sons, Inc., 1990.

Ehrlich, Paul R. *The Population Bomb.* New York: Ballantine Books, 1968.

Harper, Charles, L. *Environment and Society: Human Perspectives on Environmental Issues.* Englewood Cliffs, N.J.: Prentice Hall, 1995.

Jacks, G. W., and R. O. Whyte. *The Rape of the Earth.* London: Faber & Faber, 1939.

Lovelock, James. *Gaia: A New Look at Life on Earth.* New York: Oxford University Press, 1987.

McKibben, Bill. *The End of Nature.* New York: Random House, 1989.

Miller, Alan S. *Gaia Connections: An Introduction to Ecology, Ecoethics, and Economics.* Totowa, N.J.: Rowman and Littlefield, 1991.

Myers, Norman. *Gaia: An Atlas of Planet Management.* 2d ed. Garden City, N.Y.: Anchor Press, 1986.

Osborn, Fairfield. *Our Plundered Planet.* Boston: Little, Brown, 1948.

Raven, Peter H., Linda R. Berg, and George B. Johnson. *Environment.* Fort Worth, Tex.: Saunders College Publishing, 1995.

Rifkin, Jeremy. *Biosphere Politics: A New Consciousness for a New Century.* New York: Crown, 1991.

Robbins, John. *Diet for a New America.* Walpole, N.H.: Stillpoint Publishing, 1987.

Ward, Barbara, and Rene J. Dubos. *Only One Earth.* New York: W. W. Norton & Company, 1972.

Washington, Haydn. *Ecosol utions.* Berkeley, Calif: North Atlantic Books, 1993.

Weiner, Jonathan. *The Next 100 Years.* New York: Bantam Books, 1990.

Woodwell, George. *The Earth in Transition.* New York: Cambridge University Press, 1990.

ABOUT THE AUTHORS

EDWARD R. WELLS earned his B.S. at Slippery Rock University in Environmental Planning/Geography, his M.A. at Bowling Green State University in Philosophy, and a Ph.D. at Bowling Green State University in American Culture Studies. He is the Director of Environmental Studies at Wilson College. His areas of research and instruction are sustainable society, ecological restoration, and environmental impact assessment. He has published works on culture-nature relationships addressing the problem of overpopulation of national parks, and how U.S. agriculture disenfranchises farm workers and small family farms while favoring large-scale farms, monocultures, and the use of pesticides.

ALAN M. SCHWARTZ earned his B.S. at the State University of New York at Oswego, and his M.S. and Ph.D. at the University of Pennsylvania. He is a professor of environmental studies and founding faculty member of that program at St. Lawrence University in Canton, New York. He is an expert on U.S.-Canada transboundary environmental problems, focusing his research on the integration of science and policy in the resolution of transboundary environmental issues. His works have been published in several books and journals, including *The American Review of Canadian Studies, The Environmental Professional,* and *International Perspectives*. He has received grant support for his research from the Canadian Embassy, the U.S. Fish and Wildlife Service, the U.S. Office of Environmental Education, and private foundations. He has served as a consultant in environmental education for several U.S. colleges and accrediting boards.